Membership Essentials

Membership Essentials

Recruitment, Retention, Roles, Responsibilities, and Resources

Second Edition

SHERI JACOBS, FASAE, CAE

The Center for Association Leadership

WILEY

Cover design: Wiley

This book is printed on acid-free paper.

Published by John Wiley & Sons, Inc., Hoboken, New Jersey
Published simultaneously in Canada

For general information about our other products and services, please contact our Customer Care Department within the United States at (800) 762-2974, outside the United States at (317) 572-3993 or fax (317) 572-4002.

Wiley publishes in a variety of print and electronic formats and by print-on-demand. Some material included with standard print versions of this book may not be included in e-books or in print-on-demand. If this book refers to media such as a CD or DVD that is not included in the version you purchased, you may download this material at http://booksupport.wiley.com. For more information about Wiley products, visit www.wiley.com.

Library of Congress Cataloging-in-Publication Data:

Names: Jacobs, Sheri, author. | American Society of Association Executives, sponsoring body.
Title: Membership essentials : recruitment, retention, roles, responsibilities, and
    resources / Sheri Jacobs.
Description: Second edition. | Hoboken, New Jersey : John Wiley & Sons, Inc., [2016] |
    Includes index.
Identifiers: LCCN 2015041787 (print) | LCCN 2015046248 (ebook) |
    ISBN 9781118976241 (pbk.) | ISBN 9781118976265 (pdf) | ISBN 9781118976258 (epub)
Subjects: LCSH: Associations, institutions, etc.—Membership. | Membership campaigns.
Classification: LCC AS6 .J333 2016 (print) | LCC AS6 (ebook) | DDC 060—dc23
LC record available at http://lccn.loc.gov/2015041787

Printed in the United States of America

10 9 8 7 6 5 4 3 2 1

Contents

Acknowledgments

Writing a book is a collaborative effort. First and foremost, it could not have been accomplished without the hard work and dedication of our chapter authors. This group of thought leaders generously shared their expertise, experience, and time to the association community. We extend our deepest gratitude.

We also wish to acknowledge our friends and colleagues who were interviewed for this book and generously shared their examples, insights, and experiences: Mark Dorsey, FASAE, CAE; Stephanie Mercado; Sue Pine, CAE; Molly M. Hall, IOM, CAE; Barbara Kachelski, CAE; Jamie Moesch; Lori Hatcher; Carolyn Brennan; Lori Gracey, CAE; and Bonnie Koenig.

We would like to express our gratitude to the reviewers provided by ASAE's membership section council who challenged, guided, and helped ensure that we covered the topics essential to membership by reviewing the first edition or early drafts of this edition: Lowell Aplebaum, CAE; Susanne Connors Bowman, CAE; Denise Brown; Ozair Esmail; Andrew S. Goldschmidt, CAE; and Tony Rossell.

To Baron Williams, CAE, who kept this project on track and provided the feedback we needed to ensure we truly captured the essence of membership, thank you for your dedication, wisdom, and professionalism.

—Sheri Jacobs, FASAE, CAE

About the ASAE-Wiley Series

All titles in the ASAE-Wiley Series are developed through a publishing alliance between ASAE: The Center for Association Leadership and John Wiley & Sons to better serve the content needs of member-serving organizations and the people who lead and management them.

Introduction

By Greg Fine, CAE

Membership, or the act of affiliation, remains a core pillar of many, if not most, associations today. How an individual or entity engages in this act of affiliation can differ widely, and even the lexicon of membership (member, customer, stakeholder, etc.) can vary based on the mission and focus of the organization. Yet, one common characteristic is frequently present . . . a desire on the part of an individual to belong. This should come as no surprise. Humans are, by our very nature, highly social beings and thrive in being part of pack or group. This instinctive desire to form groups has been well leveraged by associations throughout history. In fact, many associations' first mission were simply to provide "membership" to like individuals. Often around a profession. Think guild. Over time, association professionals realized the power of the group could do much more than just affiliate, and this gave rise to common association programs of today like professional development, certification, and advocacy. Yet, all of these still relied on the traditional concept of membership. It was members who created the content that the association then monetized by selling back to members and nonmembers alike. A great model that served both associations and society well. But things are changing!

In today's world of informal connections (Facebook and LinkedIn), information overload (email and SPAM), instant communication (text messaging), and an overwhelming flood of news, data, and noise from all sources, associations are increasingly challenged to cut through the clutter to provide value in all areas, including membership. Gone are the days when simple affiliation was enough to sustain a membership base alone. Like all industries, associations are grappling with changing customer demographics, rapidly shifting market conditions, globalization, disruptive technologies, competitive pressure from new sectors, and a distracted and overwhelmed customer base. All of this is enough to make even the most positive association professionals consider throwing in the towel as they declare: "Membership is dead."

Not so fast there. While the word "membership" may have a different meaning today than in the past, the idea and value of affiliation remains a powerful concept that associations are uniquely positioned to leverage. For-profit organizations have long sought to create a level of loyalty and affiliation with their customers that associations historically begin with. Rachel Botsman, an expert on "The Collaborative Economy" has identified characteristics in the sharing economy that are quite similar to those of membership. Her thinking around the ability to harness a missing market opportunity through disruption and innovation should strike fear and inspire hope in us all. So membership is not dead; it is, like everything else, evolving.

Membership Essentials provides insight and foresight from some of the best and brightest minds in the profession today. Membership is a full-contact sport, and these individuals share their knowledge and experience on what is needed today to ensure a future tomorrow.

The Evolving Environment for Membership and Engagement

1

By Kenneth A. Doyle, FASAE, CAE, and

Scott D. Oser, MBA

IN THIS CHAPTER

- Global Expansion, Yet North American–Centric
- Economic Uncertainties with an Abundance of Options
- Work Redefined
- A Workforce of Five Generations
- A Sense of Community
- Advances in Technology
- Opportunities and Challenges
- Going Global

A search of Google for the term "MEMBER" provides 3,280,000,000 results in 0.35 seconds and a search for "MEMBERSHIP" provides 525,000,000 results in 0.47 seconds. Access to information and the meaning of the terms MEMBER and MEMBERSHIP have both changed dramatically over the last 30 years.

There was a time when being a MEMBER meant voluntarily joining a group with like interests for mutual benefit in a trusted environment. The terms MEMBER and MEMBERSHIP have been co-opted by those who often just want to sell something and use the inherent good will of the terms to break down barriers to making a sale and create a feeling of inclusion.

Previously, an association could count on new entrants to their profession or line of business to join and remain members throughout their careers. Prospective employers would not ask candidates why they were members of their association, but they would ask why you were NOT a member. You just "had" to be a member to practice your profession or craft. Not anymore.

For many associations, the reason they exist is to serve the needs of their members—a very simple statement. But you have to define who or what the "member" is before you can define needs and create benefits that would cause "membership" to be of value.

Less than two decades ago, associations easily attracted some members who were happy to pay dues for the information provided and other services generated—often called "checkbook members." Although this type of member still exists today, it is much less prevalent. The compelling reasons to pay dues to an organization just do not exist to the same extent. While much of the needed information and many services are available at low or no cost over the Internet or through other providers, there are many things around membership that haven't changed. Individuals and corporate entities still need to stay up-to-date, stay informed, connect with peers and colleagues—build a professional network, and obtain education (in some cases it's required) so there is an ongoing basic value in the association membership model.

This chapter is going to tee up the rest of the book by giving the reader some insight into the major things that have changed in the membership area over recent years.

Global Expansion, Yet North American–Centric

No longer is the typical American-based association focused on a member from the United States who is middle class, speaks English, and comes from a Judeo/Christian background. Associations are embracing members from all faiths, economic backgrounds, and from every corner of the globe. With the advent of technology, membership has become universally available and accepted, yet to a large extent, associations based in the United States still tend to be North American–centric, in spite of the outreach to the global community.

Economic Uncertainties with an Abundance of Options

The economy has always been uncertain. Inflation has been relatively tame over the last two decades, but is always a lurking threat. The United States is moving further away from an industrial economy toward a service society. But technology has allowed many middle class jobs to be outsourced to other countries where labor rates are much lower. Large corporations are now competing with national governments that are heavily promoting their own resources, products, and workforce.

The American people will drive across town to save 5 cents a gallon. Internet shopping has commoditized almost anything we buy. It has become a national game to acquire our products at the absolute lowest price, regardless of what impact this might have on the local economy or the domestic workforce.

Work Redefined

The nine-to-five job no longer exists for many workers. Work takes place in a 24/7 world. Technology has allowed us to work anywhere and at any time. We are shifting from the central office to the home office. People don't believe they will retire from the place where they started their careers. With longer life expectancy, many are opting for two or more careers rather than one and think nothing of giving up their first career and starting an entirely different one as they progress through life. Work could consist of many short-term projects. Everyone will be responsible for his own success. The employer may feel less and less responsible to pay the expenses associated with membership and participation in an association. As more people adapt alternative work styles, they will want their associations to support their new work environment and changed needs.

All this leads to greater levels of uncertainty. We will have fewer resources and less control over our future. We no longer will live to work or work to live but will balance work and life experiences. The pull between work time and personal time will be even greater in the future. Time is the only thing we have that is strictly limited.

A Workforce of Five Generations

This subject has been covered to exhaustion in recent years, but you have to address generational differences if you are going to talk about the evolution of membership. In the ASAE Foundation's 1985 publication *Future Perspectives*, Rod Geer begins his chapter with: "It's hard to read the handwriting on the wall when your back is against it, and that is exactly the predicament many association executives will be facing if they fail to prepare now for the new breed of volunteer likely to be populating our leadership mix in the future." It was as true then as it is now, but his chapter was called *Baby Boomers in Your Boardroom*.

There are five distinct generations in the workforce today. Each has its own set of values, its own drivers, and its own way of looking at the world. Despite our differences, we must all get along and work together to get ahead. The changing of the guard will occur, as it always has, and associations must adapt to the varying needs of their members and employees.

The Generations—Definitions

Traditionalists—born before 1945, also known as the quiet generation or the greatest generation. There are almost 39 million Traditionalists in the United States. They are not leaving the workforce as their parents did. They will stay active well into their 70's and will want to continue to be a member—if there is value for them. Traditionalists will want to see the world, spend time with their grand-children, and be involved in something meaningful. Organizational value to Tra-ditionalists may be received by volunteering their time (but not too much of it) and talents locally and/or staying involved with their peers with whom they have shared their careers. To keep the Traditionalists involved, associations will have to offer them a place to contribute, meet friends and feel welcome. Associations that offer rewarding experiences and comradery will continue to see participation by Traditionalists.

Baby Boomers—born between 1946 and 1964. There are almost 80 million U.S. Baby Boomers. They shaped the world we live in today, and they know it. Some Boomers are running toward retirement. They are done with work and want to dedi-cate the last third of their lives to experiences. They grew up believing that hard work and saving were the only way to prepare for another Great Depression. Now they have security and just want to enjoy their lives. Those associations that provide experiences and opportunities to give back may have a chance of keeping this type of Boomer involved.

Another portion of the Boomers don't want to stop working. Work is part of who they are; heck, for many, it IS who they are. They just want to work less so they can enjoy life a little more. They have money and will spend it on retirement homes, healthcare, and on experiences. Many will work as something to do and for the extra income to pay for special events and travel.

You will have to pry many Boomers out of their positions. They will not want to let go. They have no urge to move out of the way and let the younger genera-tion have their turn. Associations that provide a place to belong or an economic benefit will find it easier to keep Boomers involved, so long as the cost is not perceived as too high and the Boomer feels personally connected with others in the organization.

Generation X—born between 1965 and 1980. There are over 60 million U.S. Gen Xers. Initially viewed as whiny slackers by the hard-working Boomers, Gen Xers think of themselves as wide-eyed realists. They were never promised a rose garden and they are living life, not to conform to Boomers expectations, but to their own. They learned that hard work was not the path to riches; it is just hard work—time spent not doing what they really wanted to do. They understood that nothing will come easy to them.

This is the most misunderstood generation by everyone, including themselves. They are squished between the Boomers who will not get out of the way and the Millen-nials, who want the top jobs NOW! Misunderstood or not, Gen Xers will become the leaders of organizations as the Baby Boomers start to retire.

Associations will have to engage the Gen Xers in new ways. Not quite digital natives, Gen Xers are generally tech-savvy, but not all are as savvy as others. They have a dif-ficult time trusting others, and they are obsessively self-reliant. They don't see them-selves as "joiners" of traditional associations or organizations, nor do they attend meetings as other generations did/do.

To attract Gen Xers' attention, associations will have to have a compelling offer, one that includes economic benefit, personal enrichment, and (at least the perception of) potential new opportunities. To earn Gen Xers' time and dollars, associations will have to focus on delivering value every day and will not be able to rely on a reputation of overall value developed over time.

Millennials—born between 1981 and 2001. There are almost 84 million U.S. Millennials, a larger cohort than Boomers. They grew up with nothing but prosperity in their future and believed that everything would come to them. As teens, they walked through the mall and every store they went into an employee asked, not if she could help them, but if they wanted a job. Then the great recession hit and they became bewildered. As twenty-somethings, they graduated with bachelor's degrees and ended up working in the mall at the job they turned down as a teen. No wonder they have been confused. Money matters to Millennials, but in a different way. Boomers stored money like nuts for the winter, Millennials have a confidence that everything will work out and money is best spent or stored in something they can use to experience life.

Besides making money, Millennials want to make a difference. They want to give of their time and enthusiasm, but will not tolerate being ignored. If not cultivated, Millennials will pack up and text someone to go do something else. Their chapter is not yet written; however, associations will have to address Millennials as members and workers. This generation grew up with computers and is responsive mostly to screen-oriented promotions.

New Generation—born after 2001 and totally in the Internet era. At the time of this writing, there are more than 45 million of them in the United States, and the number is continually increasing. This group contains the real digital natives. Screens, screens everywhere, they grew up with access to an unlimited amount of data and information. Their options are limitless, but their time is not, so they have adapted to quickly sifting through content for what is relevant to them. They have what has been termed as an 8-second filter, which older generations see as an attention span problem. They seek acceptance through social media, where they may have different personas depending on the audience they are playing to. For an association, these future members and employees strive to avoid the bad rap the Millennials got and want to work hard and prove themselves. They are really very pragmatic and plan to be very adaptable given the uncertainties they have had growing up after 9/11 and the great recession. It may be too early to knowingly plan for how this generation will impact the world. But it will be up to them to fix the problem the earlier generations have created.

A Sense of Community

Despite all of the changes that have taken place in the world, and in the association space in particular, one of the things that has not changed is the members' desire to be part of a community. Community has always been a driver of association membership, and that need continues to be especially strong today. The biggest change in community that impacts associations is that it no longer needs to be face to face and in-person. That sense of belonging that all humans desire can now be fulfilled in different ways. You can be "friends" on Facebook with people all over the world you never talk to or see, but you can still "feel" connected to them. Thus, community can be created online as well as in person, and that creates both challenges and opportunities for associations.

Opportunities

Since association members no longer "need" to be face to face to be part of a community, associations can become more productive from both a staff and financial perspective. With the ability to get together virtually and form community without the need to be together at one physical location, associations won't incur the cost of the marketing, implementation, and staff resources necessary to hold an in-person event. In addition to a reduction in travel expenses, the association staff will also be able to focus on other areas of responsibility, since they will not be out of pocket as often as they had been in the past.

Challenges

The ability to create, manage, and maintain a virtual community is going to be critical for associations moving forward. Since many members are now expecting virtual community, the association needs to be in tune with their wants, needs, and preferences so that they can serve this expectation accordingly. If associations do not provide the right type of virtual community, it will have a negative impact on member retention, which is something that all associations want to avoid. (See Chapter 14 for more information on private online communities.) The good news is that there are a number of different technologies that association staff can utilize to fill this member need.

Advances in Technology

If anything has had an immense impact on the way associations do business and what members expect, it is technology. There have been incredible technological advances, which has impacted almost all areas of associations.

Amazing how things have changed since the 1988 edition of ASAE's *Principles of Association Management* when the question of what to automate, and when, was answered by the statement: "Once you know the basic rules of buying a computer, you must be sure you need one in the first place." (Chapter 8 provides a good overview of association database management systems.)

Technologically Savvy

Just how technologically savvy the member is will determine how information can be delivered. These variations in technological savviness will lead an association to utilize multiple delivery systems to reach members and potential members. Marketers will have to use a form of digital target marketing and have been called "marketing technologists." As of now, this means that the marketers have be very tech-savvy themselves, but in the future, as the software evolves, marketers will revert to marketing and allow the technology to personalize the delivery to the member.

Associations will have to segment members by how tech-savvy they are and then tailor the offering to the level of the target audience. Some members will want it simple and straightforward; others will regard that as rudimentary and not worth their time. One size will not fit all.

Technologically Savvy Users—Definitions

Minimal Tech User—This group can turn on the TV and change channels but cannot use the DVR. They can make calls on their mobile phones and sometimes answer a text, but the rest of what the phone can do is lost on them. They have learned how to Google, shop online, and use Facebook. One-click shopping is the best for them.

Basic Tech User—This group has slightly more advanced digital skills. They can use the DVR and most any app on the phone/tablet. If the computer stops functioning, they can reboot, but if that does not fix the problem they buy a new computer. Basic Tech Users have an extensive list of websites that they frequent and use. When motivated, they will really dig deep using Google, but are easily discouraged and will quit fairly quickly. Several options on the same web page works, as long as everything is very easy to find.

Any Tech User—The next level of digital savviness consists of people who can set up their own home networks and enjoy the challenge of making all the technology work. When the computer quits, they can reinstall the original software and bring it back to life. Members of this group are the ones whom the Minimal and Basic Tech Users call for home tech support and to figure out how to set up and turn the Apple TV on. They will figure out how to get what they need from the web and will call the help desk for assistance, if needed, to figure out how to get to the right place. They will find what they need on the web, even if it takes many searches. They enjoy multiple options on the same web page to ease their decision making.

High Tech User—This level sets up the office network, can do some coding if needed, and jail break their phones. They know how to run the server and make changes. When they go to your website, they know whether your software is running slowly or whether it's their Internet connection. They, too, enjoy multiple options on their web pages, but technical specifications become more important to them.

Technophile—This is the top level of sophistication. When they go to your website, they know how to change it without your permission. The Technophile looks like the people in the movies who write code against a stopwatch while taking shots of tequila. This group writes the apps you use, and they think any website found on Google is too basic.

Member Expectations

Members have always expected a lot for their dues, but with today's technology those expectations have shot through the roof. Members now expect you to communicate with them how they want, when they want, where they want, and about what they want. They also want the communications to be personalized. "Dear Member" is now a slap in the face to many members, as it doesn't show them that the association cares about them as individuals.

The Gamer

Millions of people are avid online game players. One of the very popular games is Halo, a military science fiction first-person-shooter video game.

When logged onto Halo online, players have performance ratings based on past play. They enter the matchmaking area, where an algorithm takes this rating and offers players a chance to join teams of other similarly rated players who are online at that moment. They form a team and challenge another group to play. Headsets allow for audio interaction in real time among teammates. They set up a plan and go into action.

Generally, these teams play matches until one team wins or time runs out. The whole experience lasts about 30 minutes. Contestants do not know who they are playing with, and players can be from all over the globe. As people become better players, they move up the ranks to more challenging play.

These "gamers" expect to be able to join a group, have a clear objective that is pursued aggressively, quickly rise in the ranks, and then move on to the next level, all in one session.

The traditional association committee structure is similar to playing Halo. One starts out joining the committee and then engages in active committee work. If that work is good enough to be noticed, the next step is moving up the chairs to committee leadership. However, this structure takes two to five years to go through this one cycle.

How can this traditional association process, which takes so long, ever satisfy someone who is used to the entire process happening in 30 minutes?

Opportunities and Challenges

With the explosion of devices that can be used for communication, associations now need to address their members through multiple mediums and using multiple mechanisms. Members are now using laptops, tablets, smartphones, desktops, hybrid computers, and more to access information and communication. Members are reading emails and direct mail, print and digital publications, are active on Facebook, LinkedIn, Twitter, Instagram, YouTube, and respond to text messages. There is probably no one device or method of communication that will satisfy the need of every member in an association. It is therefore going to be critical going forward that associations understand what their members', prospective members', and customers' preferences are when it comes to the device they are using, as well as in what format they want to be communicated.

A big question that associations are going to have to answer is which channels they will need to use and incorporate into their communications strategy. And do they have the infrastructure to support it? Since everyone wants to serve all constituents equally, some difficult decisions are going to have to be made because most associations simply won't have the financial or human resources to support every type of device and medium that is out there.

The Bar Has Been Raised

As has always been the case, associations are competing with for-profit companies for their members' attention. Many times for-profit companies like Amazon (targeting and volume of offerings), Apple (innovation and branding), and Zappos (low prices and incredible customer service) do things that most associations are currently not able to do. Members are exposed to the advanced things that the for-profit companies can do and expect their associations to be able to do the same thing. It is an unfortunate reality that many times associations are not able to provide the same kind of 24-hour service and communication people are expecting, so this puts associations at a slight disadvantage when it comes to getting members the access they want when they want it. Associations are going to have to take steps to level the playing field if they want to survive and thrive. The good news is that there are ways they can do that.

Continuous Two-Way Access

As mentioned above, there is no longer just one way that members are receiving information. They are accessing information, and receiving information, in every conceivable location, including their offices, their homes, their cars, public transportation, on airplanes, and more. With the technological advances that have occurred, there is nothing stopping a member or prospective member from trying to connect with you from almost any location. Associations need to be aware of this and provide content accordingly. Remember, your members shop on Amazon, read books on the Kindle app, and receive up-to-the-minute updates from news apps such as CNN on their mobile phones. Because of this, expectations and even value may fall short if associations are unable to deliver a comparable experience.

Personalized Offerings

This is perhaps the most important change that has happened within association communication over the last 10 years or so. Members are no longer willing to accept content and promotions that are not targeted to them. Members expect you to "know" them and therefore expect you to serve them with content and product and service offerings that are primarily appropriate to who they are and their unique needs.

In the past, associations were able to send every member the same thing because databases and technologies didn't exist to allow them to provide different information to different members. This is definitely no longer the case, and members have been trained by online retailers to expect personalized communications. Targeting content and offerings based on unique characteristics of your members requires different staff skills than in the past. It also requires a strong technological backbone as well as the member data you will be using to create customized communications. If associations fail in any of these three areas, members may hold them in a negative light. The good news is that there are some very cost-effective ways to develop processes and systems that can help even the smallest association resemble a company like Amazon.

Technology and how associations use it, or don't use it, and how cutting-edge companies use it impacts almost every aspect of an association. Whether we like it or not, expectations are being set that we need to measure up to or risk appearing outdated.

These are critical decisions as they affect associations internally (staff, technology, revenues and expenses, marketing, etc.) as well as externally (members' and non-members' perspectives, brand perception, volunteer activities, advocacy, etc.).

Going Global

The world has definitely become a smaller place over time, and that has allowed associations to attract a membership that includes both U.S.-based and international members. The ability to more easily communicate with audiences in other countries has expanded membership rosters and resulted in a much more robust membership experience for many associations.

While the ability to attract members from across the globe can have a very positive impact on an association, it also generates many questions that need to be answered. (See Chapters 4 and 6 for questions and considerations with respect to global initiatives.)

Just because technology and other changes in the world make it easier for you to attract members from across the globe doesn't mean you have the knowledge, staff, technology, or services to do so. Having a multicultural association requires a strategy to be in place so that you serve those members, or member companies, located outside of the United States as well as you do those that are based in the United States. This strategy needs to answer the questions above and more. It is also important to keep in mind that global members will have the same demands and expectations as U.S.–based members, so it is important that you are able to meet or exceed them.

Conclusion

Members want to be treated as individuals. Big companies have lavished millions on systems that suggest products and services we might want based on our previous behavior. What these companies suggest is tailored and targeted to an individual's specific wants and needs. That is what we have come to expect.

Associations will also need to know who their "members" are and their members' preferences. They have to know the individual member's likes and dislikes. Once members' preferences are known and understood, an association has to provide the RIGHT communication to members. More is not better. We have the means of utilizing customer-centric technologies to engage members in the digital age. Some have referred to this as "member experience engineering." Associations will have to embrace the concept and become good at it.

It is very hard for an association on a limited budget to compete on the same level as the big companies. But organizations have to do what they can, such as by "bucketizing" members and prospects by things like type, length of engagement, and what they purchased. The member has to be given the tools to access the association's products and services he or she wants to utilize. Associations must understand the life cycle of a member and life cycle of a member service or program.

Associations must engage members on a consistent, personalized basis. Don't just try to sell them transactions. An association cannot be all things to all people, so it needs to decide what it is, and what it is not, going to be.

References

Ernstthal, Henry, *Principles of Association Management*. Washington, DC: ASAE Foundation, 1988.

Future Perspectives. Washington, DC: ASAE Foundation, 1985.

About the Authors

Kenneth A. Doyle, FASAE, CAE, is president of Doyle Association Consulting, LLC, and a fellow of ASAE. He has four decades of association management experience as a CEO, business strategist, and organizational efficiency specialist helping associations grow and adapt to the future. Email: Doyle4000@gmail.com.

Scott D. Oser, MBA, is president of Scott Oser Associates. He has over 18 years of marketing experience in the association and publishing industries. His career has been focused on creating effective membership, marketing, and sales programs with the ability to align resources and operations to consistently achieve and exceed goals. Email: info@scottoserassociates.com.

Strategic Planning as It Relates to Relationship-Building, Engagement, and Affiliation

2

By Kristine Metter, CAE

Most associations work from a strategic plan that outlines what the association hopes to accomplish in a given period of time. In this chapter, we will cover starting strategic planning, establishing a process, engaging constituents, using metrics to measure success, and addressing challenges to strategic planning for membership professionals.

Making the Case

Your association sits down for its periodic strategic planning discussion, whether it is annually, every three years, or when someone finally suggests that the strategic plan needs to be revisited. What is the focus of the conversation? Is it the next big educational program? Is it diversification of funding streams? Is it about your advocacy efforts? Or maybe, just maybe, it is about membership and providing member value. Membership may not be a pillar of your strategic plan in and of itself, but by putting membership at the center of the conversation, you are setting the best possible focus for your strategic planning efforts.

We all have a mission statement that provides a road map for our work. Most of us cannot quote it on the fly but, in general, we know why our association exists and strive to fulfill that mission on a regular basis. Just like putting membership at the center of your strategic planning, I hope your mission has at its core a focus on members. By focusing on priorities that provide value to members, you will have a way to evaluate how you use your association's resources and to maximize the effectiveness of your efforts. And with that laser focus on member value, you should have an easier time attracting members who enable your association to grow and thrive.

A Member-Centric Mindset Leads to Growth

Mark Dorsey, FASAE, CAE, former CEO of the Professional Ski Instructors of America–American Association of Snowboard Instructors (PSIA–AASI) and current CEO of Construction Specifications Institute, takes to heart the mantra of being member-centric, but he does so with a twist. He believes that, while membership is a component of strategy, the staff and board are clear that membership in and of itself is not the goal. Rather, he advocates the association exists to help members achieve their own goals and to create excitement about snow sports. To this end, while at PSIA–AASI, an education association with more than 31,500 individual members dedicated to promoting the sports of skiing and snowboarding through instruction, he challenged his board to think differently about membership from a strategic perspective. Members are but one group to be served by the mission. The general public, vendors, marketing partners, industry associations, and other stakeholders must be considered. "Members" is often a label or demographic and distracts from the notion that individual behaviors—not labels—should drive and inform activities that assure the association has a strong brand identity, keeps the focus on mission, and is a trusted source of information. This encourages the association to be more nimble, more inclusive, and more focused on value. As a result, PSIA–AASI has seen remarkable growth in revenue and membership.

And while growth is a key component of every membership discussion, let's come back to the premise that it is not just growth of members. It is also growth in member engagement, growth in association activity to support the industry, and growth in providing value. If you are not growing and changing, then your association is likely to contract and very possibly become irrelevant. So it follows that your strategic

Figure 2.1. Ski Areas Compared to Membership

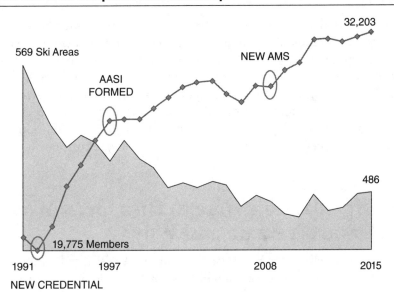

planning efforts should also seek to identify member-centric activities to keep your association growing. These can range from identifying opportunities for your association to provide leadership in a new and emerging direction for existing members to identifying new member segments for which new programs and services need to be developed.

Who Do We Really Serve?

During its most recent strategic planning process, America's Essential Hospitals, then called the National Association of Public Hospitals and Health Systems (NAPH), reviewed its advocacy strengths and scope of services in conjunction with consideration of how the Affordable Care Act was driving changes in the healthcare environment. As a result, a robust discussion about the association's membership ensued. Ultimately, the decision was made to broaden membership from just publicly governed hospitals to add private nonprofit hospitals with similar missions, patient profiles, and services as the original core members. Today, with a new name, new branding, and crisp understanding of how it delivers value to members, the association has seen 30 percent growth in two years and is recognized as a leading advocate on a number of critical issues important to vulnerable patients and the hospitals that serve them. By focusing the strategic planning discussion on membership, America's Essential Hospitals was able to set a way forward that ensures the association remains relevant to long-term members while also introducing itself to a broader set of hospitals. With this broadened membership, the association can better achieve its mission to "champion excellence in health care for all, regardless of social or economic circumstance, and advance the work of hospitals and health systems committed to ensuring access to care and optimal health for America's most vulnerable people."

Adapting Your Focus

Just as America's Essential Hospitals redefined its universe of members, your association may need to look at its member categories in relation to the mission and the services it provides. At times it will be necessary to refocus the organization based on the current environment and context within which it operates. At times there will be new entrants into the market, such as for-profit companies, that are non-traditional competitors. At times the association may decide to service non-members such as key stakeholders and industry partners in addition to members. The possible scenarios are vast; therefore, a strategic conversation becomes necessary.

If the Organization Were to Disappear, Would Anyone Start It Again and Why?

The National Association for Healthcare Quality (NAHQ) faced a rapidly changing environment where healthcare quality was once the domain of a well-defined group of quality professionals and today everyone within the healthcare system has responsibility for quality, and quality professionals are not easily identified. Faced with this changing landscape and broadening scope, the association had to refocus its work or risk becoming lost in the sea change that was happening within the industry.

Stephanie Mercado, executive director for NAHQ, started her strategic planning efforts from day one on the job. She engaged a number of members by asking, "If the organization were to disappear, would anyone start it again and why?" She found that most members struggled to answer the question. The board ultimately concluded that the organization needed to focus on the profession and not the professional. This new interpretation of their mission allowed them to focus on how to best serve their core members as well as consider who should be their members going forward. As Stephanie puts it: "NAHQ built the quality superhighway and now there are many new on-ramps that bring in new players to the quality profession such as doctors, data analysts, and even engineers and process improvement (like lean/six-sigma) leaders from the auto industry." By focusing on current and future members, they were able to reinterpret and tighten the focus of their mission. They now have clarity about their work and a renewed sense of direction.

Strategic planning often leads to uncomfortable but important discussions about how the association intends to deliver on its mission and brand promise.

Are there programs that need to be reshaped or discontinued? Are there member categories that need to be redefined? Are there stagnant member categories with which the association needs to relate differently? These can be risky propositions and, with most association volunteer leaders being risk-adverse, it becomes all the more important to engage a wide variety of members in strategic planning to build loyalty to and ownership in the association and its strategic direction.

Engaging Members in Strategic Planning

The most successful strategic planning processes are data-driven. By using data to evaluate past activities, you set a rational basis for exploring where the organization should be going. Whether your association is small or large, you either have a robust set of data points already available or you can easily capture relevant information by engaging members throughout your organization.

Sue Pine, CAE, chief staff executive for the National Association of Professional Organizers (NAPO), takes member engagement in the strategic planning procesess seriously, seeking the voice of the membership through member exit surveys, focus groups, conference evaluations, and the like. She also mines data to build member profiles and identify a variety of metrics that help guide her strategic planning process. Staff are responsible for collecting and synthesizing the member data and feedback.

She takes great care to include those outside the leadership circles in order to make sure that the rank and file membership's needs are met in addition to the needs of those who are in the "inner circle." Many associations also closely look at outside stakeholders as key sources of information needed to inform the strategic planning process. These may include exhibitors, sponsors, regulators, and even the general public. By widely casting the net, a well-rounded picture emerges on how groups relate to the organization through membership or other affiliation.

Pine also strongly believes in the value of understanding trends and their impact on association strategic planning. By committing to regular scanning of the environment and listening for weak signals that may become strong signals, associations will be better equipped to meet member needs. This work also enables associations to engage members in a variety of ways:

- *Focus Groups*—roundtable discussions of random groups of members focused on new initiatives the board is considering
- *Trends Wall*—physical wall to gather member feedback at their annual conference, then aligning member feedback to global trends
- *Chapter Visits*—board visits with local members to share information and solicit feedback
- *Volunteer Engagement Survey*—survey compiled with four to six questions from every committee chair

In many ways, collecting data to support your strategic planning is an ongoing process. Every event can tell you a great deal about how you are delivering on your brand promise and can point you in the direction of future member needs. Similarly, most of us operate in a digital world, so it is important to take advantage of your website and social media platforms as a source of information to collect member feedback to inform your strategic planning.

Metrics

The old adage is that you manage what you measure and measure what you manage. This is particularly true when thinking about your organization's strategic plan where there is a delicate balance between being inspirational in your strategic goals and counting things. There is no doubt that dashboards are important, but how do you decide what is meaningful to measure and track? And who is responsible for those measures?

Some basic member-oriented metrics are always valuable:

- Rate of membership growth,

- Retention rate, and

- Lifetime value of a member.

You also might want to routinely assess member and stakeholder satisfaction through periodic surveys and program evaluations. You need to know what programs, people, and services impact your satisfaction metrics and then apply the appropriate strategies to increase satisfaction.

And finally, make the most of your database. Tracking activity and behavior can help the association identify predictors to joining, renewing, and dropping membership. As we outlined earlier, it is important to keep a long horizon to your work through a constant scan for leading indicators, rather than being caught flat-footed when the environment changes or member preferences mature.

Hard quantitative data is most effective when married with qualitative research that adds richness to the analysis. We all pore over the open-ended comments from our event evaluations and rely on the hallway conversations we have with members, stakeholders, and industry partners. But data is only part of the answer. Your intuition or gut feeling also matters. It is valuable to take a pulse to see whether the data simply makes sense. If not, perhaps you have a mismatch with what you are doing and what you are measuring.

As you decide what to measure, look, too, at who is accountable. It is important to embed membership metrics as organizational goals with staff and volunteers at all levels having ownership. For example, a staff-wide, year-end bonus could be based on the dual metric of meeting a financial performance level AND a defined member satisfaction rate. If it is just the membership director's job, then there will be insurmountable barriers to successfully achieving your member-oriented strategic goals.

Challenges

Now that you have committed to incorporating membership into your strategic planning process, what might come as a surprise or challenge? First, you need to take steps to teach your volunteer leaders about membership best practices. Generally, they are experts in their respective fields. They are not experts in association management or membership. Start with the basics and spend time getting them acclimated:

- Talk about member retention practices.
- Outline member engagement strategies.
- Encourage open conversations about member growth.

Remember that they are not thinking about the association's business every day like you are. Give them the tools they need to quickly and easily digest the information and make smart decisions based on that information.

Next, encourage your leaders to take time to think about the association broadly—and not only from their personal lenses. Some leaders will consider their position an avenue to advance a pet project or personal priority. A smart association executive will channel his or her leaders' egos, steering them away from individual interests and toward a focus on what is best for the association and/or the industry. Leaders are emotionally vested in their organizations, so it is productive to take maximum advantage of this perspective. Set this expectation early and use every opportunity to remind your leaders they have a fiduciary responsibility to the organization.

You may also encounter challenges with sustainability and/or constrained resources. It is hard work to be continually scanning for new trends and engaging members in an ongoing strategic planning process. It takes both financial and human capital resources to effectively conduct these activities. A commitment to them, though, is essential to your organization's long-term health.

Another resource challenge comes with deciding between existing programs and service lines and developing new offerings. Most associations are deeply wedded to products and activities they have been doing for years or decades. But with limited association resources and limited member bandwidth to participate, it becomes essential to thoughtfully and intentionally bring to a close those offerings that no longer meet member or stakeholder needs. It always comes back to delivering value to the right audiences at the right time in the right format and for the right price.

And a final challenge comes hand in hand with the relentless availability of information. There are endless sources, viewpoints, and commentary, whether they are CNN, Twitter, the latest blog, or your association's newsletter. Cutting through that cacophony of data points is exhausting and at times confusing to you, your staff, and your volunteer leadership. What do you pay attention to and what do you dismiss? How do you pull out those weak signals that will become strong signals that impact your association's ability to deliver member value in the coming months and years?

In summary, if your strategic planning does not have a connection to members or membership, you have a higher likelihood of missing opportunities, going down a rabbit hole, serving too narrow an audience, or another similar situation. And in the worst-case scenario, you may even experience organizational demise.

Key Membership Questions for Strategic Planning

- What challenges do members face that will be solved by the association?
- What are the key activities that help build the value proposition?
- What resources are needed to fulfill the value proposition?
- Which trends will most likely have an effect on my industry and how can the association create new value based on these trends?
- What are the association's audience segments?
- Are there programs that need to be reshaped or discontinued?
- Are there member categories that need to be redefined?
- Are there stagnant member categories with which the association needs to relate differently?
- From whom do you solicit feedback on the association's offerings?
- What do you measure? What data points (internal and external) matter the most?

About the Author

Kristine Metter, CAE, has worked in the nonprofit and association industry for nearly 30 years, primarily in the health care arena. She is currently vice president for member services with America's Essential Hospitals, a national trade association that represents hospitals serving vulnerable populations. As a key member of the association's senior management team, she is responsible for strategic planning and program management for activities related to membership and education. Prior to joining America's Essential Hospitals, Ms. Metter was a senior leader for the Visiting Nurse Associations of America (VNAA), AcademyHealth, and the National Association of Student Personnel Administrators (NASPA). She has also worked in the health services field with organizations such as the American Red Cross, the National Institutes of Health, and the National Marrow Donor Program.

Ms. Metter has served on a variety of ASAE councils, sections, and ad-hoc activities, including the Research Committee, Health Care Committee, Membership Council, the Greater Washington Network, the *Associations Now* writers' pool, and the CAE Immersion Course. She earned her CAE in 2006 and has a BSBA in marketing from the University of Missouri and an MS in nonprofit management from the University of Maryland University College. Email: kmetter@essentialhospitals.org.

Defining Value

By Jay Karen, CAE

3

IN THIS CHAPTER

• The Value of Association Membership

• Benefits and Answering the Question: "What's in It for Me?"

• Communicating Value Received

• Are Your Benefits Relevant, Effective, Both, or Neither?

• Ways to Improve Value

• New Member Value

What is value? Seems like an appropriate question for a chapter on "value proposition." In general, value is an equation that people run in their minds when they encounter a potential purchase or investment of time and energy in exchange for something. The equation looks something like this:

"What will I get or what will be the result?" (the benefit) –

The investment I have to make (money or time) = Value

We will soon get to how this applies in the context of membership organizations. But to make my point in a somewhat simplistic and a bit ridiculous fashion, imagine you are an avid or occasional coffee drinker and walk into a local coffee shop. The sign indicates that your eight-ounce cup of the local roast will cost $8. Instantaneously, you are running the value equation in your head: "I'm going to get a cup of coffee if I give them $8. I will likely not feel too good about the value and will subsequently feel either ripped off or dissatisfied in some way. I am not likely to buy."

Before we jump to such a conclusion, there are many factors that complicate the pieces of this seemingly simple equation. First, let's examine the benefit side. The benefit received would be the same for every patron of that coffee shop purchase, right?

An eight-ounce cup of coffee. But, what if you hate coffee? Will that $8 be an even bigger waste of your money? Of course. What if the coffee was organic? Some people's feeling of benefit would now be different (I feel better about myself by supporting an organic farm), and for others there would be no change. What if the coffee was grown on a farm in an area of the world that needs investment? How would that change the "benefit"? Do I need caffeine at this particular time? The more I feel the caffeine jolt will help me, the more benefit I hope to receive. What if it was a locally owned coffee shop, instead of a location from within a multinational, billion-dollar corporation? What if you had just read a Harvard medical study that indicated drinking a cup of coffee every day is good for your health? Is the coffee shop a cool or hip place, or is it nothing really special? Will it validate me as a cool person if I'm in that coffee shop, or seen by my friends in that coffee shop? The benefit received can be much more than the enjoyment of the hot beverage inside the mug. It could also be a feeling of satisfaction received as a result of that purchase. Every person walking into the coffee shop brings different tastes, desires, sensibilities, mores, and knowledge. Thus, the "benefit" of one cup of coffee will vary greatly from patron to patron. This will be no different when we examine the benefits of membership.

Now let's look at the investment of time and money. Eight dollars is eight dollars, right? Wrong. Eight dollars to a minimum wage worker, as opposed to a corporate executive, is a different share of available assets to spend. In the membership context, will the payment of dues come out of the wallet of the person considering membership, or will his or her employer pay the membership fees? The answers to these questions alter the equation. Can you walk two blocks to the coffee shop, or do you have to drive eighteen miles? And it's not just the time it takes to realize the benefit, but the opportunity cost as well. What *could* I have been doing otherwise with my time? The investment of time will influence the ultimate value of that cup of coffee. This will be no different as people consider renewing or joining a membership organization.

And last, what is the end result of "value"? Ultimately, it is the answer to the question "Is it worth it?" And the answer to this question will be neither standard nor consistent across all the people considering the question, due to all the variables and variations of the perceived benefits and investment of time and money. As a membership professional, your job is to understand that the value proposition really is different for every single member or member prospect. And this makes it challenging when communicating the value *proposition*. The proposition is what you propose the value to be. Not an easy task, when the value perceived is so subjective!

The Value of Association Membership

Before we examine why people join associations and the value proposition question for membership professionals, it is important to understand why "memberships" are something sold in the first place. Trade and professional associations in general exist to accomplish lofty goals on behalf of an entire industry, profession, or segment of society. Associations need resources to accomplish those goals, such as people, influence, money, and so forth. Membership—paying a fee to be a "member" in an association—is a construct that facilitates an association's ability to gather the needed resources to accomplish its mission. If the mission and objectives (as well as a strategic plan) are crystal clear and are in alignment with what the industry or profession needs or wants, then you have the ability to create strong value for members.

When members and prospective members are looking to see what they get from your organization, they generally go directly to the member benefits page of your website (or to the membership brochure, if you're a bit old fashioned). That is where they hope to determine value, and that is where the value equation will be run. They will see the dues they are being asked to pay and the benefits they will receive in return. And thus they have the necessary components to run the value equation mentioned earlier. But since there could be several factors that influence (and rightly so) value, it is likely that you will be more effective if you are offering something other than a "one size fits all" membership.

Chapter 10 on Membership Categories and Dues Structures informs you about the ways in which you can segment your membership, which is a way of also segmenting and customizing value. A student member is going to examine value proposition quite differently than how a 20-year veteran in the industry will. By offering a graduating tier of benefits along with a graduating price model, you can offer a choice of value possibilities to your members. One example is with the Association for Independent Hospitality Professionals (AIHP). They have a standard membership offering for innkeepers of small lodging properties, and a higher-priced option that includes more benefits, such as a registration to their annual meeting, special recognition, and invitations to exclusive receptions.

Benefits and Answering the Question: "What's in It for Me?"

As people consider joining or renewing their membership in your association, and before they hit the "Submit Payment" button on the screen, they are going to think about what they get from the organization. And yet, as research findings in ASAE's book *The Decision to Join* point out, people are nearly evenly split on how much they value individual benefits and how much they value the work an association does for the common good of that industry, profession, or cause. Therefore, do not underestimate or understate the importance of the work that benefits everyone in your association's universe—not just the dues-paying members.

What kinds of "benefits" does your association facilitate or support that benefit the collective, rather than just the individual? Does your organization engage in lobbying or advocacy work on behalf of your industry or profession? If so, what victories or efforts have happened? Keep in mind that the efforts you are making with advocacy can be just as important as actual victories. Do the knowledge base and education you offer influence not only the dues-paying members, but an entire sector of society? When marketing your benefits, don't fail to mention the impact this work has on the greater collective. Unfortunately, after a review of many well-known association websites and their member benefits pages, most associations only tout the benefits received by the individual, dues-paying members.

As an example, think about the positive impact nurses have on our world—no matter the specific discipline or geography. And now think about how the world benefits from the successive improvements in nursing over time, due in no small part to the learning and advocacy that occur in nurses associations. Don't you think the associations should be touting the greater impact they are making on the world and how dues-paying members help make that happen? If ASAE reports the collective good is slightly more important to people than individual benefits, you would think more organizations would be spotlighting this. Many associations write about the collective good in their mission and vision statements. Don't assume members and prospects will read those statements. Articulate the collective benefit on your member benefits page, in your presentations, and anywhere else it makes sense. For example, CTIA: The Wireless Association lists among its member benefits "media exposure" and "public policy representation," which will benefit the industry as a whole at least as much as any individual member.

While some people are pleased and satisfied with the collective good an organization supports and facilitates, others are looking for more individual benefits. They want programs and services that help them in their careers, their businesses, and sometimes (directly or by extension) their personal lives. An accountant will typically join an accounting association, so that she may be better at being an accountant. The benefits and services offered through the association should help her achieve that. The programs and services may include online learning, a journal or magazine, conferences, and access to vendors that specialize in her field. An association of hardware stores may offer safety classes for the employees, as well as savings on industrial shelving or liability insurance. These are things a general manager of a hardware store may need to run a more stable and efficient operation.

In a successful association, members will feel that the total membership experience cannot be distilled down to a "dues for benefits" transaction. They will feel as though they are contributing to something greater than themselves, and yet also receiving something in return. These members may not blink an eye when renewing their membership. They may not feel the need to run the value equation in their minds, because they assume the value will be there. But not all members will feel such an ambiguously good feeling. Others will want to know exactly what you are doing for them. Communicating the value received is another important aspect to understanding membership value.

Communicating Value Received

The benefits you offer for the price you charge assumes the member or prospect will receive fair or good value. How do you communicate the value actually received by each member? Do you communicate this throughout the year? Just at the time of renewal? Do you communicate it at all? Some association executives may use the phrase "return on investment" (or ROI) when articulating to the member the value received.

ROI is a term often used in the financial world: What was my ROI on this investment of $10,000 in XYZ mutual fund? Did I receive an 8 percent return? In the association world, when communicating with your members about what they are receiving in return as a result of their membership dues, consider using a phrase like "total member value" or TMV. By using a term often used in the financial world, like ROI, members may only think about what financial return they have seen from their dues dollars. If you communicate it to them in this fashion, they may limit their thinking to this fashion. Financial return could or should only be part of what a member has received.

When should you communicate this total member value, and how? The answer to "when" is: more often than just at the time of membership renewal. Reminding members in subtle and creative ways about what they are receiving (either the individual benefits or the collective good benefits) helps members feel good about their investment during the duration of their membership. Yet, renewal time is a good time and an opportunity to give a comprehensive report on the value they are receiving. Most members may have little or no idea about the level and depth of what you're doing for them . . . so tell them! Don't be bashful about this. In addition, be sure you communicate all that you have done or offer, even if the member receiving the communication didn't avail himself of all the benefits. Just knowing what's available to a member can make that member feel good about the value, even if he or she didn't take advantage of all of it.

Discounts, products, and services that are included in the cost of membership are easily communicated to prospects and members alike in terms of dollars and cents. When describing the value of tangible benefits, you might say: The value of membership really adds up. From a $200 discount on our annual convention, to a free subscription to our monthly magazine ($45 value), to your complimentary listing in our industry guide (normally $149), it's easy to see how your $299 dues investment pays for itself.

Intangible benefits aren't necessarily less convincing than tangible benefits. But describing them does require more thought and creativity, and understanding them takes more effort on the part of the member or prospect. Consider how you might describe the value delivered to your members by your association's role in helping convince a senator to pass legislation that protects your members' interests. And don't forget that, even if the legislation hasn't passed yet, communicating the fact that you are working on it can be nearly as impactful to your members' judgment about their dues investment.

Underestimating the ability of your members and prospects to comprehend intangible benefits can weaken your value proposition. We all understand that everything in life can't be counted in dollars and cents, and you can play up the fact that some things your association does are priceless. When describing the value of intangible benefits, you might say: "Through our public service campaigns and the 40 million media impressions that followed, we helped increase public awareness of the important role you play in the business world. How can you put a dollar figure on that?"

If your members are by and large looking for a financial return, you can try to assign a dollar value to intangible benefits. In the case of your association's role in getting the senator to pass legislation, you could quantify the benefit by determining how much a member might have spent independently to lobby for the bill. Or if the bill ultimately resulted in a savings of time or resources for your members, estimate the dollar value of the savings. How do you measure the value of a contact made at a networking reception? What value do your members receive when your association helps portray their trade or profession in a favorable light though the media or trade press? Can you assign a dollar figure to increased knowledge that your members gain through all association programs? Communicate in terms of dollars, if you believe it will be effective. But also be mindful that, by doing so, you are also training your members to view value only in terms of dollars. Nonprofit associations do not typically exist, nor receive their tax-exempt status, for the purpose of delivering a financial return to members.

Here are a few ways you can communicate total member value (TMV) to your members:

- Attach a TMV report to the renewal notice that illustrates and spells out all of the great benefits and services. The more you can personalize this, the better. If you can customize each report in ways that demonstrate the value you know he or she received, that will be impressive (if the value is good!).

- Member check-up calls. If you have the staff or volunteer capacity, consider calling your members on the phone at least once a year. Not to sell them on coming to the conference. Not to just remind them that they are late paying their annual dues. Just a "How are you doing?" call, during which you can slip into the conversation any good news about the value of membership.

- Share video testimonials of your members explaining what they receive from being a member. Embed the videos in your emails, social media, and website.

- At your meetings, be sure to have members behind the microphone remind your audience about the good work you are doing.

See Chapter 15 on Membership Communication to discover other ways to directly communicate value, or places where you can shoe-horn it into other conversations or communications.

Benefits vs. Features

Is access to your association's membership directory a benefit of membership? Are networking events a benefit of membership? What about a compensation report? The answer to all three questions is no. All three are features. When describing benefits of membership, it's crucial to put yourself in the shoes of the prospect or member. When communicating about any program, the benefit is more powerful than the feature, because it defines the outcome or result for the user or participant. By connecting the dots for the prospect or member, you are getting to the heart of the value proposition faster and more effectively. If you just list the programs and features you offer, and don't explain the benefit, the value proposition may be lost on many.

Feature	Benefit
Membership Directory	Locate peers in your profession with whom you can solve problems, discuss ideas, or capitalize on opportunities.
Networking Events	Develop and strengthen contacts to help you advance your career, or give back to your profession by meeting people new to the field. Enjoy the fellowship of your peers.
Compensation Report	Make informed compensation decisions and requests based on the latest research.

Are Your Benefits Relevant, Effective, Both, or Neither?

Your value proposition is helped greatly by having benefits that are highly relevant to the purpose of your organization. But if those benefits are seen as ineffective by your membership, then the value proposition could be weak. Therefore, it's helpful to analyze which benefits are relevant, which are effective, which are both, or which are neither. The less relevant and the less effective your programs are (or are perceived to be), the weaker your value proposition may be.

If you want to take inventory of your programs in this way, you can survey your members and ask them one question about each and every benefit or program. For example, for an association of professional coffee baristas, you could ask them: "When thinking about your membership in the Professional Coffee Barista Association, how effective is this program or service?" To analyze how relevant the benefits are to the mission of the organization, consider running a similar survey with either your board of directors or all the various volunteer leaders in your organization. Your most involved members are more likely to be familiar and in-tune with the mission of the organization and should be better judges about the relevancy factor. Ask them one question about each benefit: "When thinking about the mission of the organization, how relevant is this benefit to achieving our mission?"

Figure 3.1 is a grid you can use to analyze the relevancy and effectiveness of your membership benefits (or potential benefits you are considering or working on). Using the barista association example again, the association may have a disability insurance program that is seen as highly effective, but not very relevant to the mission of the organization. Therefore, that benefit would be plotted in the upper left box. Also, the magazine published by the association, which is meant to be an educational tool, may be seen as highly relevant but not effective (maybe because the editorial content is written by the advertisers and not very insightful). That service would be plotted in the lower right quadrant.

Figure 3.1. Grid to Analyze Relevancy and Effectiveness

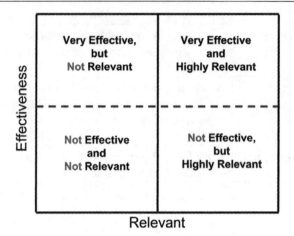

For any benefits that land in the lower left quadrant, you should strongly consider getting rid of them completely. Even if members don't avail themselves of a benefit that is neither relevant nor effective, just having that among your benefits could be a signal that you are out of touch with what your members need.

Ways to Improve Value

If value is an equation of "benefits minus price," the two basic ways to improve value for the end-user include altering the benefits or changing the price. And frankly, association executives should be analyzing both price and benefits all the time for everything from tweaks to wholesale change.

Although there are times when this may be prudent, rare is the association that is open to considering a total dues reduction for the same benefits. Lowering price as a tactic to gain more members will seem risky, since there is no guarantee the end result will actually be more members. Yet, if your value equation is "out of whack" (very high price for not much benefit), a big change to your pricing could be highly advisable.

If you are going to consider a new dues model, be sure to engage members and member prospects in the due diligence process. Test the waters. Survey. Interview people. Run hypothetical numbers and situations, including potential impact on attrition or recruitment. When you ask members or prospects for their opinions on pricing, be sure to ask the right questions in the right way to find the answer you need, which could be different from the answer you were looking or hoping for.

Let's assume the current price is $159 for the existing portfolio of benefits, which will not change under a new dues model. Here are different ways to answer the question about what price members or prospects would pay to be in your organization:

Bad

Based on the list of benefits above, which of the following prices do you want to pay for membership in the organization?

$99

$139

$199

Asking what price someone wants to pay will skew the prices to the lower side. After all, who WANTS to pay higher prices?

Better

Based on the list of benefits above, which of the following prices is as much as you will pay to feel like you are getting a fair or good value?

$99

$139

$199

Offering a choice of prices, while asking how much would they be willing to pay, could still skew low.

Good

Based on the list of benefits above, tell us what price you would pay to feel the following:

- Membership would be a fair value, if the price was no higher than [enter a number here].
- Membership would be a good value, if the price was no higher than [enter a number here].
- Membership would be a fantastic value, if the price was no higher than [enter a number here].

This allows the respondents to do more critical thinking about what they would pay, and it gives you some feedback on what might be an easy sell (fantastic value) and what might be a harder sell (fair value).

This last questioning method is akin to the "Van Westendorp Price Sensitivity Meter," which has customers revealing their sensitivity levels to various prices, for example: How low is so cheap that the product must not be good? How high can the price be to seem too expensive? This concept is worth exploring to get your pricing as effective as possible, while also demonstrating as a membership professional your mastery of the subject!

Another "good" approach would be to create different surveys and send them out to sections of your audience. This is a form of "split testing." Let's say you have a list of 1,500 people you want to survey about this potential dues change. You could divide the list into three sets of 500 people each, and ask the question in the following ways:

Set 1

Based on the list of benefits above, would you be willing to pay $99 for membership?

Yes or No

Set 2

Based on the list of benefits above, would you be willing to pay $139 for membership?

Yes or No

Set 3

Based on the list of benefits above, would you be willing to pay $199 for membership?

Yes or No

When analyzing the results, you may be surprised to find that just as many people in Set 3 answer Yes as in Set 2 or even Set 1. The number of people who answer No could give you a feel for both the attrition rate you might expect and the resistance you would have from member prospects to joining. Understanding price resistance, as opposed to just price acceptance or pricing desire, may give you the ceiling you are looking for, and the additional confidence to price in a way that gets you the resources you need.

Be sure to collect meaningful data on the respondents as you gather this information, so that you may run valuable cross-tabulations in your results. For example, "People early in their careers indicated X as the best target price for membership, whereas people who have been doing this 10 years or more indicate Y as the best target price."

The second way to improve value is to keep the investment steady, while increasing and/or improving the benefits. What if that coffee shop included a pastry with that cup of coffee, and for the same price? Obviously, the value would change for a lot of people—well, at least the ones who like pastries or who like to share pastries! Improving benefits is something not to be overlooked, as quality and quantity of benefits are part of this value equation. If the coffee house started using a higher-end bean or a better roaster, the experience of that cup of coffee might appreciably increase. Thus, the value improves. Let's say you've been operating a relatively old-fashioned email listserver community. You then upgrade the online community experience to a system with a slick online user interface, great search tools for archived conversations, and file sharing, and still maintaining an email-only option. Value in membership for many might now be greater.

In order to increase value, don't just add a smattering of new benefits without first having put them through the "relevancy and importance gauntlet." And be sure you have or will have all the necessary resources (staff, volunteers, technology, money) to manage the new benefits.

New Member Value

It is widely known in the membership profession that the toughest members to keep are often the newest members. Determining value is difficult for people who have never been in your organization and who are figuring it out for the first time during that first year of membership. Using another non-association analogy, the local golf course charges $75 for a round of golf. How would someone feel about that value who has never played the game or who is just dipping his toe in the water? And how would someone feel about that who has been an avid golfer for 15 years? One has already experienced the product or service (or in this case, the game), and is more willing to see value in the transaction.

There are a few things you can think about with regard to improving the value for those who might have the most difficult time seeing great value. First, you can offer a different price or special discounts for new members. That's a simple way to approach this. By offering a lower fee for entry, you're encouraging people to give it a shot. Lowering the investment lowers the perceived risk. You could also increase the benefits offered to new members, as a way to improve the value proposition. "Join by August 15th, and we'll also throw in. . . ." By doing this, you are maintaining price integrity. You're not lowering the threshold for entry, but you are trying to increase the perceived value proposition.

Taking the opposite approach, the Association of Otolaryngology Administrators offered a 10-month free trial to new members and removed any financial barriers to joining. This allowed practitioners to experience the association for long enough to understand and use the benefits. After running this trial in 2014, approximately a quarter of the "free" members renewed at the prevailing dues rate. The AOA reported that the renewal results fared better than any marketing campaign.

And last, you could do neither and just have a unique, strategic sales and marketing approach to your new members. You can alter the value proposition by educating people. Value proposition is greatest for the people who actually understand and use the benefits. It takes time to get to that point. Not until after attending conferences, engaging in the online community, reading the magazine, and making some association friends do people feel the highest value. If your prospective members understand the benefits before trying them on for size, they may get to that "higher value" mindset more quickly. Are your member prospect communications clear and effective in getting people to that higher value mindset? Are you using videos, testimonials, and effective language (that is, benefits versus features)? Are you available via phone, email, and online chat to prospects, so they can have their questions answered?

Conclusion

Getting back to the coffee shop example, just think about two different people looking at the price of a hot cup of Joe for $8: same price, same drink, and possibly two very different conclusions on value. Being a member of an association is not a one-size-fits-all, one-price-works-for-all proposition. Understanding this allows you to craft a benefits and pricing strategy that could work beautifully for your organization.

About the Author

Jay Karen, CAE, is CEO of the National Golf Course Owners Association (NGCOA), an organization representing owners and operators of golf courses throughout the United States. Prior to joining NGCOA, Karen was CEO of the Select Registry. He has been a speaker at ASAE conferences and served on ASAE's Executive Management and Membership Section Councils. Email: jay@ngcoa.org.

Governance as It Relates to Membership

4

By Charles W. L. Deale, FASAE, CAE

IN THIS CHAPTER

- Governance Is Not Management
- Translating Purpose into Focus
- Membership Functions for Governing Bodies
- But Danger Potentially Lurks
- How Membership Staff Can Support Their Governing Body

In developing the focus for this chapter, there were two approaches to the topic of governance and membership that are relevant and important to discuss, both of which could not be adequately addressed in the space limitations of the book.

The first approach was to delve into the myriad of roles that are commonly accepted as being appropriate for association governing bodies to engage in . . . and, conversely, those that generally are frowned upon and viewed as "no-no's" because they more properly fall into the realm of staff functions.

The second approach flips the governance-membership "coin" over and examines it from the perspective of the myriad roles that members play in the governance function: how members elect their governing bodies, the manner in which member perspectives are reflected on those bodies (representational versus at-large boards, for instance), where and when decisions can be vested with members versus boards (dues rates and increases, for example), opportunities by which members can become actively engaged, the distinctions between governance (fiduciary authority, corporate powers, etc.) and volunteerism, and so on.

Ultimately, the decision was made to address the myriad roles commonly accepted for governing bodies, largely because of its specific focus on how membership is integrated into so much of the deliberative work of governing bodies and, to play off this book's title, how *essential* that membership-related governance focus is in all aspects of association functions. This approach also better serves the primary audience of this book—association staff and those relatively new to the membership arena—many of whom may not be familiar with the role delineation between boards and staff, by providing suggestions for how staff can support their governing body.

As anyone with any measure of association management experience is well aware, there is *not* one size that fits all organizations when it comes to any association-related topic. Governance and membership certainly are not exceptions to this rule.

So it would be impossible and an exercise in futility to attempt to address every possible permutation in this chapter. Readers simply will have to accept that there are countless exceptions to what is presented and apply their own experiences and perspectives to the topics in the pages that follow.

Governance Is Not Management

Association consultant Robert C. Harris, CAE, issued a New Year's "resolution" for association boards that succinctly captured the overarching role that volunteer leaders should play. The affirmation from Harris read: "In 2015, I resolve to focus on the association's Purpose, Plan, and Performance."

By that, Harris meant that an organization's *purpose* or mission statement should frame board discussions; that board meeting agendas should be built upon organizational *plans* that serve as a multi-year roadmap and guide to resource allocation; and that *performance* measures or metrics should be established to gauge success.

Another thought leader and expert on the topic of governance, Glenn H. Tecker (2014), chief facilitator of ASAE's CEO Symposium and co-author of *The Will to Govern Well*, also concisely summarized a board's key function when he wrote that: "Your job is to look at what the organization is trying to accomplish and whether or not those things are getting done" (p. 26).

Finally, in timeless remarks offered 30 years ago, corporate CEO and nonprofit leader Kenneth N. Drayton (1986) stated his strong conviction that "Governance is governance. Management is management. Governance is not management. Every organization must clearly distinguish between them if it wants the two to work in harmony to achieve the institution's mission."

The ASAE Foundation's 2013 book, *What Makes High-Performing Boards: Effective Governance Practices in Member-Serving Organizations*, benchmarked governance practices at more than 1,500 associations. Out of that study group, only a small number (11 percent) received the highest performance rankings (half of those, interestingly, had annual budgets below $750,000).

According to researcher and book co-author Beth Gazley (2014), there were three things that set these top-tier associations apart from other organizations, one of which was a strong strategic orientation. Gazley wrote on the AssociationsNow.com website: "High-performing boards were twice as likely to invest substantial board meeting time to strategic considerations. Fully 99 percent of these boards were operating under an organizational strategic plan."

Translating Purpose into Focus

How do you take Harris's "purpose, plan, and performance"; Tecker's key board function; Drayton's "governance is governance"; and Gazley's strong strategic orientation and translate it into what association's governing bodies should focus on, specifically as it relates to the membership function?

Simultaneously, how does an association professional metaphorically draw a line in the sand and make it clear to elected leaders that the execution of policy—the day-to-day management of the organization—is properly left to staff (this is predicated, of course, on the assumption that an association has paid staff or has contracted with an association management firm and is not an entirely volunteer-run organization)?

Refrain from Intruding on Management's Domain

Certainly the most fundamental answer to the preceding questions is to ensure that clearly defined roles of elected (and other volunteer) leaders are articulated in the association's governing and other policy documents.

The ASAE Bylaws are one such example of this no-doubt-about-it definition. Article IV states in straightforward terms (with emphasis added here) that, "The governing body is the Board of Directors, which has authority and is *responsible for governance* of ASAE. The *Board establishes policy* and *monitors implementation of policy by ASAE's staff* under the direction of the President & CEO."

But even prior to taking a board seat—during the election cycle (and, where applicable, during the nominating process)—individuals should understand what are permissible and appropriate governance activities and where restraints exist. This then carries over into the on-boarding process so that, hopefully and ideally, a clear and unambiguous picture has been painted by the time an elected leader sits for his or her first meeting.

The Energy Education Council, Springfield, Illinois, takes this process of enlightenment a step further by having its directors sign a document reflecting their acquiescence with the commitment they are making.

The agreement, reprinted here as Exhibit 4.1 with the permission of the Council's executive director, Molly M. Hall, IOM, CAE, includes a clause that the board will not intrude on management's domain (administrative issues). And apropos to this chapter, the directors state their dedication and accountability to the Council's membership; their willingness to "actively promote" membership; and their desire to understand members' "common concerns."

Exhibit 4.1. Energy Education Council, Board of Directors Commitment Agreement

Mission Statement: The Energy Education Council creates a safer, smarter world.

As an elected member of the Board of Directors of the Energy Education Council, I state my commitment and dedication to the mission, to the membership, and to my colleagues on the Board and the staff of the Energy Education Council in carrying out this mission. I understand that my duties and responsibilities include the following:

- To understand and define the organization's mission, values, and purpose.
- To receive no financial gain for service on the Energy Education Council Board of Directors and agree to disclose any actual or possible conflict of interest.
- To understand my accountability to the Energy Education Council membership and will exercise leadership in making sound judgments in the best interest of Energy Education Council.
- To refrain from intruding on administrative issues that are the domain of the management.
- To hold in the strictest confidence any and all subjects of discussion, business and related communications designated as confidential by the Energy Education Council Board of Directors.
- To actively promote membership, both by recruitment and emphasis on retention in Energy Education Council, and encourage fellow colleagues to become active. I will continually make myself familiar with current activities of Energy Education Council and will encourage and support the staff.
- To attend and participate in Energy Education Council Board meetings, and respond to Board communications. I will come to Board meetings prepared and ready to participate in a meaningful fashion, will arrive on time, and not depart until the meeting is adjourned.
- To share in the fiscal oversight responsibility for Energy Education Council with all other Board members. I will maintain a familiarity with the Council budget and take an active part in reviewing, monitoring, and supporting the approved budget.
- To understand that the Board shall speak with a unified voice on behalf of the organization, and will seek to understand and share the membership's common concerns. I understand that others may construe my comments to represent the policies and members of Energy Education Council, and will be informed and speak with care accordingly.

I understand that the Energy Education Council Board of Directors may ask me to resign from the board if I cannot substantially fulfill these responsibilities or may remove me from the board per the directions specified in the Energy Education Council bylaws. I understand the importance of the expectations listed above and by signing below I accept this commitment.

| _____ | _____ | _____ |
| Printed Name | Signature | Date |

Now, does what has just been described mean that directors are not and should not be (to varying degrees) "doers"—rolling up their sleeves and undertaking tasks? Are their functions merely, though not inconsequentially, limited to governance and policy (as per the ASAE Bylaws)? Absolutely not! There certainly are hands-on functions that directors can and should undertake, both to fulfill their duties and to advance the organization that they represent. Indeed, a number of specific examples now follow.

Membership Functions for Governing Bodies

Henry L. Ernstthal, CAE, wrote in *Principles of Association Management* (2001) that "Almost every decision made by an association . . . has some bearing on membership . . . [and] cannot be made in a vacuum; they must be integrated into the overall decision-making process so that every action is analyzed for its membership consequences" (p. 62).

Even though countless new models have emerged in the decade and a half since Ernstthal penned those words, the fundamentals have remained constant: membership stability remains critical to the well-being and sustained viability of almost all trade and professional associations. As such, it is incumbent upon governing bodies to remain closely attuned to and, more often than not, active "players" in the membership arena.

Following are a number of key membership-related subjects or functions in which governing bodies (primarily referred to here as "boards") typically are or should be engaged in a strategic, policy, and/or oversight capacity, and in which individual directors can be actively engaged.

Dues Structures

Membership dues structures typically are a function or offshoot of organizational type—for example, a flat rate for all members (individual membership organizations, or IMOs) or an escalating rate based on attributes (trade associations) . . . or perhaps some combination thereof when an organization has a mixture of membership types. The seventh edition of the *Membership Marketing Benchmarking Report* (2015) published annually by Marketing General Inc., Alexandria, Virginia, noted that IMOs are evenly split between an everyone-pays-the-same dues structure and dues based on specific attributes, while three-fourths of trade associations report that dues are based on attributes (p. 58).

Governing bodies need to regularly review, and modify as necessary, their organization's existing dues structure to ensure it remains in sync with prevailing practices in its particular profession or industry.

An example of an association that reconfigured its structure is the Washington, D.C.–based American Alliance of Museums. The AAM, which has four membership categories, shifted its model to provide three "tiered" offerings for its museum member category—Full Suite, Enhanced Access, and The Basics. The most creative aspect of this approach is that the low-end tier has no set dues; rather, museums opting for The Basics are given the choice to "pay what you want."

Active Engagement

Barbara Kachelski, CAE, executive director of the American Academy of Cosmetic Dentistry, Madison, Wisconsin, believes that a key theme for board members is for them to be "magnets" for the organization, attracting and not repelling members and future volunteers by their words and actions, both when their volunteer hats are "on" and when they are not.

Association consultant Douglas C. Eadie cautioned against board members becoming overly involved in hands-on work at the expense of governing. Eadie (2004) stated that organization boards have "effectively involved their members in the following activities without diluting their governing work" (p. 70). Examples he listed were:

- Visibly participating in key organization events to signal the board's commitment.

- Making key presentations when member or client support is a critical issue.

- Playing a leading role in implementing initiatives involving key stakeholders.

7 Measures of Success (pp. 74–75) noted that remarkable associations engage board members as a set of eyes and ears for the organization, asking what members need (as opposed to "good" associations, who decide what members need) and talking *with* (versus *to*) members at every opportunity. "We found a commitment to mining data from just about every encounter with members. The staff and leaders at remarkable associations are constantly listening to members and sharing the information they glean from those contacts" (p. 39).

And the *Associations Now Volunteer Leadership Issue* (2015, pp. 57–58) described board members' roles as including being a "membership influencer." "Board members can play a key role in membership recruitment and engagement by virtue of their position and influence," wrote Joe Rominiecki. Association CEO Mark Golden, FASAE, CAE, added that "the board has a degree of credibility and direct touch, and a lot of times it can say things far more convincingly than staff. Golden also noted that directors often see more members (and potential members) face-to-face than staff can ever reach.

Data from the Marketing General *Membership Marketing Benchmarking Report* (2015) validates the preceding perceptions. Responding associations—both individual and trade—overwhelmingly indicated that word-of-mouth recommendations (which, of course, are inclusive of, but not limited just to, board members) are the recruitment marketing channel that generates the most new members (p. 23).

So, to circle back to Barb Kachelski's belief and the data that support it, associations should actively engage their governing body members as "magnets" to help the organizations grow.

Marketplace Expansion

Increasingly in recent years, associations—and the boards that govern them—have been analyzing and often acting on options that seek to expand their penetration into markets not previously a part of their core membership base. Most prevalent is geographic expansion, particularly the decision to pursue a global orientation, although there also are associations that traditionally were state or regionally based and decided to "spread their wings."

Both Ernstthal and Sarah L. Sladek, author of *The End of Membership As We Know It* (2011), summarize a variety of issues that must be considered by associations when deliberating an international strategy: dues payments (amounts and acceptable currencies), services to be provided, electronic-only services or provision of all services (including print), organizational capacity to effectively take on the expansion, relationship of traditional benefits (advocacy, for example) to the newly targeted constituents, and potential for alienating the core membership base (perception that they're being overlooked).

Still other associations seek to expand horizontally or vertically within their long-standing membership base—an example being hotel and motel associations absorbing other elements of the travel and tourism sectors and rebranding themselves. To cite one specific organization as an example, the Virginia Hospitality and Travel Association now encompasses hotels, other lodging, restaurants, and travel destinations/destination marketing organizations.

So whether it's necessitated by contraction within the traditional marketplace; the emergence of new markets; a desire to absorb existing sectors; a strategic initiative to expand geographically; or some other factor(s), governing bodies need to regularly deliberate on "who" and "what" issues—who they want the association to represent and what they want the organization to look like.

Membership Categories or Models

Sladek declares in *The End of Membership As We Know It* that many of the traditional association memberships "For hundreds of years . . . have been cut from the same cloth" (p. 95) are, if not dead, then at least in critical condition. Sladek adds that "membership associations are introducing a variety of operational models" and that "Innovation is a must." In Chapter 6 of the book, she describes five emerging models in particular and cites a variety of associations that have instituted these new approaches to membership.

If your organization is confronting what Sladek describes as "the choice between survival and extinction" (p. 94), or some middle ground between, then your governing body would be well-served to undertake a journey of exploration to discover whether any existing categories should be jettisoned, new ones unveiled or—most dramatically—an entirely new model for the association should be crafted.

Dual Memberships

Many associations have dual (national and regional or state, for example) or multi-layered (national, state, local) membership arrangements. For example, REALTORS® first join a local real estate association, and that automatically extends their membership to the state and national associations. There is no commonplace standard in this area; practices vary widely.

Similarly, there is no prevalent practice in terms of dual memberships being optional or mandatory. Ernstthal in *Principles of Association Management* (pp. 61–62) advised associations contemplating a chapter-based structure (or examining the continued viability of an existing structure) to "consider whether membership will be integrated—that is, whether a member must belong to the national organization in order to belong to a state or local chapter. The alternative is empowering chapters to take on local members who have not joined at the national level. Either situation has significant potential for turf battles and competition for members between the parent organization and the chapters." Truly a two-edged sword that governing body members must deal with delicately and diplomatically!

Dues Rates

Policies vary widely among associations in terms of stating specific prevailing dues rates in governing documents and also in establishing who has the authority to create and adjust those rates (i.e., the board or the full membership).

Several examples are illustrative of this:

- National Press Photographers Association, representing visual journalists— NPPA's policies and procedures document specifies the current rates for each membership category, meaning that any rate adjustment requires an amendment to the document (such amendments are approved by the board, not the membership).

- CFA Institute—The bylaws for this global association of investment professionals state: "CFA Institute shall have the right to establish and collect dues for members of CFA Institute." Note that the language is purposely vague in terms of to whom that "right" is granted—the Board of Governors or management.

- NATSO, Inc., representing America's truck stops and travel plazas—This trade association's bylaws read: "The Board of Directors shall have the power to fix a schedule of dues for and within each class." Again, no specific mention of current rates and no involvement of the membership in establishing those rates.

- ASAE—There is no specific mention of or reference to dues in the bylaws.

Besides determining rates (or recommending those rates to the membership for consideration, where required) on an annual basis, governing bodies often deliberate on a host of other rate-related issues: sliding scale or set amount (according to the previously cited Marketing General study, the majority of trade associations have a sliding scale; IMOs do not); same, higher, or lower rates for international members versus domestic members (for U.S.-based associations); accepting only a single currency (for example, U.S. dollars) for payment of dues or allowing multiple currencies when non-U.S. members are involved; determining what dues will or will not cover (what programs and services will be included, and what will be unbundled); establishing dues maximums or "caps" for large corporate members; and others.

That last issue—caps or maximums (not unusual at organizations where the largest members have dues running well into six figures)—can, according to Ernstthal in *Principles of Association Management* (p. 56), "present problems if the industry is consolidating. If a member paying maximum dues absorbs another member, the organization loses the latter's dues completely." So governing bodies need to be prepared to address what potentially can be a politically divisive issue that, if handled poorly, can have long-term negative financial and reputational implications for the organization.

Dues Increases

Much like dues rates, practices vary widely among associations in terms of to whom the authority is invested to approve adjustments in dues rates. The 2015 *Marketing General Benchmarking Report* reports that 22 percent of IMOs and one-third of trade associations increase their dues annually. But by strong margins, 63 percent and 57 percent, respectively, both types of associations only raise dues as needed.

Boards need to determine the approach they will take in approving—or, again, recommending to the membership for approval—dues adjustments: an ad-hoc, as needed approach (if so, based presumably on appropriate data to justify the hike) or an automatic escalator, perhaps based on the Consumer Price Index.

Special Assessments

These are not common among associations, especially individual membership groups, but the need periodically does arise in certain circumstances to impose them—for example, for a legislative battle, headquarters building fund, or public awareness initiative (such as the National Association of REALTORS® Consumer Advertising Campaign).

Special assessments—by the very nature of the word "special"—obviously require careful consideration by governing bodies (as do all financial-related matters, of course) before their authorization. Groups also need to determine whether the assessments will be mandatory or voluntary. In other words, if the former, will failure to pay the assessment result in revocation of membership?

And boards also should decide that, even if they are granted the authority to institute an assessment (as, for example, the American Gas Association's board is as per the AGA's bylaws: "The rates of membership dues *and the amounts of any special assessments* shall be fixed by the Board of Directors"), would it be prudent and appropriate to present the "case" for the special assessment to the membership for discussion and, possibly, a vote?

Dues Reporting Oversight

Typically, when dues payments are on a sliding scale based on some unit(s) of measure (sales, locations, volume, etc.), associations rely on the honor system. In other words, they trust their members to be accurate in their self-assessments and pay the appropriate amount of dues. The Russian proverb "trust but verify" that became a well-known phrase by President Reagan seldom comes into play with associations and dues payments.

But if boards have questions or doubts about the veracity of some members' payments, they can opt to monitor the situation more carefully and seek to validate (or adjust) the information.

At one trade association for which I held a membership position earlier in my career, the elected officers chose to review the units of measure that members had self-reported (dues invoices were generated based on the information that members submitted). The officers unilaterally bumped up some members' units based on their knowledge of the members' operations—and, surprisingly, not a single one of those members objected when they received their invoices reflecting a higher dues amount! So, at times, perhaps "trust but verify" *is* a course of action that boards should take!

Adjudicating Violations

This is, admittedly, very dangerous terrain on which associations must tread extremely carefully and which has the potential for serious legal implications. It is one thing when members voluntarily resign membership or allow that membership to lapse. However, it's quite a different matter when a member is alleged to have violated an organization's code or standards and potentially is subject to disciplinary action. In some cases, the governing body acts as judge or jury and metes out, as warranted, sanctions. In other instances, the process might be handled by a board-designated body, such as an ethics or judiciary committee, with the board acting in an appellate capacity.

Seeking the advice of legal counsel and ensuring that proper insurance protections are in place for those serving on governing bodies certainly is advisable for associations engaging in adjudications procedures.

Monitoring Results, Trends, and Projections

The landmark research project commissioned by ASAE and its then-existing Center for Association Leadership that resulted in the best-selling book *7 Measures of Success: What Remarkable Associations Do That Others Don't* (2006, 2012) had as a key measure, data-driven strategies.

The authors wrote: "If there's one phrase that sets remarkable associations apart from their counterparts, it's 'Data, data, data.' They gather information, analyze it, and then use it to become even better. Research . . . is always put to use, not put on the shelf" (p. 38).

In a similar vein, *Race for Relevance: 5 Radical Changes for Associations* written by Harrison Coerver and Mary Byers, CAE, and published by ASAE in 2011, stated that a first step for competency-based boards is to "analyze the major challenges and opportunities for the association in the next five to 10 years. What high-impact trends or developments will affect the membership, the members' market, or the association's environment?" (p. 34).

This "data, data, data" mentality should be a recurring and constant practice for governing bodies—studying performance dashboards (results versus goals; market penetration; year-over-year trends; long-range projections; environmental scans;

and so forth) and all other available data, and discussing the implications of that information, so that properly informed conclusions can be reached and decisions made.

But Danger Potentially Lurks!

Board members may—indeed, typically do—have the best of intentions and genuinely feel that they are a microcosm of the "typical" association member, and thus can accurately represent what all members are thinking.

Oh, the danger that often lurks in that mentality!

Consultant Douglas Eadie (2004) related the frequency with which he has witnessed board members "confusing wishful thinking with reality" (p. 71). Eadie cited the example of an organization's board being "flabbergasted" by the results of a membership survey (a survey the board had questioned the need for since they were confident of the members' deep satisfaction) that uncovered profound skepticism about the value of the organization. Eadie described this as the "all-too-common tendency for self-deception."

Involvement and Personal Perspective

The Decision to Join (ASAE, 2007) did a comparison of different levels of involvement of individuals—governance; committee; ad hoc; nonparticipants—on a number of questions. A brief summary of the researchers' analysis follows.

People involved at the highest level may take on a more collective view of the association's activities, one that reflects their leadership responsibilities and thereby differs with the personal perspective of most other respondents. This concept may account for the differences in the way leaders at the governing level rank the importance of these activities as compared with other respondents.

Several important observations stem from this comparison. All of them are conjectural but worth raising for discussion:

1. The first has already been made. Leaders do have a different perspective, and it is one that indicates greater concern for the good of the order, which is both laudable and an expectation of leadership.

2. The second is that governance-level people who think they don't need empirical data on the way rank-and-file members evaluate the importance of programs, because as elected leaders they are in touch with the rank-and-file that elected them, might be well advised to look closely at the difference between their views and nearly everyone else's.

3. The third may be a small point, but the extreme difference between leaders and everyone else on the importance of "gathering, analyzing, and publishing data on trends in the field" is curious. Why is there such a difference? This is a strength of many trade associations, and many observers have noted that individual membership organizations could do a better job of this. Perhaps the rank-and-file in individual membership organizations agree.

Similarly, frequent ASAE speaker Jeff De Cagna, FASAE, wrote in *Associations Now* (2013, pp. 48–50) that "Board members often do not fully appreciate that for the majority of stakeholders, the experience of association membership is not nearly as immersive and rich." He added: "most association boards 'don't know what they don't know' . . . and many believe their associations are already doing the right things." Consultant De Cagna concluded by cautioning that boards need to avoid a "willful blindness" and stressing that they have a duty to "build a deep understanding of the organization's existing business model . . . and ensure the model is sustainable."

Still more: Mark Golden (2015), FASAE, CAE, executive director of the National Society of Professional Engineers, Alexandria, Virginia, stated in *Associations Now*: "Most board members are so engaged with their associations, and have been for so long, that their perceptions and values are far different from the rank and file" (p. 57).

What, then, are the answers or solutions to this "wishful thinking" or "willful blindness" mentality?

For one, Golden, a key participant in the *7 Measures of Success* task force, harkens back to the "data, data, data" commitment and strategy so that boards make informed decisions based on solid research. As the book states: "Remarkable associations also face the facts: They're not so arrogant as to presume that they know better than what the data tell them" (pp. 39–40). So when a board member says: "I know what the members want," diplomatically ask him or her to back up the claim with quantifiable facts.

And for another, since it can't be assumed that elected leaders correctly can identify the priorities of rank-and-file members, arm them with the information they need. For example, ASAE's 2007 study *The Decision to Join* remains a go-to resource for understanding the fundamental reasons why people join associations (or don't). The study includes a companion guide, *Supporting the Decision to Join: What Association Boards Should Know and Do About Membership and Affiliation.*

How Membership Staff Can Support Their Governing Body

You now have a better understanding of the wide range of membership-related issues with which governing bodies must regularly or periodically grapple and the impact that their decisions and actions can have on organizational effectiveness. How, then, can you contribute to this important function for which volunteer leaders are responsible, and facilitate their success in fulfilling that duty? Here are several tips that enable you to provide added value.

- First, start internally and obtain guidance from your association's CEO (if you are not serving in that capacity) or your immediate supervisor in terms of the extent, if at all, you are allowed or expected to interact directly with members of the governing body. Can you contact them directly on membership-related matters, or must the flow of information come from someone to whom you report? Many associations are very particular about this issue!

- Once that internal operational issue is resolved, and assuming you have permission to work directly with your board, seek to become a trusted advisor to your leaders—and for them to be valuable sources of knowledge to you. You bring to them the type of expertise in membership marketing that they likely lack. Concurrently, they possess knowledge on the industry or profession that your organization represents, so express your interest in and appreciation for the insights they can share. In short, complement and supplement one another!

- Be forever mindful of the fact that things happen on *their* schedule, not *yours*. You are paid to do your job; this is a volunteer "job" for them. So be sensitive to the amount of time they can commit, when they can do so, and the volume of information they can handle that you might send their way.

- And speaking of information, provide regular statistics, research results, etc.—but make sure it's concise and actionable. Offer your interpretations regarding what the data mean, the implications, possible actions that can be taken, and so forth. The board members (both individually and collectively as a body) will reach their own conclusions and decisions, but you can help inform that process with appropriate analysis.

- Just like you, volunteer leaders like to know which membership activities have worked well previously and which have fallen short of expectations. Share lessons learned with them so that they have the ability to build on prior successes and avoid replicating failures.

- When board members are asked (or expected) to take specific actions—for example, contacting new members, calling members who are up for renewal, or visiting in person with prospective members—make sure that they are supplied with adequate and appropriate collateral material that will facilitate their efforts. An example could be providing a concise (1 to 2 pages) briefing paper that summarizes key background information on a potential member with whom the board member will be meeting.

- Finally, have in place easy-to-use feedback and after-action follow-up mechanisms. Make it simple to learn (via a phone call, email, text message, or short form) what resulted from the volunteer leader's action, and also ensure that timely and thorough follow-up takes place. Leave nothing to doubt!

Consistently support the members of your governing body with these tips—and other ideas you might have—and you'll likely find that you have allies who will be willing and eager to advance your association's membership cause.

References

ASAE. *7 Measures of Success: What Remarkable Associations Do That Others Don't.* Washington, DC: ASAE, 2006, 2012.

Bowers, Ashley, & Gazley, Beth. *What Makes High-Performing Boards: Effective Governance Practices in Member-Serving Organizations.* Washington, DC: ASAE, 2013.

Coerver, Harrison, & Byers, Mary. *Race for Relevance: 5 Radical Changes for Associations.* Washington, DC: ASAE, 2011.

De Cagna, Jeff. *Associations Now,* March 2013.

Dignam, Monica, & Dalton, James. *The Decision to Join: What Association Boards Should Know and Do About Membership and Affiliation.* Washington, DC: ASAE, 2007.

Drayton, Kenneth N. Speech to Independent Sector Leadership/Management Forum, 1986. Independent Sector Monograph, 2001.

Eadie, Douglas C. *High-Impact Governing in a Nutshell: 17 Questions That Board Members and CEOs Frequently Ask.* Washington, DC: ASAE, 2004.

Ernstthal, Henry L. *Principles of Association Management* (4th ed.). Washington, DC: ASAE, 2001.

Gazley, Beth. www.AssociationsNow.com. February 2014.

Golden, Mark. *Associations Now Volunteer Leadership Issue,* January/February, 2015.

Marketing General. *Membership Marketing Benchmarking Report.* Alexandria, VA: Marketing General, Inc., 2015.

Sladek, Sarah L. *The End of Membership As We Know It.* Washington, DC: ASAE, 2011.

Tecker, Glenn H. *Associations Now,* January/February 2014.

Tecker, Glenn H., Frankel, Jean S., & Meyer, Paul D. *The Will to Govern Well: Knowledge, Trust, and Nimbleness.* Washington, DC: ASAE, 2002.

About the Author

Charles W. L. "Chip" Deale, FASAE, CAE, is executive director of the National Press Photographers Association, Athens, Georgia. A career-long association executive, Deale is the former chair of both the ASAE Executive Management and Membership-Marketing section councils; a past member of the ASAE Board of Directors; and was the inaugural recipient of ASAE's Professional Performance Award.

Membership Is a Team Sport

Working with Other Departments

By Sara Miller, MBA, PMP, CAE

5

IN THIS CHAPTER

- Your Association's Goals
- The Membership Department
- Member Benefits
- What Do Other Departments Do? (and How Can You Help?)
- Say No to Silos
- Transforming Actions into Value

I f you took snippets of membership publications over the last few years, you might be scouring LinkedIn and contemplating a career move. From the retirement rate of Boomers to the changing needs of the Millennials, membership isn't what it used to be.

- In 2011, Coerver and Byers released *Race for Relevance.* They presented five radical changes that successful organizations must make to thrive in this new world, including refining the membership model to better reflect today's market and a specific audience: ". . . the days of the broad-based association's or professional society's ability to add value to diverse and complex member markets is coming to an end" (p. 76).

- According to Jamie Notter and Maddie Grant in *When Millennials Take Over,* "Every 20 years or so, a new generation enters the workforce, and the rest of us, quite frankly, freak out about it" (p. 2).

- Sarah Sladek's *The End of Membership as We Know It* focused on rebuilding the association to reflect the new business environment. She talks about revisiting the needs of all members and rethinking the membership model: "Membership associations that refuse to implement change and interest younger members have a 10-year life-span—at most" (p. 71).

Are you wondering whether it's 5 o'clock (somewhere)? Don't fret. Membership organizations need to change, but there are rewards for those who do so successfully. To grow, you need to understand how the association and other departments view and value membership.

Your Association's Goals

Some nonprofits are working toward a clear end, for example, eradication of a certain disease, and they will happily disband when that end becomes reality. This outlook may not apply to your association, so make sure you understand the organization's purpose. After all, if you're going to evolve the membership structure, you need to know where the organization is going. Even if you've been in your position for a while, it's important to take a step back and re-learn the organization. This means looking outside the confines of membership. Table 5.1 provides some questions to ask.

You have to understand what the association is trying to accomplish. This sets the stage for all the work to come. When you see the big picture, you can be more strategic and increase membership's likelihood of success.

Table 5.1. Association 101

Resource	Sample Questions
Vision and/or mission statement	Where is the organization trying to go?
	How is it going to get there?
"About Us" section of your website	How does the association translate the vision/mission?
	What accomplishments are cited as examples of organizational impact?
Strategic plan	What new initiatives are on the horizon?
	How do they relate to membership?
Recent annual reports	How important is dues revenue to the annual budget?
	Where is the recent growth in organizational revenue?
Survey data	What do members want and how has that changed?
	What products/programs/services are most popular?
Environmental scans	Who are your association's major competitors?
	How has the landscape changed over the last few years?

The Membership Department

If you want your organization to truly be part of the Membership Economy, start with the team and the culture. You need to have the right people and prioritize the right values.

(*The Membership Economy*, Robbie Kellman Baxter, p. 33)

Regardless of your industry, you need customers. We can talk about the impact of Boomers retiring or how hard it is to connect with Millennials or what to make of the forthcoming iGeneration. But, at the end of the day, your association needs people if it's going to succeed.

Enter the membership department. You need to find, engage, and keep your customers. Your goal is to make a member out of every customer, to convert individuals from free to fee. You've probably heard (even said) the phrase "membership is everyone's job," but if your department's name includes "member" or "membership," then you're not like everyone else. Membership starts with you.

Understand How the Executives See Membership

Membership departments are as different as the associations they represent. Structures, responsibilities, and size vary greatly. It's important that you understand how and where you fit in the organization. If you reviewed Table 5.1, then you understand what the organization says and how it presents membership. Now you need to understand how staff work with and feel about membership. How do you do this? Start by interviewing the executives and/or leadership team. Here are some of the questions I asked when I started a new position:

1. What do you think our members want? Don't want?

2. Why were you a member of the association?

3. Do you have any ideas for the membership department?

4. Do you have any advice for me as the (new) membership director?

5. Here's an example of a recent membership recruitment email. What do you like? What don't you like?

If you're new, these questions can help guide the conversation. If you're a tenured staffer, the questions can help you take a fresh look at the organization. In either case, it's important to let the conversation advance naturally.

Understand How Other Departments See Membership

The next step is to understand where membership's work intersects with other departments. This overlap can occur in at least two ways:

1. Internal functions that are split or shared by multiple units:
   a. Example: Membership enters refunds, but accounting has to review and process.
   b. Example: Publications creates the monthly journal, but membership sends the monthly mailing list to the printer.

2. Products/benefits that are created by one department then promoted by membership:
   a. Example: Publications creates the monthly journal, but it's promoted as a primary feature of membership.
   b. Example: Meetings/events plans and manages the annual conference, but it's primarily attended by members and the registration discount is a key feature of membership.

While membership may be responsible for both benefit creation and delivery, it's unlikely that this is true for all products, programs, and services. Instead, membership needs outputs from around the organization to continually reaffirm the value of the association and belonging.

Shared Internal Functions and New Opportunities

The membership team relies heavily on other departments to deliver the promised member experience. Key cross-department functions include Accounting, IT, and Publications. It's important to understand what other departments do broadly and how that work impacts membership specifically. (See Table 5.2.)

Table 5.2. Identifying Connections Between Membership and Other Departments

Function	Membership's Role	Other Departments	Dependencies/ Opportunities
Dues Processing	What is the membership department doing for these specific areas?	What are other departments doing for these specific areas?	Where are the intersections between membership and the other department(s)?
Customer Service			
Marketing			
Engagement		How does the work tie to specific member features?	Where are opportunities to further support each other?
Volunteers			
Sales			
Events			
Groups			

Although you could complete the above table on your own, resist the temptation. Get out of your office and go talk to your colleagues. Grab coffee or meet for lunch. Have an in-depth conversation that doesn't center around today's crisis or upcoming due dates. What are the opportunities for collaboration between departments? How can the groups benefit each other? For example, your Publications department produces a monthly journal. That journal is an important member feature. What are new opportunities to further promote the journal's content to increase membership? You need to understand how the departments are connected. You will quickly see that success in one area filters through to the rest of the association.

These meetings should not be a one-time occurrence. As you become more comfortable in your position, it's easy to be caught up in daily activities. Don't get stuck! Consider scheduling these meetings with your colleagues every 6 (or 3 or 1) months to talk big picture about projects and potential opportunities.

> If your organization isn't comfortable with this type of collaboration, you may need to ease into it. Start with someone you know who is open to the approach. If you've been at the association for a while, then you probably know who to call on. If you're new, wait a month or two, giving yourself time to understand the culture and find your allies.

Understand How Your Team Sees Membership

There are two parts to this. The first is more short-term: What is the team doing on a daily basis? What are the routine tasks? The second piece is long-term: What are the new projects you want to work on? What does membership look like in 1, 3, or 5 years?

Membership's Daily Activities

If you don't already have it, spend time documenting everything the membership department does. Mind maps are incredibly useful for this type of brainstorming. According to Wikipedia, a mind map is "a diagram used to visually organize information" (https://en.wikipedia.org/wiki/Mind_map). The map is helpful because it lets you brainstorm with structure as each node focuses on a different area with the flexibility to drill down as much as you need.

The goal is to think through everything your department is working on. The diagram should be comprehensive, with only as much detail as needed to make the item clear to all participants/readers. You could write a paragraph to describe your department's work, but the image works better.

Creating the diagram makes for a good team exercise as people get to share what they do. An added benefit is that you will probably identify immediate takeaways and improvements as people find duplicate functions or share tips for automation.

You can create a mind map on a whiteboard or piece of paper, but there are plenty of free online tools as well. Coggle.it can help you create a simple, starter mind map, like the one in Figure 5.1, in less than 10 minutes. It's important to find the medium that works for you and your team.

Membership's Strategic Planning

With so much change in the association world, the future seems unclear—except for the fact that we all need to evolve. I often hear executives ask: "What would this association look like if we were building it today?" It's a good question. With changing demographics, the growth of online communities, and the opportunities that come with globalization, what would an association founded today look like?

Taking the mind map of daily activities, consider a world 2 to 5 years from now where those tasks are no longer necessary (because they're being done by robots, obviously). It's not a stretch to envision a world in which many of the tasks that keep us busy today are no longer on our plates. And what will your team do then? It's time to re-imagine what "membership" means in the modern world. Start talking with your team about the future.

You need to spend time understanding how your department sees membership. It is very difficult for others to understand membership if your department isn't on the same page.

Figure 5.1. Mind Map of Membership's Daily Activities

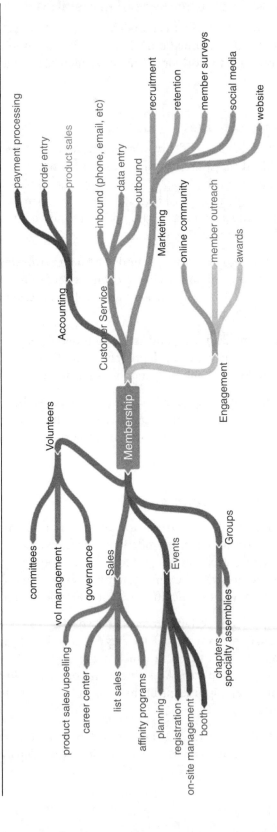

Member Benefits

Benefit creation, benefit delivery, and benefit promotion are not always housed in the same department. Success then depends on the various parties agreeing to a game plan and holding each other accountable. You need to understand your member benefits—what they are, where they come from, and who promotes them. See the sample in Table 5.3 from a previous association that highlights member offerings and which departments are involved at various phases.

Table 5.3. Ownership of Member Features

Member Feature	Creation	Delivery	Promotion
Journal/magazine	Publications	Publications	Publications/Membership
Annual meeting	Meetings	Meetings	Meetings/Membership
Online community	Membership	Membership	Membership
Product discount	Publications	IT	Membership
Component groups	Membership	Membership	Membership
Voting rights	Governance	IT	Governance/Membership

Conducting a similar audit in your association will reinforce the considerable dependencies across program areas. If the other departments ceased to exist, membership wouldn't be far behind. You rely on the products, programs, and services they provide. Create a work environment that supports the efforts of all parties.

What Do Other Departments Do? (and How Can You Help?)

From your meetings and collaboration with other departments, you'll learn what your colleagues are trying to accomplish. Spend time thinking through how you can help them. See the sample in Table 5.4.

Table 5.4. Membership Department Promoting Other Departments

Issue	Education department wants to promote a new product.
Opportunity	The membership department is talking with members on a regular basis.
	If you have an on-boarding series for new/renewing members, you could feature this new product. It would be great if the product is member-only or if members receive a price discount, but that's not needed. You can highlight the product as yet another example of the association's commitment to advancing the profession.
	Assuming you're sending invoices on a regular basis, you could include a buck slip about the new product. Buck slips don't typically increase postage costs unless you are already close to the weight limit. If you're concerned that the insert could depress results, consider testing packages with the buck slip against your control.

(continued)

Table 5.4. (Continued)

Issue	Publications department wants to increase page visits.
Opportunity	The journal (and/or magazine) is likely a top benefit of membership. As such, it makes sense to increase promotion around the periodical to both new and lapsed members.
	At past associations, we successfully used a journal incentive to renew members via a telemarketing campaign. The incentive was a PDF of the top 10 articles from the last year. It's true that individuals would have access to all the articles when they re-joined and it's true that, depending on when they lapsed, they may have had access to/read all of the top articles. Still, people liked the exclusivity and convenience of the resource.

Issue	Events department is concerned with the possibility of low attendance at next year's annual meeting.
Opportunity	Low attendance hurts the membership department too, as many members renew around the meeting.
	Consider joining forces (and budgets) and starting recruitment campaigns months before the meeting. You can target areas close to the meeting location (perhaps within driving distance). The focus is on all that the association has to offer year-round that culminates in the annual meeting, which is right in their backyard.
	If you have chapters/affiliates/sections, you can work with them to offer a special discount to members they recruit for the meeting. You could even make this a fun competition, with the winning component (bringing the most attendees) receiving national recognition and/or a financial incentive.

This collaborative approach works in reverse, too. There are likely issues you're struggling with and your colleagues could help (Table 5.5).

Table 5.5. Other Departments Promoting Membership

Issue	You want to reach out to non-members and upsell them membership or, at least, convert them to a qualified lead.
Opportunity	Look at all the ways individuals can sign up for information from your organization. Work with the online team (or marketing team) to onboard those names into a multi-part series that includes a free content and a membership ask.
	If you sell materials, for example, books, review what is currently shipped in each package. Usually, for a nominal fee, you can include a buck slip or insert about membership. You can test different messaging and offers. The return may be low to start, but so is the risk. The individual has already paid for the product, so this doesn't affect the sale. The more the person is exposed to membership benefits, the greater the likelihood of eventual conversion.

Issue	You want to expand your market segmentation, which requires benefits that resonate with each audience.
Opportunity	Reach out to your internal subject-matter experts to better understand current workforce trends. Discuss the specific needs of each segment. (If you don't already have them, work together to create personas for the target audiences.) The subject-matter experts can also help you align current product offerings with the needs of the audiences. While you can work through the logistics of the campaign, it's very helpful to partner with in-house experts on the copy/pitch.
	At American Public Health Association, we had an in-house advisory group of staff who were members before being employed by the organization. We could run ideas by them, ask questions about the field, etc., all in safe space. Although this isn't the same as running a true member focus group, the advisory team was incredibly helpful.
Issue	You're interested in partnering with another association to offer joint membership.
Opportunity	For the partnership to be successful, you have to provide relevant products and benefits.
	Work directly with the education team to identify products that will resonate with the new audience.
	Talk to the publications team about special journal features tied to this group.
	Partner with the website team for special promotions during program launch, plus ongoing pushes of relevant content.

Success in one area can lead to success in all areas. Look outside of your department and explore new opportunities.

Say No to Silos

Remarkable associations generally do not exhibit what's typically referred to as the silo mentality—organizational fragmentation by department or responsibility. When asked about signature products, for example, employees of great associations usually gave the same answers no matter what department they worked in or what their supervisory level. They shared a common view of who the association was and how it served its members.

(*7 Measures of Success*, p. 45)

It's not all about you. Membership is an important part of the association, but there are many important departments doing important work. While there may be times when your priorities are moved to the top of the list, more often than not you'll be struggling along with everyone else to make the most of limited resources.

Don't monopolize conversations and make what you need or what membership is doing the sole focus. It should always be a two-way street. Invest the time to understand what your colleagues are struggling with and find ways in which you can be of support. Why? The association's activities are connected. Internal disconnects won't stay within the confines of your building. Before you know it, you'll see a negative impact on your association's membership, programs, and revenue.

Figure 5.2. Connectivity Between Departments

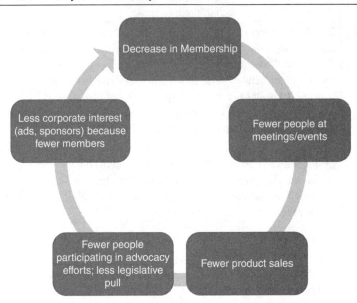

It's worth noting that this cycle doesn't have to start with membership. Given the strong connection between these elements, an issue or decline in one area will impact the rest of the organization. Success, therefore, benefits everyone and requires broad input from across the association. You will not achieve your membership goals in a vacuum.

Identifying the Silos

According to www.investopedia.com, the silo mentality is "An attitude . . . that occurs when several departments . . . do not want to share information or knowledge with other individuals in the same company." While some people are naturally geared toward this approach, that isn't true for the majority.

Are you wondering whether you suffer from a silo mentality? Answer these quick questions:

- Can you name three recent accomplishments of other departments?
- Do you routinely see an issue from a perspective other than your own department?
- When do you share member input with the rest of the organization?

Did you answer no/never to these questions? You may have a silo mentality. If you read the above questions and answered that you are perfect, but everyone else in the organization falls short, then you may suffer from silo mentality. Finally, you may also be in a silo if you are routinely surprised that the seasons have changed or you walk around the office and don't recognize anyone.

Sometimes the silo mentality starts with something as innocent as putting your head down to focus on a project and, before you know it, you've lost track of the world around you. The dangers of the silo mentality are always lurking just beyond productive teamwork. Best intentions can fall by the wayside with sudden staffing changes, scope creep, important deadlines, or decreases in your line of business.

You need to continually keep your "mentality" in check to make sure you are focused on the collective best interest of the organization and how your department can help.

Addressing the Silo

Addressing the silo doesn't mean you have one of *those* meetings where everyone gets together and brainstorms what *you* can do to grow membership. This is about pulling people together to talk about mutually beneficial opportunities that help everyone reach his or her goals. You should be open to the feedback of others and vice versa.

"Team" does not mean the same to everyone, and we've all seen the word abused. If you are going to create meaningful change, make sure you're living the "team." If your department or organization is having trouble coming together and silos continue to rule, you need to address the behavior (and make sure you're not part of the problem).

When there are successes, pull together everyone who had a role in the victory. Work with the other department heads to surprise the joint team. You need to celebrate the victories and process the misses. You can reinforce the team approach by maintaining togetherness in good times and bad. Some companies have received media attention for celebrating mistakes, going so far as to reward the biggest mistake of the year. This may be too outside the box for your association, at least today, but it does show that organizations should embrace change and not be afraid to fail. If the association is going to revert back to the blame game and protecting the silos, you're limiting your potential before you even start.

Transforming Actions into Value

Simply put, it takes more time to gather input from your stakeholders, to be inclusive of other departments and ideas, and to balance your priorities with the work of others. You could probably move faster if you put your head down and focused exclusively on your own work. But "faster" doesn't mean "better." So invest in others, just as you invest in yourself and your team.

You're now meeting with the executives/leadership, other departments, and your team. You're connecting membership's activities to projects around the organization and you're planning for the future. You're bringing people together and resisting silos. What's next?"

Enter the dashboard. There are frequent posts in ASAE Collaborate about dashboards and how to report on your activities. Infographics are also a popular option for showcasing information. Common data points include:

Table 5.6. Dashboards 101

Marketing	Membership	Customer Service
Overview of recent campaigns	Total number of members	Total number of calls
Results	Total retention	Top issues
Pending activities	Total recruitment	Historical information; YOY comparisons
	Total lapsed	

Since membership affects the rest of your organization, you should provide data on a regular basis. At the Association of periOperative Registered Nurses (AORN), we share monthly dashboards. For a hot topic in the customer service team, a weekly report is provided to select staff.

The shared data should be easily digestible and not require years of membership experience to understand the impact/relevance. You can always maintain more comprehensive information for your eyes only.

Also, the raw numbers are important, but they're not the whole story. Since you're one of the departments with frequent member contact, you need to share the voice of customer with the rest of the organization. It can be a difficult conversation, especially when the feedback isn't positive, but this is why you've built good relationships and operate in a silo-free environment. Your reporting should also highlight where you've partnered with other departments. It's great exposure for them and reinforces your role as an aggregator.

Summary

Membership is a team sport. You rely on other departments for new content and offerings. They rely on you for steady communication of the benefits and continued growth.

- You need to know what the association is focused on and the role membership plays in that goal(s).

- You have to build relationships that allow for honest and open communication around what's best for the association (and not what's best for an individual or a specific department).

- You must understand and embrace "teamwork" in your association and never compromise—whether times are good or bad. Don't build a silo.

- You should create feedback loops and share member knowledge via dashboards and other tools so the organization can make informed business decisions.

Success is possible, but only if everyone is working together. Ignore the fact that there is a "me" and an "I" in membership and work closely with your colleagues to achieve meaningful change.

> Coming together is a beginning, staying together is progress, and working together is success.
>
> (*Henry Ford*)

References

Baxter, Robbie Kellman. *The Membership Economy: Find Your Super Users, Master the Forever Transaction, and Build Recurring Revenue*. New York: McGraw-Hill, 2015.

Coerver, Harrison, & Byers, Mary. *Race for Relevance: 5 Radical Changes for Associations*. Washington, DC: ASAE, 2011.

Notter, Jamie, & Grant, Maddie. *When Millennials Take Over: Preparing for the Ridiculously Optimistic Future of Business.* Idea Press Publishing, 2015.

Sladek, Sarah L. *The End of Membership As We Know It.* Washington, DC: ASAE, 2011.

About the Author

Sara Miller, MBA, PMP, CAE, is the director of membership at AORN, the Association of periOperative Registered Nurses. She has more than 15 years of experience working with nonprofits and associations, including management positions at Challenger Center for Space Science Education, the Humane Society of the United States, and the American Public Health Association. Email: hello@saramiller.info.

Managing a Global Membership

6

By Andrew Calhoun, CAE

IN THIS CHAPTER
- Global Considerations
- Volunteer Leadership
- Support of Chapters
- Marketing and Communication
- Case Studies
- Closing Thoughts

An increasing number of associations and societies are expanding their reach into markets outside the United States. For some organizations, the growth occurs without a planned strategy; it happens because of interest in the U.S.-centered activities of the organization, or in reaction to events. Does it make sense for your organization to take a more active and concerted approach to grow membership, increase product sales, and expand your reach in countries outside the U.S. to help you to achieve your strategic goals?

Global Considerations

Some membership organizations attract a small percentage of members who reside outside of the United States, because they value their information and benefits or they wish to attend a conference or event held in the United States. Although members may live around the globe, the organization may not be considered a global organization if the vast majority of its benefits are U.S.-centric.

Ask yourself whether the products or services that your organization represents have appeal to individuals outside the United States, because they are a globally recognized

Figure 6.1. Population Trends

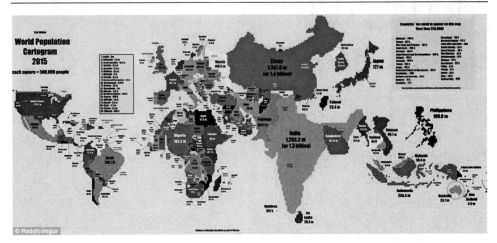

Copyright ODT Inc. Reprinted with permission. For maps and other related teaching materials, contact ODT Inc., P.O. Box 134, Amherst, MA 01004 USA; (800-736-1293; Fax: 413-549-3503; Email: odtstore@odt.org; Web: www.odtmaps.com)

standard, or if the industry is truly without boundaries, such as pharmaceuticals, IT, or consumer goods. If the answer is yes, then your leadership should be mapping a global strategy. This chapter explores some of the opportunities and challenges that are different for an organization that is growing in markets outside the United States.

According to the World Bank, by 2025 six major economies—Brazil, India, China, Indonesia, South Korea, and Russia—will account for more than half of all global growth. Although these countries show where the population growth is trending, they should first be evaluated for their potential before becoming primary targets for global growth. Overall population numbers are not an exact determinant of the potential market for your products and services. The infographic in Figure 6.1 paints an interesting and perhaps unexpected picture of where potential constituents live.

Historically, members from outside the United States may have joined a U.S.-based association because there was nowhere to go locally for the professional information they needed, but that is no longer the case. With the advent of digitally delivered information, education, and in-person events that are held with competing organizations and for-profit companies, you must be able to position your current offerings in ways that may be consumed easily. This includes translations, new delivery mechanisms, and an appreciation for cultural differences.

Cultural Differences

- How important is punctuality? Is the scheduled time frame for a meeting set in stone, or does it allow for some flexibility?
- Hierarchies (titles) may have a great influence on the communication style in your new surroundings, so it is important to be aware—understand who the decision-maker is.

- Professionals in large markets, such as India and China, place a high value on certifications; the value of "membership" is less important.
- In some countries, such as India, there is a high importance by individuals that they at least believe that they obtained a "discounted price" on product or services.
- In countries such as Japan, people typically speak softly and are more passive about sharing ideas or making suggestions.
- Some cultures have much of the decision-making authority with one person. Other cultures, notably the Japanese and the Chinese, stress team negotiation and consensus decision making.

If you are early in your expansion, consider developing criteria to help guide your launch. A geographic focus will make near-term success easier. Look at countries where you have a significant number of members and constituents/subscribers, and where English is widely used as a business language. Look first to countries where the economy is strong enough for the members or their employers to pay for membership and products. The longer-term play may be driven by establishing yourself in emerging economies, which show the largest potential for growth, perhaps in cooperation with local institutions to gain early credibility. According to the World Bank, emerging economies have some characteristics of developed markets, and are in the process of moving from a closed economy to an open market economy while building accountability within the system. Introduce products that provide the greatest chance for early wins and recognition. In more places than not, these will be internationally research-driven intellectual property (IP), not the membership "product."

Additional Considerations

Member/customer support changes a bit for organizations that make a significant move into non-U.S. markets. More communications will come from individuals for whom English is not their primary language, living in regions that may be many time zones removed from your office. This requires planning, patience, and, ideally, people on staff with conversational fluency in major languages, such as Spanish. You will find additional insights in the Marketing and Communications section.

Legal Considerations

States in the United States have different laws and regulations and, naturally, so do countries around the world. It is critical that you budget time and money to assess potential legal risks. These include registration, chapter bylaws, product fulfillment, privacy, and operational rules. For example, some countries prohibit telemarketing, even if it is to your former members; and some laws in some countries allow chapters to dismiss or exclude members without what we would consider "just cause." If your organization provides certifications, you must be aware of special requirements in the countries where you offer them. Copyright and trademark protections also may be different. Taxes in some countries may mean that you need to be prepared to take a financial loss in order to gain the potential "political" gain from holding that event where your constituents may live. Your entire tax-exempt status may not be available or may be extremely limited in some countries.

Of note is that in the 21st century, the legal system of the United States has become so different from that of other countries that virtually no other jurisdictions, including other Common Law countries, look to the United States for legal precedent on any subject. The vast majority of countries in Asia, Latin America, Africa, and Europe have European Civil Law systems. Consult with local counsel.

Currency

Will you allow members/constituents to pay in the local currency or through a local institution? In some countries, many transactions are by wire transfer, which can be expensive on both sides of the transaction. One option is for a chapter to aggregate funds from members in local currency and remit payment every month back to headquarters. Are there restrictions on repatriating your earnings, and does that matter? Would reinvesting them to build the local infrastructure be just as useful?

Perceptions

Do the countries in which you are investing view the concept of a not-for-profit organization the same way we do in the United States? Must the country's government play a role, or are there other options? Are members familiar with the concept of volunteering and volunteer leadership? China is a good example of a culture that is vastly different from the United States, because it is hard for them to understand why a person would perform services as a "volunteer" for no payment.

General Considerations When Communicating with a Global Audience

- Be mindful of geographic locations when referring to seasons—"summer" in the United States is "winter" in Australia.
- Be cautious about relying on online translating applications too much, because of accuracy concerns.
- When translating messages, be aware of text expansion. The same word in different languages might be markedly longer in length.
- Remember to use the international date format with the day first, such as 25/6/15.
- Do not use slang, contractions, or colloquialisms in your communications.

Go mobile. Ensure that your information is viewable and scaled for mobile platforms. An increasing number of people conduct a majority of their work and financial transactions on mobile phones and pads. See Figure 6.2.

Figure 6.2. Growth of Mobile Technology

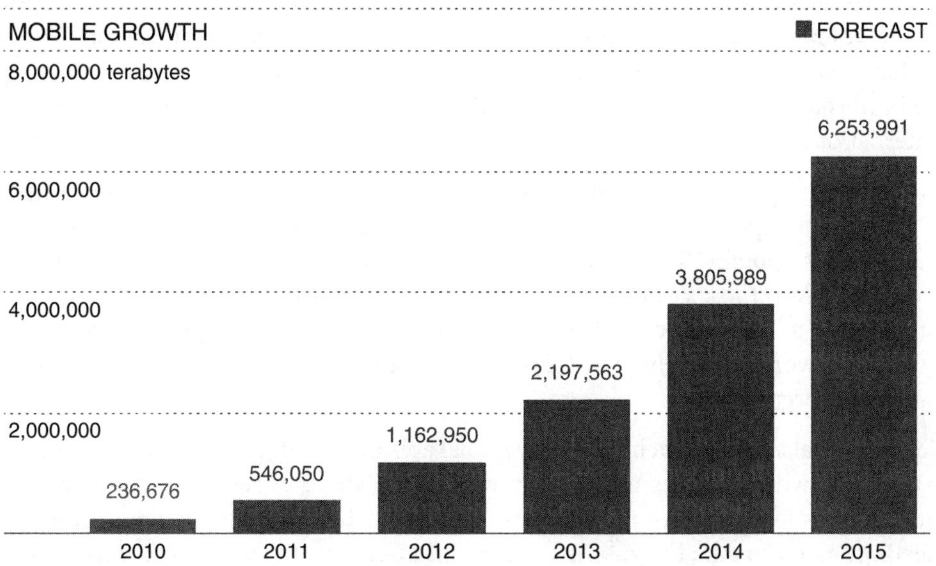

MOBILE GROWTH ■ FORECAST

8,000,000 terabytes

					6,253,991
				3,805,989	
			2,197,563		
		1,162,950			
	546,050				
236,676					
2010	2011	2012	2013	2014	2015

6,000,000

4,000,000

2,000,000

Volunteer Leadership

Volunteers at the International Level

A key element of success for not-for-profit groups is the volunteer support they have at both the international and the regional/local levels. International positions include those on the board of directors, committees, task forces, and working groups. They generate ideas, provide counsel, and make recommendations on actions that should be taken on a global and sometimes regional basis. These positions are important on a personal level for your members, because the leadership roles contribute to the members' professional growth. For these reasons, it is important to have a robust, but manageable number of these volunteer groups to achieve goals.

Whether or not your organization has a more traditional committee structure of annual terms with a hierarchical reporting structure or a more nimble system of subject-driven working groups with a limited time commitment, there are important considerations for organizations with a significant global presence, or those trying to get there. You need to establish a process for soliciting interest from your membership on areas in which they are qualified and where they have interest. You might even consider non-members as part of your pool, for non-decision-making, expert advisory groups. You will gain a wider perspective of opinions, as well as adding credibility for having external opinions. An example is a group that is convened to provide input on the future of cloud computing. Naturally, you need to have a volunteer management system, even if the information initially is on an Excel spreadsheet that is transferred to your database.

In addition to finding volunteers with the necessary skills and experience, geographic representation is important, both from a "political" vantage point and from practical standpoints. If the breakdown of your membership has measurable representation from regions outside the United States, those regions should have representation on the volunteer groups. Even if you aspire to grow in certain regions, but do not yet have the members there, it is important to demonstrate your understanding of the importance of their input. That extends all the way to the make-up of your now "international" board of directors.

Diverse geographic representation also provides you with perspectives from leaders with different experience. The best way to understand what your members in Brazil may want, as opposed to those in India or in China, is to learn from executives who live and work in those countries. Research and survey data are important sources of information to help you chart the course, but direct input from the various regions around the world will help you use that data to make recommendations on how to direct your organization.

Nothing speaks commitment to a truly global approach better than locating meetings in countries where you currently have members, or where you see good future opportunities. This includes meetings of your international board and possibly committee meetings. Look to take the volunteer meetings another step and co-locate them with your major conferences. Bringing in your top volunteer leadership to the same place as your larger conferences allows you to leverage their presence as a draw. Arrange for a Spotlight Stage that gives visibility to members of your board during a larger, paid event. Volunteers also can play an active and important role with members on the local level. A great way for smaller organizations to gain additional exposure in areas outside the United States is to partner with another, complementary group that already has a presence. When approaching a potential partner, you should be prepared to demonstrate that you are bringing something of value to the event. This might be access to a different kind of attendee or a cross-marketing opportunity for both groups.

Corporate trade associations also see the need to be active in the different areas where their members reside. The Advanced Medical Technology Association (AdvaMed) represents medical technology manufacturers from around the world. Its largest MedTech Conference moves to a different major city in the United States every year, but they were conscious of the need to hold events in overseas locations as well. One example is their Global MedTech Compliance Conference that has been moving to different cities in Europe. The event is co-organized and run by a European counterpart organization to maximize the penetration and chance for success.

Support of Chapters

Some organizations with a global membership operate exclusively out of a central headquarters, without offices or affiliates in other countries. In these cases, partnerships and alliances with similar organizations can provide access and local connections. However, especially for groups that are individual member based, chapters/ components are important contributors to the organization for three major reasons.

1. Chapters serve as a local connection point for your members, for meetings and the distribution of information.

2. Chapters support the larger organization in gaining greater recognition and visibility in the region where they are located.

3. Chapters drive revenue growth for membership and product sales.

Well-run chapters can be a key to your organization's success; however, the relationships you have with them are not always trouble-free. They are a face of your organization and can be viewed by members and others in the community as *the* face, meaning that, if they are received well in the area in which they operate, that is a positive reflection on the organization as a whole. The opposite can happen as well.

Peggy Hoffman, president of Mariner Management & Marketing, says that her survey data and years of experience specializing in management of local, state, and regional associations show her that a chapter can have an urgent need for something that national doesn't see as a top priority. She adds that often national and individual chapters have different strategic agendas. If the two sides don't meet on common ground, or make the assumption that the agenda is the same on both sides, miscommunication and frustration are common results. The chapter also may be promoting something that goes contrary to the philosophy or even the statutes of the association. For example, it may misrepresent a training course that was developed entirely by the parent association, to be used a specific way. Frequent communication and a clear understanding of expectations are the easiest ways to prevent actions of your chapters from affecting you adversely.

Although active volunteer leadership may not garner the same response as it does in the United States, local support is key to a strong global organization. Chapters, or components, are a primary vehicle for your organization to interact with members and can be the voice of the organization with government. Chapter structure and support are important areas to plan and manage.

Chapter Structure

If you are in the beginning stages or are refining the relationship you have with your chapters, you should connect with and gain the advice of association executives who manage groups that are similar to yours. Obtain their advice on the things they've done before. There are many important considerations. Here are a few to consider:

Do you want your chapters to be independent, as a small business, or should you have a closer, franchise-type arrangement?	Yes or No
Will you have affiliation agreements with other organizations?	
Are you considering the different ways that you may have to organize chapters in various countries? Be cautious when considering organizing chapters in different ways, because this will establish precedents that can be hard to rectify.	
What kind of regular reporting will you require of the chapters and how frequently?	
Will you require a certain type of governance/leadership structure at the chapter?	
Can the chapters decide how many positions they need beyond the chapter president, such as a marketing director, education director, or a secretary, etc.?	

(*continued*)

Will you create model bylaws? What exceptions will you allow, based on restrictions in certain countries?	Yes or No
How often will you review the bylaws on a chapter-by-chapter basis, and what is the consequence for non-compliance?	
How often and to what detail will you review chapters? Chapters that grow to a certain size or fail to thrive may present governance and financial risks that should be considered.	
Should the chapters have required standards, such as the minimum number of events they hold per year, a mix of events to attract different interests, a minimum number of formal meetings, audited financials?	
Will the chapters be run exclusively by volunteers, or will you encourage paid administrative staff for the chapters that can afford this?	
Should headquarters subsidize any paid staff?	
Will chapters have a physical office? In some cultures, you need to have an office to be considered legitimate.	
Have you developed a process for new chapter formation? Will new chapters form organically, with help from headquarters, or will headquarters form chapters in areas that are of strategic importance, even if a sizable number of members are not currently in the area?	
How active a role will the chapters have in advocacy on the regional level?	
Do you have a documented process for assisting chapters during their vulnerable first two years?	

Chapter Support

Your chapter volunteers are the most committed members you have, but they also have day jobs. They may not have a management, marketing, or leadership background, so provide learning opportunities and access to tools to make running the chapter easier. Help them to understand how the activities of the chapter will help to achieve their professional and your organizational goals. What types of support might you look to provide to your chapter leaders?

- Customer support—Having the right type of people is important. Chapter relations staff must be good communicators and also savvy with volunteers from diverse cultures and varied personalities. The job requires managing and delivering tools to help the leaders to grow the reach of the association.

- Chapter website—The pages on your website where volunteer leaders can go to find a host of resources to help them are critical. It can be the primary repository for useful information and it should be password protected. You might include some of the following resources:
  - How to market and run a good event
  - How to generate statistical reports on your chapter membership
  - How to build your board
  - What reports are required for HQ
  - How best to communicate with your members

- What awards are available and how to win them
- Ways to attract younger professionals

- Regional leadership conferences—Plan to hold leadership conferences to assist with professional development and the sharing of best practices. Decide whether HQ pays for these or the chapter leaders themselves pay to attend, using chapter money.

- Hosted chapter websites—Will you plan to create hosted websites for your chapters to use, or allow them to create their own and establish a data feed?

- Regular communications—Coordinate messages coming from other departments to chapter leaders.

- Awards—What individual and chapter achievement awards make sense?

- Publications—Is there a publication targeted to volunteer leaders?

- Translations—Is everything coming from HQ in English? What commitment to translated intellectual property (IP) and marketing copy are you willing to provide?

- Affinity offerings—Are there discounts on products or services that you can offer?

- Advocacy support—Utilize the connections that your chapter leaders have with government officials, but recognize that they probably do not have much experience with government affairs.

- Local office—Which chapters should have a physical presence?

- Should headquarters open a regional office?

According to ASAE survey results in *Achieving Global Growth*, 20 percent of associations currently have one or two offices outside the United States and "growers" (high-achieving associations) make up nearly all of these respondents.

It is critical to run great chapters, with an open eye to innovation, because the environment is changing and you may need to modify your structure and delivery to maintain loyalty and increase engagement. The traditional chapter model may not be sustainable, because of things such as easy access to networking groups from other places and availability of information from multiple sources online. Look at things such as more online content, volunteer groups that are established with clear time commitments and a clear goal, and self-investing or partnering with other organizations to have experts in the region who have connections and knowledge to support the volunteer efforts.

Marketing and Communication

Be cognizant of ways that your audience wants to receive information, so they know what you have to offer. If they don't know you have it, they will not use it and, consequently, will not value it. Use multiple channels to deliver your message. People in different countries value different things and like to receive them in different ways. Your product portfolio may be robust enough, but the delivery and positioning may have to be modified for the markets you are in and the markets you are trying to reach. People in Latin America still value printed material more than other cultures do; social media is huge in Southeast Asia; locally managed chapter websites help to ensure that the right copy and visual impression are made.

Another key to ensuring that your communications are read is to have them come from someone your audience recognizes. That might be a volunteer leader at the chapter, or a message delivered by a partnership that you have established. Credibility and trust take time to develop, so utilize relationships that already are established.

Translating your intellectual property (IP) into target languages can be expensive, but it is important and critical to do it right. In addition to IP, you might also consider sending some of your shorter communications in the native languages where you have a significant population; this effort may increase your open rate. Overall, it is a relatively small expense to deliver a better customer experience.

Your members will respond to email and even paper mail, but what other methods of communication will enable you to penetrate your target markets? Look into introducing a chat function to augment your communication channel. That may encourage greater communication from segments of your membership who are reluctant to participate in other ways. You'll gain insights from your members and provide a quick, positive customer experience.

Although social media platforms can sometimes be seen as a threat to the traditional association model, they provide a no-cost opportunity for networking and information sharing. Social media communication is an important delivery channel and should be used to build relationships through real-time, two-way conversation. Know that they need to be monitored to ensure that you are aware of and appropriately respond to any unfavorable messages.

Marketing Product Support

When chapter leaders are holding local events or attending industry conferences, they will need marketing supplies, such as printed material, giveaways, or signage. In addition to sending marketing collateral, or even sending the files for on-site printing, you could provide your chapters with a budget every year and allow them to order what they want. This could be promotional items with the chapter name printed on them. This all can be done by establishing a relationship with a fulfillment house with a number of ordering and delivery options.

Research

What do your members, prospects, volunteer leaders, and the business communities want, and are you delivering it? Surveys could come from the headquarters office if the chapter does not have the resources to conduct one on their own. Staff from the headquarters office, however, can provide guidance from your communications and marketing team on how chapters can create effective questions to send out on their own. Survey applications themselves are readily available online. You might include a member satisfaction survey, an exit survey for non-renewing members, and surveys

Figure 6.3. Quadrant Chart Showing Opportunities for Change

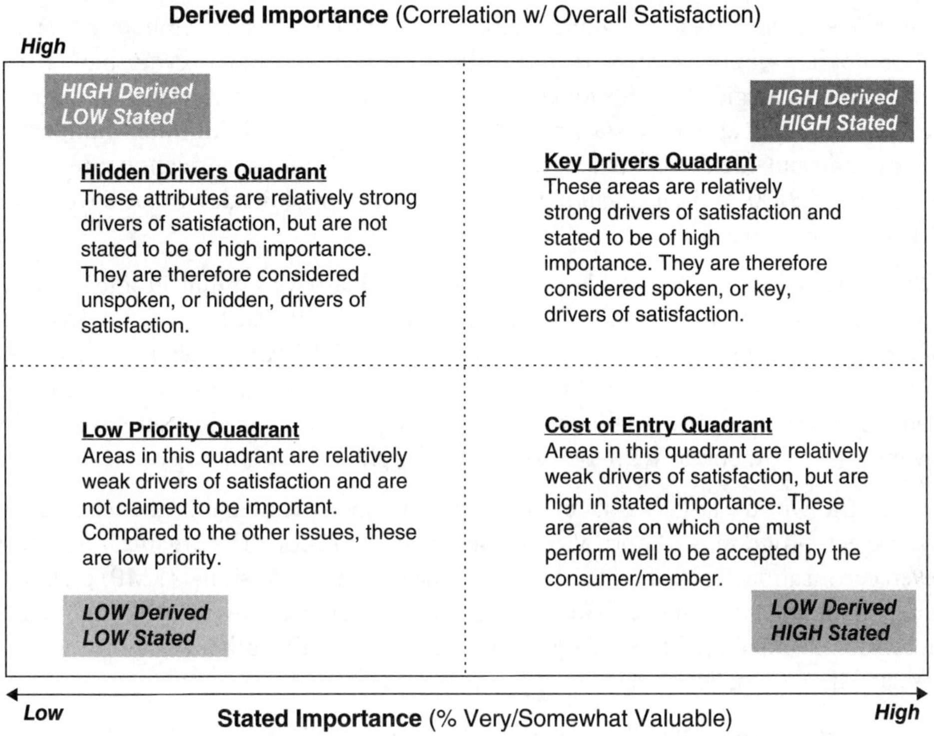

Derived Importance (Correlation w/ Overall Satisfaction)

High

HIGH Derived LOW Stated	HIGH Derived HIGH Stated
Hidden Drivers Quadrant These attributes are relatively strong drivers of satisfaction, but are not stated to be of high importance. They are therefore considered unspoken, or hidden, drivers of satisfaction.	**Key Drivers Quadrant** These areas are relatively strong drivers of satisfaction and stated to be of high importance. They are therefore considered spoken, or key, drivers of satisfaction.
Low Priority Quadrant Areas in this quadrant are relatively weak drivers of satisfaction and are not claimed to be important. Compared to the other issues, these are low priority.	**Cost of Entry Quadrant** Areas in this quadrant are relatively weak drivers of satisfaction, but are high in stated importance. These are areas on which one must perform well to be accepted by the consumer/member.
LOW Derived LOW Stated	LOW Derived HIGH Stated

Low **Stated Importance** (% Very/Somewhat Valuable) *High*

targeted to specific initiatives or groups, such as students. One chart that is driven off of survey data and paints an excellent picture of what members value and where future opportunities exist is the quadrant chart shown in Figure 6.3.

Product development is another key to building and maintaining your relevance. That includes regular updates to your current portfolio of products and services, but also means active investigation into new areas, where you can leverage your current strengths. Read more about this in the Case Studies section.

Perhaps you should address needs of your membership around the globe through a revised membership structure or pricing model. Make the organization an attractive fit for them. Structure and modeling options are covered in another chapter.

Start from the marketplace and dive deeply into the problems and questions that your constituent/member bases are facing, to deliver solutions that meet them. Instead of promoting a product, promote the result that the product will solve. How will it help your constituents to grow in their careers? Elizabeth Engel and Anna Caraveli point out in their whitepaper on Leading Engagement that, if we shift our focus to outcomes, we can more successfully engage our stakeholders to help co-create the future. When you determine where your members are trying to go and what obstacles are preventing them from getting there, you can actively engage volunteers in the community in the creation of products to fill their needs.

Case Studies

Your current exposure to the global market may be subscribers, members, or certification holders who have come to you without active marketing on your part. However, if your strategic plan calls for concerted expansion, you must take an active role. Success can be at all levels, starting with smaller groups with a limited number of constituents outside the United States, to larger organizations, with annual revenues in excess of $100 million. Included are examples of organizations that have taken deliberate steps to grow.

When you look at examples of larger associations that have significant international operations, such as the Project Management Institute (PMI), ISACA, the Institute of Electrical and Electronics Engineers (IEEE), and CFA Institute, you see that a key to their success has been their focus on market-driven economies. Your organization may be significantly smaller than these; however, you can glean useful ideas by reviewing best practices. We'll look at a few examples.

PMI is the world's largest not-for-profit professional membership association for the project, program, and portfolio management profession. The organization offers seven certifications, including the Project Management Professional (PMP) certification, which is held by more than 590,000 practitioners worldwide. Although many factors have contributed to PMP's growth, here are a few that other organizations can emulate, if on a smaller scale.

PMI recognizes the importance of support for its chapters and volunteers around the world and have staff dedicated to this, both in the field and out of headquarters. It participates in the annual planning process for the chapters to provide advice and check progress toward goals. One initiative is the Chapter Innovation Program to recognize successes and to share transportable ideas among chapters.

PMI is conscious of cultural differences and recognized that constituents in Latin America have a greater preference for receiving information in printed format than in other regions. PMI also utilizes SMS texting for renewal campaigns and telemarketing in many other countries where it is allowed.

ISACA is a professional membership association that provides guidance, standards, certifications, and career progression and other effective tools for professionals in information systems in the areas of audit/assurance, risk, governance, and security. Since its formation more than 45 years ago, the organization has grown to 140,000 constituents in 180 countries, with more than 200 volunteer-led chapters. Existing business lines of IP, certifications, training, and membership continue to provide steady positive growth, but this organization is referenced here because of its recent strategic push to move into a new market to capitalize on a large opportunity and global unmet need.

Through research and planning, ISACA developed forward-looking strategic objectives that would help support continued success. One of the primary findings was in the need to dive deeper into the cybersecurity area and develop a comprehensive innovative training and certification portfolio. By leveraging existing capabilities on the product side, the organization is positioning itself as an innovator ahead of other groups and for-profit alternatives.

We also see smart, long-term growth with organizations that are a bit smaller in size. The predecessor of the Association of Fundraising Professionals was chartered in 1962 and had 197 members. It began in the United States and grew by way of alliances, partnerships, and organic growth. Within a year after its founding, the first chapter was formed in partnership with another organization. Membership grew from there, and now stands at 26,000; additional chapters were added in the 1970s and now are at 169; certifications were formalized in the 1980s; and attendance at its largest conference grew, now eclipsing 40,000 attendees. Along the way, AFP looked to international markets as a natural extension. In addition to its U.S. and Canadian chapters, AFP now has 11 chapters in six other countries/regions. Alliances also have been formed and reciprocal arrangements have been established with similar organizations in dozens of countries.

Closing Thoughts

Whether you are an individual membership organization, a corporate-based trade association, growing your membership and product sales in other countries requires numerous considerations. Look first at your current membership distribution in other countries and also in which countries you want to grow. Start where you will have the greatest chance for success.

Should you always lead with membership? A full bundle of services, packaged in a membership, is not always what people in every country want to buy—that includes the United States. Maybe lead with the products or services that will be well received. In many countries, your IP, recognized certifications, and training are what will be of interest, so you may use membership as a loss leader. Your products may be far more salable and allow you to achieve a goal of expanding your exposure and influence.

Have a longer-term perspective on investment and patience, so you can invest in products and services that will serve your members better. You do not have to submit quarterly growth reports that are scrutinized by Wall Street. By becoming truly global, organizations are better positioned to weather turbulent economic conditions that have buffeted the United States over the past years. By building in those markets, they also are positioned to ride growth as the economies mature.

Seek advice and look for alliances or partnerships to increase your exposure and decrease your risk. Begin with communications that show your constituents that you understand that their interests may be different than what is delivered to your U.S. audience. Here are a few additional thoughts that may help.

- ASAE's Foundation Research Series publication on *Achieving Global Growth* supports strong consideration for going global: "The more an association dedicates resources and specifically designs products and programs to international members, customers, and prospects, the more likely the chances of success and sustained growth over time."

- Some cultures will not openly provide input or criticism, so when you hear responses of "yes," "okay," or "good," they may be simply recognition that the person heard you or they may be one of politeness. Be clear on expectations and agreements.

- Some cultures will be more comfortable in providing you with feedback than others. You may need to consider when to use focus groups or online surveys.

- Social and professional hierarchy are more distinct in some countries than they are in the United States. This may affect a member's willingness to take on certain roles and responsibilities.

- Remember time differences and religious holidays when scheduling calls or webinars. Consider times that work for different regions or, for webinars, you might plan on holding several on the same day to provide more customer-friendly access. You certainly could record an earlier webinar and replay it, put there really is something to be said about a "live event" when people can contribute to the ongoing discussion, if even by a chat function.

- Start holding meetings outside the United States.

- Consider delivery challenges of materials to particular countries and restrictions to embargoed countries.

- Provide payment options that make it easy for your constituents, but do not leave your organization unduly at risk.

- Consider working with an association management company (AMC) that already has an established office with a support staff in the markets you want, especially where it is challenging to run operations and the cultural differences are substantial.

As Sheri Jacobs of Avenue M Group often says, it is not necessarily the ability to pay, but rather the willingness to pay that matters. The audience may believe in what your organization stands for, and even that it has the resources to assist them, but you must demonstrate that what you provide is better than the next best alternatives that are competing with you. Think critically with your strategic plan and increase your global reach into markets where you can expand the impact your organization makes. "Going Global" can make a big impact on the future strength of the organization.

References

ASAE. Foundation Research Series publication, *Achieving Global Growth*, p. 17.

Engel, Elizabeth, & Caraveli, Anna, *Leading Engagement from the Outside In . . .*, whitepaper by Spark Consulting and The Demand Network, 2015.

Hoffman, Peggy. Mariner Management & Marketing, http://marinermanagement.com.

How to Grow Your Association in Emerging Markets Using Strategy and Tactics, GLOBAL STRAT and MARKETING GENERAL, 2012, p. 11.

About the Author

Andrew Calhoun, CAE, joined ISACA in October 2014, as the director of membership services, overseeing an international constituency of 140,000+ in 180 countries and chapter relations activities in support of 208 chapters. ISACA members and certification holders represent a variety of professional IT-related positions, including audit, risk, governance, security, and cybersecurity. Calhoun has more than seventeen years of association management experience, supervising areas including membership, chapter relations, non-dues revenue, conferences, and marketing. Email: andrewtcalhoun@gmail.com.

An Overview of Membership Research

7

By Dean A. West, FASAE

A few years ago, the Clinical Laboratory Standards Institute (CLSI) was suffering declines in membership and membership revenue. They identified the following barriers to membership retention and acquisition.

- *The current membership structure was too complicated.* Complicated membership structures make it more difficult to attract and retain members. Complicated structures with a multiple of options create choice fatigue, making it difficult for individual decision-makers to determine which membership option is best for them or their organization.

- *Individuals who participated with CLSI through their standards process (a critical product line) were not involved in the membership decision.* Anecdotal evidence suggested the membership decision was team-based, but CLSI was not sure who made or influenced the decision.

- *Members and nonmembers as well as volunteers and non-volunteers indicated that there was confusion over the meaning of membership.* Some individuals did not know whether or not they were members, and some believed that activity in the standards process made them members and thus assumed that others active were also members.

- *The CLSI standards, the primary reason for the association's existence, as currently published, were challenging to understand and use.* Participation in standards development and sale of the finished standards product were essential to association revenue.

Clearly, the CLSI faced a complex, difficult series of challenges, yet addressing these issues involved substantial financial and reputational risk. The greater the risk to the association and the more long-range the consequences, the more research was considered a vital, strategic imperative.

To address these challenges, CLSI implemented a comprehensive analysis of the market, including the development of a membership market simulator designed to test the response of CLSI's market to different membership offers at different price points.

- The CLSI Simulator highlighted necessary changes from the current model.
  - What benefits to include.
  - How to structure those benefits.
  - How to price the benefits.

- Research also identified an *unmet need* that could only be addressed through offering an individual membership.

- Two years later, the association began implementing the results of decisions made using the research.

- Restructured and simplified organizational membership (reduced from 25 to 6 options).

- Aligned categories by constituent groups (markets).

- Added benefits at higher price points to increase the member value proposition.

- Created an individual membership level for volunteers and professionals to participate in CLSI.

Today, the number of members and membership revenue is increasing after several years of decline. Within approximately 2 years, more than 300 people have joined as individual members, creating a new revenue stream for the association.

The bottom line? Making informed decisions based on sound research can deliver substantial results.

This chapter provides an overview of the membership research process, guidance on the use of membership research, and examples of how associations use membership research to improve decision making. While by no means a comprehensive treatise on research, it provides association executives with the basic insights necessary to establish a methodical and effective membership research process for their associations.

Why Membership Research Is Important

Membership research is defined in this chapter as the planning, collection, and analysis of data relevant to membership decision making and the communication of the results of this analysis to staff and volunteer leaders. The association can study many different constituencies to address a wide range of potential issues. Membership research often takes priority for the following reasons:

- Members represent the primary market of the association.

- Members represent a sample of the potential market of the association.

- Members represent an accessible, definable audience for research activities.

- Decisions affecting members have the greatest potential return on investment for the association.

The ongoing collection, analysis, and use of membership information are critical for sustainable association growth and success, and the ability to manage this process is a fundamental competency of the membership executive.

What Goals Are You Trying to Achieve?

The starting point for all research activities is desired outcomes. For example, is your most important goal membership acquisition or member retention? The decisions you make and the information you need to inform those decisions are impacted by this choice. Based on your desired goals, you can identify the decisions you need to make. For example, if membership acquisition is a goal, then an important decision is which potential market you target first. The following are common membership outcomes:

- We want to increase the number of members.

- We want to increase the number of members at our annual meeting.

- We want to improve our retention rate of members.

- We want to improve the satisfaction of our members.

If you have a clear understanding of the outcomes you hope to achieve, you can identify the areas of inquiry important for a research process to address. You can also evaluate the return on investment of your research activities.

To begin, list all the potential membership outcomes you think are important. Then talk with your staff or key volunteer leaders to prioritize which outcomes should drive the research. Some outcomes might be complementary. For example, a customized membership value proposition supports both acquisition and retention goals.

Key Questions Membership Research Can Address

Common membership outcomes generate a series of key questions that are often answered through membership research:

- Whom do we represent, and how is the membership divided into different markets and constituencies?

- What are the issues and problems with the greatest impact on our members?

- What are the personal, professional, and organizational goals or outcomes that are important to members?

- What are the programs and services that help members achieve their outcomes and thus represent the most value?

- How can we improve the marketing and implementation of our programs and services?

- What competitive influences or alternatives have the most impact on our members?

- What opportunities exist for our association, and how do we take advantage of these opportunities?

Establishing a Research Management Strategy

By developing an ongoing process to answer these questions, the association creates a research management strategy providing decision-makers with the information and insight necessary for the association to create long-term, sustainable growth. When establishing the association's ongoing research process, consider the following questions.

Who Is Going to Use the Research Results?

Associations often serve many different audiences. As a result, research activities are often designed to serve a wide variety of decision-makers working on a range of potential outcomes.

In 2013, the National Association of the Remodeling Industry (NARI) conducted a comprehensive environmental scan and membership needs assessment and used the information collected through it to provide:

- Guidance to the board for the association's strategic renewal initiative.

- Guidance to individual staff department heads on program improvement.

- Guidance to volunteer leaders of committees to improve programming and members' access to function-specific special interest group meetings.

This example represents only a portion of the decisions that were supported by this research project. Good research supports multiple objectives within the association.

NARI has established an annual process for collecting membership information for both staff and volunteer leaders. Today, they are beginning to see the benefits of this annual benchmarking process, as it highlights changes in the environment within which their members live and work and the corresponding changes in their needs for the association.

Different groups within the association have different roles and responsibilities. Each group needs information for different types of decisions. By understanding who will be using your information, you can make sure that the information collected addresses their needs.

What Is the Venue(s) for Decision Making?

There are three main venues for decision making within the association. The needs of decision-makers within each venue should guide research efforts of:

- Volunteer leadership groups (e.g., board of directors)
- Staff/volunteer leader combinations (e.g., membership committee)
- Staff groups (e.g., staff meeting or budget committee meeting)

Information at its most strategic level regarding the association's membership and the member environment is necessary to support board-level decisions about organizational strategy. For staff/volunteer groups, information must help these groups make decisions within their areas of influence, such as chapter development, conference education, or member marketing activities. Staff-directed groups need tactical information to guide execution of programs and services by improving the configuration and marketing of these efforts.

Although information collected through the research process should be reconfigured to meet the needs of decision-makers within each venue, information used in each venue is not mutually exclusive. Volunteer groups may also need tactical information, and staff groups will also need strategic information.

What Is the Time Frame of the Decision?

Some decisions are made on an immediate basis, while others are considered over a long time frame. For planning purposes, three general timeframes may be used.

- *Long term*—greater than one year. Long-term decisions relate to the ongoing assessment of the member market and the evolution of the association over time to serve members within this market. Decision-makers must anticipate how factors will affect members three to five years in the future and prepare accordingly. Environmental scanning information to guide strategic planning is an example of information supporting long-term decisions.

- *Annual*—Annual decisions relate to the annual planning and implementation of the association's programs and services, for example, budget development and approval. These decisions are predictable and important to effective allocation of resources. For example, an annual satisfaction study could provide insight into which programs or services are expanded, reduced, or modified.

- *Short term*—less than one year. Short-term decisions may take place at a committee or staff meeting and guide the direct implementation of association programs and services. Staff needs specific information relevant to these decisions. An example might be insight into how to improve the rate of renewals during the membership renewal process.

By understanding the time frame of decisions, you can establish specific tactics for data collection and analysis to ensure that information is available when the decisions are being made.

What Is the Impact of the Decisions Being Researched?

The value of research is in the application of data, not the collection of data. If the association is not going to use research, then conducting research is a waste of time and resources. Depending on the impact of a decision, the association executive can determine the relative worth of a research process supporting a decision.

The association executive should consider not only the beneficial outcomes of better decision making but also the opportunity costs of continuing activities based on incorrect assumptions or knowledge. Consider the following simple analysis for a sample association.

The association has a budget of $1.5 million and represents 3,000 members with a dues amount of $200 per person. The association's retention rate has been a steady 80 percent for many years.

Each year the association conducts a fall and spring new member campaign, mailing 1,000 membership brochures to prospective members. The brochure outlines the key membership value proposition and member benefits, and the two mailings cost a total of $6,000 (excluding staff time).

Unfortunately, since the brochure is based on the wrong member value proposition, the performance of the promotion is not as effective as it could be. Instead of finding 100 new members each year from this campaign, the association acquires only 50. Table 7.1 highlights the costs of this reduced performance.

Table 7.1. Performance, Expenses, and Lost Revenue

Year 1 Lost Revenue	Year 2 Lost Revenue	Year 3 Lost Revenue
50 new members @ $200 = $10,000	40 retained members @ $200 = $8,000	40 retained members @ $200 = $8,000
	50 new members @ $200 = $10,000	40 retained members @ $200 = $8,000
		50 new members @ $200 = $10,000
$10,000	$18,000	$26,000
Year 1 Direct Expense	**Year 2 Direct Expense**	**Year 3 Direct Expense**
Campaign Costs = $3,000 (1/2 are wasted)	Campaign Costs = $3,000	Campaign Costs = $3,000
Total Opportunity Cost	**Total Opportunity Cost**	**Total Opportunity Cost**
Net costs = $13,000	$21,000	$29,000

The total costs for this decision error are $63,000 over three years. In addition, this example demonstrates that the costs increase for each year the association fails to correct its mistake. Finally, in this example, we've only considered a single promotion. Since the fundamental understanding of the member value proposition is incorrect, every new member promotion is flawed, so the total cost of this mistake is amplified.

This is a simple example, but it illustrates how using membership research effectively can have substantial short- and long-term benefits that must be considered when making decisions about the annual research investment of the association.

Saving $15,000 in the direct costs of a quality research study fails to take into account the opportunity costs and direct impact of decisions based on a flawed understanding of the market. As the potential opportunity costs of making the wrong decision increase, the justified investment in research also increases. If in doubt about the decision to conduct research, simply ask yourself if you can afford to be wrong. The more strongly you answer no, the more important research to support your decision becomes.

Areas of Inquiry for Membership Research

Research can be as simple or as complex as your budget and time frame allow. Based on the assumption that the association does not currently have a robust research program, there are four key areas of inquiry that represent common areas of inquiry for membership research.

By collecting information in each of these areas, the association creates a comprehensive picture of the membership and the factors with the greatest impact on membership strategy. These four areas of inquiry should not limit the association's exploration of potential research topics, but should begin providing the necessary context about which areas might be most useful to study, given limited resources and the association's distinct research goals.

Market Identification

Who do we represent? A key step in membership analysis is to create a membership profile identifying the individual and organizational characteristics of your membership that are important to decision making. Individual characteristics are demographics related to the person, for example, age or gender. Organizational characteristics are demographics related to the employing organization within which the person may operate, such as the number of employees or gross revenue. The purpose for creating an audience profile is to clearly identify primary audiences for service, their unique characteristics, and similarities and differences between audiences.

Understanding the characteristics of an audience is essential to customizing the association's service to these audiences. In addition, this audience definition helps leadership prioritize between audiences so that resource allocation decisions can be made openly and objectively, given the strategic priorities of the association.

Membership Marketing Strategy

Membership Environment Assessment

What is the environment in which members operate? The impact of the environment on your members will shape their relationship to the association. The purpose for researching this area is to collect the evidence necessary to identify the concerns and challenges facing or anticipated by the association's members. By understanding the problems of the target audience; your association can produce, modify, or expand programs that address these problems.

Environmental analysis can range from macro-factors, such as immigration or changes in technology, to micro-factors specific to the individual, such as a personal desire to limit business travel. Five distinct areas should be considered for analysis:

1. *External environmental factors.* External factors are defined as issues completely outside the members' industry but with an impact on their company or profession. An example of these factors might include new technology, economic conditions, or even international conflict.

2. *Industry factors.* Industry factors are defined as issues within the industry in which your members operate. An example of industry factors might be consolidation or new entrants into the market.

3. *Company factors.* Company factors are defined as issues within the employing organization of your members. An example of a company factor might be changes in staffing models or new technology.

4. *Professional factors.* Professional factors are defined as issues within the profession represented by your members. An example might be government-mandated changes in credentialing or continuing education.

5. *Personal factors.* Personal factors are defined as issues that directly impact the individual. An example might be personal reluctance to travel or commute.

By creating a comprehensive understanding of the environment within which your members operate, you can identify what changes or threats might represent opportunities for the association.

Association Performance Assessment

What is the relationship of members to the association, and how is this relationship reflected in their use of association programs, products, or other association initiatives?

Members join an association to receive some determined value. How they receive this value is reflected in their choices for participation with the association. Avenues of participation can be as complex as volunteering for a committee or as simple as purchasing a book. The goal when researching this area is to identify patterns of behavior and assess the level to which the association is successfully serving members through its existing portfolio of programs, services, or initiatives. Key factors to assess within this area include factors with the greatest impact on the decision to join and the decision to retain membership. Which factors have the greatest influence on membership value, and how do these factors differ for each audience?

In addition, information can be collected on the awareness of, use of, satisfaction with, and perceived value or perceived importance of individual association programs. This information provides a framework for assessing your association's current performance and for modifying existing programs and services to deliver improved value to your members. This area of research focuses on understanding the relationship between the member and the association. Also important to assess, separately from the distinct programs and services, is the role of the association in the life of the member and how this role is reflected in the emotional connection between the association and the member.

Competing Influence Assessment

What other organizations compete with the association and what is the impact of these organizations? No association operates in a vacuum. This area of inquiry identifies primary competitive influences and the criteria members use to make decisions relative to these competitors.

Michael Porter is considered the leading expert on competitive analysis. His seminal work identified Porter's Five Forces (listed below) that are important to the understanding of the competitive environment and the use of this information in decision making.

- *Jockeying among current providers*. This area relates to the current competition between existing providers within a market. For example, two different associations may be attempting to serve the same market with education programs delivered through a conference.

- *Threat of new entrants*. The threat of new entrants relates to the potential for new organizations, such as another association, to enter the market to provide similar or directly competing programs. The greater the barriers to entry into a market, the more difficult it becomes for new organizations to enter the market.

- *Bargaining power of suppliers*. The bargaining power of suppliers relates to the ability of suppliers to affect the organization's flexibility to configure or provide their services. The more powerful the supplier community in a market, the less flexibility the association has in configuring product or service options because powerful suppliers can dictate terms.

- *Bargaining power of customers*. The bargaining power of customers relates to the ability of customers to affect the organization's flexibility to configure or provide its services. The more powerful the customer base, the less flexibility the association has in configuring its portfolio of programs, products, and services.

- *Substitute products*. Substitute products relate to service options different from existing solutions, but which still meet the needs of customers. For example, virtual training, using advances in technology, represents a substitute educational product that reduces the market for face-to-face, hands-on training.

Understanding the relationship of Porter's Five Forces and developing specific strategies to deal with each area is central to developing a successful strategy that reflects the realities of the competitive environment.

Research Methodologies for Associations

The development of the research methodology can be simple or complex, depending on your research needs. A complete discussion of research methodologies is beyond the scope of this chapter, but some guidelines and concepts can help you narrow your focus.

A specific market research methodology balances the following:

- *Data type.* What type of information are you trying to collect?

- *Direct costs (e.g., postage, data entry).* What are the direct costs of conducting the research and are these costs fixed or variable based on the methodology?

- *Professional fees (if using external expertise).* What type of external assistance are you engaging and what will these services provide and cost?

- *Time frame (one month, several months, ongoing).* What is the time frame for conducting the study, analyzing the data, and providing the report?

The optimal market research process may incorporate different methodologies designed to balance the strengths and weaknesses of each method while respecting the financial resources and time frame of the association.

Each specific tool for market research has advantages and disadvantages.

Primary and Secondary Data

Research collects data. Generally speaking, there are two types of data. Primary data is new data collected specifically to address the problem at hand, and secondary data is data that has already been collected through another research project. Both types of data are important. The membership executive needs to evaluate the value of existing secondary data so that new, primary data collected does not duplicate this information and adds to the association's knowledge base.

Qualitative vs. Quantitative Research

There are two general methods of research. Qualitative research is not subject to quantification or quantitative analysis. Quantitative research is subject to mathematical or statistical analysis.

Qualitative research is used to help the association understand the in-depth motivations and feelings of a target audience. Focus groups represent a common form of qualitative research. Qualitative research is best used in conjunction with quantitative methodologies. Qualitative research provides the analyst with a more in-depth understanding of complex issues, which is helpful during analysis. Qualitative research is also used to identify potential response options that can be tested using quantitative tools.

Qualitative research is less effective in identifying small differences in the marketing mix that may have a great impact on the success of a project or program. A second weakness is that conclusions drawn from qualitative data may not be representative of the larger membership audience.

Quantitative research is used to provide more accurate, objective information that can be extrapolated to a larger audience. Common forms of quantitative research include mail or online survey instruments. Quantitative research allows the association to specifically test precise concepts. Quantitative research uses surveys that can be mailed, posted online, or done by telephone or even with on-site intercepts, such as at a conference. The key is that the results can be quantified.

Common Tools of Market Research

In preparing for research, the membership professional should become familiar with the following common research tools.

Data Mining

Data mining is a series of tools used to study the internal database of the association created by the association through existing activities. For example, dues collection often provides insight into demographics. Purchase history provides insight into popular educational content or preferred delivery channels.

The use of data mining and other strategic database analysis tools represents a growing resource for associations that have invested in the collection of data about members for many years as part of other initiatives that may not have been originally conceived as research sources.

Stakeholder Interviews

An executive interview is a structured or semi-structured format in which the researcher asks a series of questions to an individual selected as part of the study. This method is an excellent choice for collecting in-depth information from individuals who would be difficult to reach through other qualitative mechanisms or for which other mechanisms would be cost-prohibitive.

In-Person or Online Focus Groups

A focus group is a group of 8 to 12 participants who are led by a moderator in an in-depth discussion on one particular topic or concept. Today, focus groups can be organized as face-to-face activities or as online events. The primary advantage of focus groups is the opportunity to probe for in-depth insight or understanding of the membership audience and learn from the interaction between participants. The primary disadvantages of focus groups, particularly face to face, are the costs and the inability to quantify the analysis or extrapolate findings to the larger membership audience.

Focus groups can also be organized more informally, for example, at the association's annual conference. The key to focus groups is to establish a group that represents a diverse range of opinions relative to the research goals.

Online Surveys

Online surveys are similar to paper surveys but are administered via the Internet. The capabilities of the online format allow for a more robust data collection instrument and faster turnaround time without additional expenses for paper and postage. The primary disadvantage of online surveys exists when online access to members is restricted because of members' Internet security protocols or other technological limitations.

Telephone Surveys

Telephone surveys can be used for both qualitative and quantitative research. Commonly, members of a particular audience are contacted and led through a structured or semi-structured interview process. The primary advantage of telephone interviews is the ability to collect data very quickly. The primary disadvantage is the limitation on the number and type of questions that can be asked before respondent fatigue begins to influence the results.

Mixed Mode Surveys

A mixed mode survey strategy combines different types of surveys into a single process. For example, an online survey will be combined with a mailed survey. Mixed mode survey strategies are the most comprehensive form of data collection and provide a greater volume and quality of data for analysis. The primary disadvantages are the additional costs involved and the longer time frame for instrument development and data collection.

Survey Deployment and Analysis

The development and implementation of the survey instrument varies by method, but there are some common steps:

1. Identify whom you will survey based on the research goals.

2. Develop a list of initial questions.

3. Determine question and response format.

4. Establish questionnaire flow and layout.

5. Evaluate the questionnaire and layout.

6. Deploy the survey instrument.

7. Collect, edit, and analyze research data.

Whom Should We Survey?

The sampling plan outlines who will be included in a research study. Depending on the research objectives and size of the target audience, the association can survey a sample of the target audience or conduct a complete census, including every member or stakeholder.

There are many types of sampling plans, but the goal of all sampling plans is to identify a potential respondent group of sufficient size and with the proper characteristics to ensure sufficient data quality for analysis.

When developing the research plan, these steps should act as a guide for the creation of the specific research implementation strategy. Today, the implementation of a survey may include providing access not only to many different people, but through many different devices. The use of multi-modal surveys provides for higher response rates and improved data quality, but also creates challenges for the research. For example, some very useful research techniques such as discrete choice analysis, critical to effective pricing, are not compatible with mobile delivery due to the complexity of the question. It is thus necessary to balance research needs with an understanding of the value of multimodal survey distribution. Both are important considerations.

Sidebar: American College of Surgeons (Using Multimodal Research)

In 2014, the American College of Surgeons (ACS) needed to conduct their membership satisfaction survey. Unfortunately, they were concerned about the response rate because surgeons' schedules are generally crammed and there's not much room for downtime between patients. The demands on their time have made it historically more challenging to obtain the required response and completion rates for surveys with this extremely busy group.

The ACS was able to tackle this challenge by working with Association Laboratory, Inc., to effectively design a survey that doctors in 30 countries completed across a variety of devices—PCs, smartphones, and tablets—as well as a variety of operating systems.

The survey design, which made responding convenient, fast, and easy—combined with technology that enabled consistent responses across all devices—was just the right prescription for obtaining an effective response rate and very high completion rate with accurate insights under a tight deadline. The survey garnered more than 2,800 responses. The responses were consistent no matter what device people used to take the survey and resulted in a very high completion rate (93 percent of the people who started the survey completed it) with this hard-to-reach demographic.

How to Analyze the Results

Analyzing research results is an ongoing process that creates a dialogue among the users of data. Users should look for patterns in the data and be creative about using data for different needs. For example, environmental scanning information can be used to guide needs assessment decisions, educational content decisions, and messaging decisions.

Analyzing research data is a complex undertaking. Misinterpretation of research data—the researcher coming to the wrong conclusions—can harm the association's strategy development because it may encourage the association to pursue a strategy at odds with the realities of the marketplace. To minimize this risk, the association executive must take a common-sense, methodical approach to reviewing the information, developing conclusions, and communicating recommendations.

The development of your research process should be designed to produce quality information without bias. Three major types of survey bias or error in survey research should be considered.

1. *Sampling bias (the Wrong People)*. These are errors that result from chance variation. Chance variation is the inevitable difference between the sample value and the true value of the sample mean. This error cannot be avoided, only reduced by increasing the sample size. For the practitioner, this means you need to clearly identify the participants in your research so that their responses are as reflective as possible of the overall body of individuals for whom you are developing strategy.

2. *Systematic bias (the Wrong Process)*. Systematic bias is error that results from poor research design or execution. The development and implementation of a quality research project takes specific expertise and experience. If the project is poorly designed or executed, flaws in the data may result. For the practitioner, this means that you must carefully consider the steps in your research process to ensure that you don't inadvertently create flawed data by using the wrong research tools.

3. *Measurement bias*. Measurement bias is error that results from a discrepancy between the information being sought and what is actually obtained by the measurement process. For the practitioner, this means that you need to confirm that the information you collect is what you expected and needed to collect from the research process.

The following steps are important to the analysis:

- Determine the quality of your research data. As discussed earlier, sampling bias is addressed by managing the size and composition of the sample. Systemic bias is addressed through the creation and implementation of a quality research process.

- Review the results, given your expectations of the response to determine the extent of any measurement error. While some error is inevitable, understand the differences between your expected and collected information, take this into account, and adjust your analysis accordingly.

- Review the data objectively, without a predetermined set of conclusions or biases. This is perhaps the most difficult step in the analysis. If the researcher approaches the analysis with a pre-existing bias, the final analysis and recommendations will reflect this bias and affect association performance.

- Review the data skeptically. The researcher must understand not only what the data says but also what it does not say. Don't look for answers that are not supported by the data collected.

- Focus not just on individual pieces of information but also on patterns of information that represent a more complete depiction of respondents' attitudes and opinions.

In summary, the analysis consists of two components: what the research knows based on the data and what the research suspects based on an interpretation of the data. The final analysis must be clear between these two points of view.

Presenting Research Results to Decision-Makers

One of the most challenging aspects of research is to make the resulting information and recommendations actionable. Too often a quality research study simply acts as an impressive doorstop because decision-makers don't understand the information or don't understand how to apply the information to their problems. Membership research can fulfill three functional roles: descriptive, diagnostic, and predictive.

- The descriptive role includes gathering and presenting statements of fact. For example, 20 percent of respondents are between the ages of 25 and 30 years old.

- In the diagnostic role, data or actions of a particular target market are explained. A common diagnostic question is satisfaction. A question is used to collect member satisfaction on each of the top 10 programs or services. Programs that are rated lower in satisfaction are given priority for review.

- The predictive role involves collecting data to help anticipate future behavior. For example, a study might ask: "How critical will each of the following industry issues be to your company over the next three years?"

A good market research study helps the association balance these three areas to provide the highest quality and most useful information for decision making. To provide a quality research report, consider the responsibilities of the researcher:

- First, determine the quality of the data. Poor data or inappropriate data should not be included in your study. If you discover that respondents had difficulty answering a question, simply remove this data from the analysis.

- Second, analyze the data correctly. There are a wide variety of analytical techniques to review data, but first and foremost, use common sense. Review the data with an open, objective mind.

- Third, look for insights that lie behind the data. Consider the following metaphor. If you want to know which way the wind is blowing, you don't look for the wind. Instead you look at which way the branches or leaves of a tree are blowing. A great deal of research can be categorized as showing the leaves blowing in the trees. A good researcher asks what lies behind the research. What is driving the response?

- Fourth, present the information in context to the decision being considered. A list of tables and charts is not helpful if the information contained is not directly applied to the decision. Don't force decision-makers to configure the data to meet their needs; this is the job of the researcher.

- Finally, tell the story. You are responsible not only for providing information but also for telling decision-makers what you think it means. Provide insight, not just data.

Engaging a Research Consultant

Many associations conduct high-quality research without engaging external assistance, while others rely on external partners for virtually all aspects of their data collection, analysis, and reporting. The key is to understand the scope of your research activities and the association's internal capacity and capability to conduct research.

The market research industry is highly specialized and fragmented. A company that is outstanding at producing an online survey may have no expertise in qualitative research. An organization with substantive knowledge of one industry may have no experience in helping organizations in other industries. Within the supply chain of research there is a great deal of fragmentation. Consider the following simple example for producing an online survey.

- First, a research company representative needs to obtain the research business. This is often a company principal or related executive manager.

- Second, an analyst or researcher must design the research methodology and create the questions that will be asked.

- Third, an individual will be responsible for programming the HTML language, managing the e-mail deployment, and generally overseeing the physical creation and deployment of the survey.

- Fourth, an individual may be responsible for statistical quality control and analysis.

- Finally, an individual may be responsible for recommendations and reporting.

While a separate person may not be responsible for each step, this simple example reveals the diverse steps within a research process. The process requires a human, technological, and physical infrastructure to be successful. The more research you conduct, the more an investment in this infrastructure makes sense for the association. The more likely scenario is that the association will purchase the infrastructure and insights from an external research provider. (See Benefits of External Research Assistance.)

Benefits of External Research Assistance

- *Access to research capacity.* Few association staff members are sitting around with nothing to do but conduct research. By contracting with an external resource, the association trades financial resources for the capacity to conduct the study.
- *Specialized expertise.* Many research companies have special industry or strategy expertise. By contracting with these companies, the association gains their expertise and experience with these issues.
- *Objectivity.* An external resource looks at your information with a fresh eye. This provides new insight or ideas in areas where the association might be struggling.
- *Independence.* An external resource will be an independent voice unbiased by politics or other legacy issues that may stand in the way of effective analysis.

As the volume of research conducted by the association increases, the value of developing an internal capability for research increases. In addition, the more objectivity, independence, and specialized expertise are critical to the analysis and recommendations, the more an external resource adds value. For most associations, a combination of internal capability and external support is the best option.

To create an optimal research infrastructure, consider the following simple process.

1. Assess the past and current research activity of the association. What research have you been doing and why? What has been the result of this research?

2. Identify desired research needs of both staff and volunteer leaders. What information is required or desired to make decisions.

3. Identify gaps between current and desired research needs. Based on the gap, develop a structure to help you meet your research needs within the resources you have available.

To determine your external support needs, it can be helpful to conduct an internal research audit. See the Research Audit Questions in Exhibit 7.1 at the end of this chapter.

Membership research is a tool to help membership executives develop and implement successful membership strategy. Competent membership professionals will be familiar with the use of membership research to guide decisions and develop strategy.

Reference

Porter, Michael E.. *On Competition*. Boston: Harvard Business Press, 1979.

About the Author

Dean A. West, FASAE, is president of Association Laboratory Inc. Association Laboratory is a nationally recognized strategic research firm serving trade and professional associations through staff and offices in Chicago, Illinois, and Washington, D.C. West is a fellow of ASAE and a former board member of the Association Forum of Chicagoland. He is a former executive director and has more than 25 years' experience in association management, business strategy, and marketing research. Email: dwest@associationlaboratory.com.

Exhibit 7.1. Research Audit Questions

The following questions provide a simple process to assess the internal capacity and capability of the association to conduct research. By answering these questions, the association gains an understanding of what human, technical, and external resources might be necessary to implement an effective, ongoing research process to guide decisions.

1. What research has been conducted within the last three years?
2. What was the purpose, reason, or rationale for this research?
3. How or by whom was this research initiated?
4. What were the goals of the research?
5. What type of research was conducted?
   a. Qualitative
   b. Quantitative
   c. Integrated or combined methodologies
   d. Other
6. What tools were used to collect the information?
7. Who conducted the research?
8. Was the research a single project or is it ongoing?
9. Who were the primary users of the information?
10. How was the research used to improve decision making?
11. What is the key decision-maker or project leader's evaluation of the research?
12. What was the actual or estimated cost of the research?
13. What future research projects are currently anticipated or included within the planning cycle?
14. What challenges or opportunities are currently driving a desire for increased research, analysis, or other membership or market understanding?
15. What are gaps in the understanding of key decision-makers regarding the association's products, services, or markets?
16. What is your internal capacity and capability to conduct research?
17. What external support is necessary to conduct research you believe is essential to quality decision making?

Mission ~~Im~~possible

8

Using Data to Drive Organizational Excellence: Collecting, Managing, and Using Member and Prospect Data

By Wes Trochlil and Sherry Budziak

IN THIS CHAPTER

- Is Your Database Supporting Your Mission?
- AMS/CRM: A Prerequisite for Data-Driven Organizations
- Determining Requirements and Selecting an AMS/CRM
- Achieving a Successful Implementation
- Managing and Using Data

Is Your Database Supporting Your Mission?

Whether it's improving volunteer engagement, increasing revenue and decreasing marketing costs, or better managing member and customer data, your association management system (AMS) or customer relationship management system (CRM) should be supporting your organization's mission. CRM software is designed to manage all customers (and potential customers), including all contact information (name, address, email, phone, demographics). CRM systems allow you to track all interactions with a given customer and are often used to track the sales process (from lead to close). Traditional CRM software is not designed to manage financial sales transactions.

Association Management Software (AMS) is software customized to manage association-specific activities like membership, events registration, certification, and committee management. AMS software often has at least some rudimentary CRM functionality, and some AMS packages are built on CRM software packages (e.g., Salesforce.com and Microsoft Dynamics CRM). AMS software typically has accounts receivable functionality, allowing the association to track payments for membership, events, products, and so on.

Regardless of which database system is used, only an effectively managed one can provide your organization with the empirical data required to boost your bottom line, engage your volunteers, and ensure that your organization's mission is achieved.

In today's digital world, a centralized database system is a core asset of the organization's management capacity. It is the primary tool for managing the organization's day-to-day operations, including membership application and dues renewal, meeting logistics and registration, product sales, certification tracking, subscriptions, publications, fundraising, advertising sales, exhibit management, membership self-service, e-commerce, content management, activity tracking, reporting, and more. It tracks and accesses real-time information across functional areas.

Moreover, the modern AMS/CRM systems establish an in-house "standard" of consolidated, comprehensive demographic activity and preference data on all members, prospects, and other customers—enabling data to be analyzed and organized for developing future strategies and tactics.

AMS/CRM: A Prerequisite for Data-Driven Organizations

If data are the currency of the digital age, the foundation for creating and sustaining value is your AMS or CRM. An effective system provides a wealth of information and functionality that can improve decision making, support product development, increase operational efficiency and effectiveness, and enhance stakeholder satisfaction.

As technology continues to advance, a well-designed database system makes it possible to analyze and index all possible combinations of a member or customer's record—complete with intelligent reminders and notifications—to anticipate and customize what members or customers may want.

Even more important than collecting, organizing, and managing an individual's record, a modern AMS/CRM enables users to analyze and detect patterns, based on the behaviors and preferences of the entire customer base—setting the stage for a truly data-driven organization. Particularly when paired with a business intelligence (BI) system and integrated with other core association systems, such as the organization's content management system (CMS) and financial system, the opportunities increase exponentially to design and deliver the products, services, and experiences that provide the most value.

A well-designed and managed AMS/CRM system can help enhance value for an association's members and customers in numerous ways:

- The association can develop prototypical customer segments (personas) based on past purchase histories, preferences, expectations, career characteristics, and other relevant variables. The association can then develop targeted strategies to promote and cross-sell specific content to those segments.

- Going beyond existing product, services, and experiences, the analysis of data related to customer behavior/personas can facilitate the design of new offerings that will have a high probability of success.

- When data are integrated with a CMS, the association can personalize the member's digital communications experience. For example, when signing on to the association's website, the customer might be presented with relevant continuing educational courses, new web-based content related to topics for which he or she has expressed an interest, targeted journal articles and suggested e-books, or a discussion topic in a virtual community that is related to a particular interest.

- The AMS/CRM system can expand the potential of self-service opportunities, enabling customers to easily and efficiently handle a range of interactions with the association.

- There is an improvement in data quality, leading to reduced waste and increased operational efficiency and staff effectiveness. More resources can be focused on delivering customer value, and redundant, inconsistent data and "data islands" can be eliminated.

- As the repository of member and customer records, a well-structured, comprehensive AMS/CRM database establishes the basis for data-based decision making and BI systems.

Determining Requirements and Selecting an AMS/CRM

While there are many solutions from which to choose in the marketplace, at a general level there is a great deal of similarity among enterprise-wide association management systems. They all typically include standard modules to support functions such as constituent, committee, events and dues management, product sales, events registration, continuing education, and call center capabilities.

What differentiates systems is how well their design and specific capabilities will fit your organization, how well the AMS/CRM will integrate with your other systems, and which of your organization's operating processes will need to be adapted to fit the system.

Determining Requirements and Selecting an AMS/CRM

In addition to baseline functionality, some of the features that an association should expect from a well-designed AMS/CRM are:

- *Centralized data processing.* Ideally, all data managed by the organization should be processed through one centralized system rather than multiple databases. A centralized system minimizes data redundancy as well as provides a holistic view of members' and customers' activities. If portions of the database are housed in multiple systems, then it is critical that the systems share information—preferably in real time—so that any one data element appears only once.

- *Generation and tracking of all invoices.* A well-designed AMS/CRM serves as your organization's accounts-receivable (A/R) package—all money flowing into the organization is recorded here. It can keep track of open A/R and also provide insight into how members and customers are spending money on your organization's products and services.

- *Link to your financial package.* Once all of your A/R is in your database, you need a relatively easy way to move it from your database to your financial management system. Your AMS/CRM should allow you to create a summary export that can then be imported into your financial package so that no rekeying of data is necessary.

- *Seamless online experience.* Today's consumers expect to be able to interact with your organization when it is convenient for them. This means that your website becomes a primary point of interaction with your constituents. They expect to be able to manage their profiles as well as easily purchase your products and services. Your AMS/CRM solution should provide a strong connection between your back-office management system and your public-facing website.

- *Flexible reporting to support data-driven decision making.* The system housing your database is useful only if you can extract information from it. Therefore, it is important to have several options for analysis and reporting. In addition to cross-module reporting, the user interface should allow individuals from across the organization to analyze data and initiate complex queries relevant to their areas of responsibility. Some of the best insights can come from staff exploring the data, rather than relying on a limited number of predefined reports. Even system non-experts should be able to rely on the database to help answer questions and form strategies.

- *Tracking all member, nonmember, and customer transactions, including information collected by outside vendors.* Transactions with your members and customers often go beyond financial endeavors. Your members also will participate as volunteers and serve on committees; write for publications; speak at your meetings; and involve themselves in other, non-financial interactions. A well-designed AMS/CRM will enable you to track these "interactions" as well as your constituent "activities"—providing a holistic view of your members and customers.

- *Contact management.* Track communication between your organization and your members and customers by capturing conversations that occur by phone, social media, or email. This should also include incident tracking and resolution functionality, so that you can efficiently monitor and manage the resolution of customer issues.

- *Role-based security support.* While all staff should have access to your database, not all of them will need access to the same information or tools. A system should support setting up different roles based on the functional needs of each staff member. Therefore, it is important that an AMS/CRM system support role-based security. Staff should be able to log in and use the system as they need to use it, with full access to certain areas of the database and restricted access to others.

- *Tracking of changes (audit log).* Because the AMS/CRM will allow multiple users access to the system (including member and customer access through your website's self-service functions), you will need a way to track changes. The audit log does that, automatically capturing what changes were made to the database—including the field that was changed, when it was changed, and who made the change.

Selecting a New System

If you have an AMS/CRM system that is no longer meeting your needs, is hindering you from analyzing data, building customer personas, innovating, and moving forward with core strategies or is lacking in a well-designed user interface, then it may be time to look for new association management software or investigate whether the software can be further customized or evolve to meet current needs.

Symptoms that it is time to change might include having to manage multiple databases (e.g., Access, Excel, and Filemaker) throughout your organization, or your business processes have changed and are not being supported by the current system. Perhaps you have new programs that need to be supported, or you are struggling with your current system's capabilities. Even if your system adequately handles day-to-day tasks, you may realize it is not capable of taking you into the next generation of business intelligence and strategic data-based decision making.

Regardless of reasons, a rigorous process should be followed for determining your current and future needs and comparing them to the capabilities of alternative systems. There are more than 100 products on the market that claim to be association or membership management software systems. Selecting the right one for your organization can be daunting, but it will be much less so if you follow these six steps:

1. *Assess needs.* A review of internal business processes and system support needs—currently and in the near future—across the organization will help identify what functionality your AMS/CRM system requires.

2. *Develop a request for proposals (RFP).* Specify detailed functional requirements regarding your needs and what you expect the AMS/CRM to do in order to receive

the most accurate pricing and whether the product can meet those requirements. Be sure to ask about implementation processes, project management support and training, level of system security, ongoing support and maintenance, and prior installations in similar organizations.

3. *Identify prospective suppliers.* Consult resources like ASAE's knowledge center, events, directories, and online forums; state, regional, and local societies of association executives; and consultants.

4. *Review and score responses to the RFP, then convene demonstrations.* Based on the review of the RFP responses, identify two or three suppliers to demonstrate the software to you via a general overview or a scenario-based/"scripted" demonstration, in which concrete examples of managing or processing data are provided to determine whether a product can support your needs.

5. *Check references and select a supplier.* In addition to vendor-supplied references, talk to colleagues to identify other associations using the company's product and contact them for references. If possible, conduct an on-site visit to see the product in action.

6. *Negotiate a contract.* Pay particular attention to provisions regarding data backup and those that allow you to take control of the application and data should the vendor no longer be in a position to support you. Have a firm understanding of implementation costs during the first year, as well as ongoing fees in subsequent years and rates for additional support not included in the base contract.

Achieving a Successful Implementation

Implementation can be an arduous task. It is not just a matter of installing a system, but involves a range of activities that need careful attention. Among the most critical are:

- A detailed project governance and management plan

- An analysis of current processes and development of new standard operating procedures (SOPs)

- The design and implementation of links integrating other systems with the AMS/CRM, including single sign-on processes

- A data quality/data conversion plan

- Ensuring all set-ups, security, data, and reports are ready prior to going live with the new system

- A thorough and ongoing training plan

- A "mock" go live and debriefing process, including staff practicing their SOPs

Project Governance and Management

Successful implementation of a major system like an AMS/CRM is an organization-wide activity and begins with a well-defined project governance and management structure. Core roles may include:

- Project sponsor (a member of the senior management team, typically the individual overseeing membership)
- Oversight/steering committee (the senior management team or a designated group comprising senior leaders)
- Project manager (typically the IT staff lead, but often from membership)
- Core team/staff technology committee (e.g., cross-department business unit/functional leaders)
- Subject-matter experts (individuals involved at various stages as their specific areas of responsibility and expertise become relevant)

An appropriate oversight structure then needs to be supplemented by project management tools and processes, well-defined benchmarks and metrics, and a comprehensive ongoing communication plan.

Process Improvement and Standard Operating Procedures

Implementing a new AMS/CMS creates an opportunity for the organization to examine its current processes and look for improvement opportunities. There may be situations in which keeping an existing process and modifying the system appear advantageous for the organization. However, the more customized a system is, the more complex it becomes to integrate with other systems. In addition, following a standard upgrade path to future enhancements becomes more difficult, and the ability to receive system maintenance support may be compromised.

Along with reviewing current processes and determining which ones may need modification, staff should be documenting the new processes. This is critical both for training and in the event of staff turnover.

System Integration

The AMS/CRM will be designed as the central hub for the organization's data. That means that other third-party solutions need to feed data into the AMS/CRM, and the AMS/CRM system needs to provide those other systems with information. Whether data is flowing between the financial system and the AMS/CRM when a member enrolls in a seminar, or data transfers between the content management system and the AMS/CRM when members update their profiles on your website, the goal is to have one integrated system in which a piece of data exists only once and then is shared as needed.

Given that the typical association will have many systems from various vendors (content management, learning management, abstract management, and financial management systems, among others), a very well-planned and thought-out integration strategy is critical to success.

Integration: What You Need to Consider

When starting the process of integrating your database system with other third-party applications, there are a few guiding principles to keep in mind. For example:

- While data should flow among systems, each piece of data should exist in only one place. As a simple example, if a member's organizational affiliation is saved in two systems, the database would quickly lose synchronization.
- Ideally, data flowing to and from the AMS/CRM should be in real time. Think of a user who changes her email address. In order to maintain "single sign-on" functionality, that change needs to be communicated in real time across any other systems relying on an accurate email address.
- Data quality controls will make or break the long-term value of the system, particularly as the organization expands self-service options, user-initiated purchases, and other transactions on its website.

Some of the more specific things that need to be addressed related to the organization's integration strategy and third-party applications are:

- Accounting (accounts receivable, general ledger, etc.)
- Registration software. What information needs to be kept in your AMS/CRM?
- Website content. Will you require personalized information that will need to be pulled from the database, such as continuing education credits?
- Online member directories, such as name, business address, phone number, and email. Will a separate directory with more detailed information be required for a password-protected membership directory?
- Self-service capabilities. Will you allow members to edit their own data, and if so, what data will they be able to edit? Also, will they be able to add profile information that can be retained in the database?
- e-Commerce. Will you need to track any transactional product information from your back office database on the website?
- Event registration. How will you make sure to track membership event history if you manage your event registration via a third party? You will need a strategy for capturing this information in your membership system as well.
- Surveys. Do you want to associate survey responses with the individual member record? What analytics are available to analyze survey data?
- Advocacy. What level of engagement do you want to provide for your members to communicate with their respective legislators? For example, is it necessary to provide specific legislator addresses and salutations for template emails based on your home or business address ?

Data Quality/Data Conversion Plan

Just as an organization should explore updated operating procedures when implementing its AMS/CRM, it also should commit to cleaning its current database and establishing a data governance process to guide initial data conversion as well as ongoing data quality efforts. Data conversion often is a critical path item that is addressed too late in the process, leading to failed promises and schedule delays. It is never too early to address data conversion and data quality.

The data cleaning process may include purging old and duplicative records as well as archiving data. To convert the remaining data for use in the new AMS/CRM, it is necessary to develop standardized definitions for every data field, map data fields from the old to the new database, and train staff who enter data into the database to define each field in the same way and use the same naming conventions. During the testing phase it will be necessary to run parallel systems for a period of time to ensure that data and systems are operating as expected. There also will have to be quality checks built into the self-service center as members update and modify their own records.

Security

There are myriad potential security issues to consider when implementing the AMS/CRM. Since individuals throughout the organization will have access to the system, it will be necessary to set up a role-based security system defining access to the database and the ability to make modifications to specific fields. Staff should be able to log in and use the system as they need to use it, with full access to only certain areas of the database and restricted access to others.

The database will also have to be secure from outside attacks. As web-based systems increasingly link to the database, including through the self-service center for members, the risk of unauthorized access must be addressed.

Data Reporting

The AMS/CRM should have flexible reporting capabilities to allow individuals to explore and analyze data to develop new ways to add value to the member experience. In addition, the system will need to generate sets of standardized reports designed to support and monitor ongoing operations. From tracking member recruitment and retention efforts to reminders for follow-up action related to member inquires, each department in the organization will rely on the AMS/CRM to help keep track of core metrics and make decisions. Therefore, standard ongoing reports required by managers should be thoroughly tested prior to going live with a new system to make sure that there is no loss of operational efficiency.

Thorough and Ongoing Training

Implementing a new CRM/AMS represents major changes for the organization. It may involve changes in organizational culture, and it certainly will involve changes in operating processes. There also will be changes related to the definition of data elements used in the new system. And, of course, there is the basic task of learning a new user interface and how to efficiently navigate the system.

All the changes associated with the new system require staff training—ranging from the simple mechanics of using the system to new processes and approaches for maintaining data quality. Staff also will need to gain an appreciation for how information from the database can help them do their jobs and accomplish the goals and objectives of their specific departments.

If staff is given only short-term training on the mechanics of navigating the AMS/CRM, then the implementation will be rocky and there will be significant risk that data quality will quickly deteriorate. Instead, initiate a comprehensive, ongoing training and development program that addresses topics such as standard operating procedures, data definition/quality, the use of information, and navigating the system interface.

"Mock" Go Live and Debriefing Process

When you have successfully completed several testing cycles, new processes are ready to go, data have been converted to the new system, and everyone has experienced initial training, it is time for the final step—a mock go-live test. The test will give everyone the opportunity to examine what they have learned, apply sample scripts/ scenarios for interacting with the database, confirm data flow and system integrations, and ensure operating processes are understood and applied as designed.

The most important part of the mock go-live is the evaluation process. There should be a thorough "action" debriefing process leading to a "go" or "no go" decision. While any glitches should have been identified in earlier rounds of phased testing, if unexpected issues arise, the mock go-live provides the final opportunity to discover and fix implementation problems, whether related to the system itself, integrations with other systems, training, or new operating processes.

Managing and Using Data

The payoff from having a well-functioning AMS/CRM comes from the way the organization manages and uses data, transforming it into meaningful information to support data-driven decision making and enhancing value to members and other customers.

The competition for a member's time and attention is fierce. To be successful in communicating a message and providing value to members, it is increasingly imperative to target timely information that is valued by the specific member, and to do so when and how the member wants to receive it. Discovering that "right" mix of content, timing, and distribution can be facilitated by the database.

For example, understanding the purchasing behavior of member segments/prototypical personas can help the organization make resource allocation decisions related to new product development. It also can lead to more focused marketing efforts, as well as a personalized experience when members interact with the organization's website.

The data from the AMS/CRM also can be used to develop likely profiles of prospective members. For example, a non-member may interact with the organization by purchasing a product or enrolling in an educational activity. The type of interaction and what is learned about the customer's preferences may suggest the individual fits a segment that also might be interested in joining the association to gain access to other specific products/services or collegial networks. That creates the opportunity to develop focused tactics specifically targeting and cross-selling to that segment. However, the process of cultivating prospects can be a long one. Fortunately, a database is the ideal way to manage and monitor a long-term strategy for cultivating prospects.

One particular group of prospects that many associations find problematic are graduating students entering the profession. Many associations have student members, and may extend full membership to students for one year after graduation, only to discover that most simply drop from sight after the complimentary year. An analysis of the database may discover patterns among those who do join, which then can be extrapolated to develop approaches to products, services, interactions, and communications, which may improve conversions.

Another scenario could be that a significant cluster of graduates return later at a certain career stage rather than joining right after graduation. Again, that information could be translated to develop appropriate marketing strategies and tactics.

Using the Data to Measure Engagement

Measuring member engagement has become increasingly important to associations over the past few years. But what is member engagement? From the book *Maximum Engagement*, written by David Gammel, CAE, and published by ASAE, member engagement is defined as ". . . the result of a member investing time and/or money with the association in exchange for value." It's a very simple definition, but very powerful. Engagement is the exchange of time and/or money for value. Engagement could be volunteer time, attending a conference, responding to a survey, or dozens of other activities.

There are four keys to measuring member engagement:

1. *Identifying the data you do and do not have.* The first step in the process is knowing what data you have and where it's kept. Next is identifying data you don't have and determining how you'll collect that and where.

2. *Identifying significant engagement points.* What data points best demonstrate engagement? How long an individual has been a member? Which events he attends? What kind of volunteer service she does? Each association will have a different list.

3. *Scoring the engagement points.* For most associations, different activities have different value. For example, service on the board of directors may be more significant than attendance at a local meeting. Each data point should receive its own "weight" or value.

4. *Review periodically.* Just like data management itself, the process by which you measure engagement should be reviewed periodically to ensure that you are collecting and measuring the data points that are most relevant to member engagement.

Using the Data to Measure Engagement

For the past four years, Grantmakers for Effective Organizations (GEO) has been measuring member engagement using the data they collect in their database, which includes event registration, interactions between staff and members, and website activity. GEO was interested in learning how engaged their membership is and whether there was any correlation between level of engagement and membership retention.

GEO identified 36 data points within their database that they believed demonstrated engagement. These points included in-person engagement, volunteer service, how long the organization had been a member, content and resources use of the website, and much more. Because GEO is using a fully integrated data management system, all of these data points were available in one system.

GEO extracted these data points, weighted them (gave different values to different activities) and scored all 400 of their organizational members. Here are a few things they learned:

- There is a positive relationship between engagement score and renewal rate. For example, members in the top 30th percentile of engagement scores are nearly 100 percent likely to renew their memberships the following year. Conversely, members in the bottom 20 percentile of engagement scores are least likely to renew their memberships.

- Despite an overall increase in membership over three years, total engagement scores have remained steady (that is, as GEO grows, members remain engaged, rather than becoming less engaged).

More importantly, GEO is able to use this data to proactively engage members, especially those members in the bottom 20 percent who are most likely to drop membership. GEO has developed new programs to engage these members, including quarterly webinars, orientation webinars for new members (to help them understand and take advantage of all of GEO's products and services), and more direct outreach from GEO staff (for example, scheduling in-person meetings with "at risk" organization members when GEO staff is traveling nearby).

Path to Success: Culture, People, Process, and Technology

One of the more common mistakes that associations make following implementation of a new data management system is the assumption that, once a new system is live, the work on data and data management is "done." In fact, much like strategy and ongoing association operations, data management is never done. The most successful associations understand this and implement processes for actively managing their data in order to ensure it is as up-to-date as possible and as useful to the association as possible.

Every good project manager, for any project, will tell you that success begins with a supportive organizational culture and involves the three core pillars of people, process, and technology. Managing your database and getting the most from your data are no different.

Culture

Maximizing the value of your database begins with having an organizational culture that respects and encourages proactive data management and data-driven decision making. As with all culture, creating a culture for effective data management and use must come from the top, from the executive director/CEO, as well as the other members of the senior management team.

Creating a Culture for Effective Data Management

Here are some examples of how CEOs and senior managers create and demonstrate a positive data management culture:

- During all staff meetings, include an agenda item that addresses data management and the data management systems. The agenda item isn't for solving data management problems, but to keep the staff updated on what is being done in the area of data management and to not so subtly communicate to staff that data management is important in the organization.

- The CEO and senior staff should have processes in place for tracking important member interactions in the database. One association has a process in place whereby the CEO and senior staff email the CEO's assistant about meetings they have with members, and the assistant enters these meeting notes into the database. A process is in place so that these notes are entered uniformly and can be easily viewed or queried by all staff.

- The organization includes a budget line item in its annual budgeting specifically dedicated to technology and services related to data management and system maintenance and improvement.

Organizations that invest money in their data management not only communicate that they value this activity (create a culture for data management), but also tend to be more successful with their data management efforts.

People

In order to be most effective, associations must have people with the proper analytic skills to know how to work with the data—how to "ask" the right questions of the data and, just as importantly, how to communicate what they have found in a way that can be understood, prioritized, and used by management.

Process

Associations need the right processes in place for incorporating insights from the data into "normal" day-to-day operations and decision making at all levels across the organization.

Technology

Associations must have the right systems and analytical tools in place that allow them to discover patterns in the data that will lead to insights and innovation (business intelligence tools).

Actively Managing the Data

Managing data is much like maintaining and weeding a garden. If you keep a garden, you can choose to weed the garden frequently, periodically, or never at all. A garden that is never weeded soon becomes unusable. A garden that is weeded only infrequently is very difficult and time-consuming to clean up. But a frequently weeded garden is much easier to maintain and keep productive.

The same is true for your database. Frequent "cleaning" of the data will ensure that your database is much more usable to staff and much more effective for marketing and communications purposes.

Tools for Keeping Your Data Current and Up-to-Date

A multitude of tools and processes are available for maintaining data cleanliness, including:

- *National change of address (NCOA) services.* The NCOA database is a database of mailing addresses maintained by the U.S. Postal Service, tracking when people and businesses change addresses. There are services available that will match the NCOA database against your current data set and update addresses when needed. In addition, first-class mail sent by your association is automatically returned or forwarded based on the NCOA database, which presents another opportunity to update your data.

- *Online update campaigns.* Most members and customers won't actively go to their profile on your website and update their contact and/or demographic information. But if you remind them via an email campaign, many of them will. A secondary benefit of an online campaign is that any email that bounces can be investigated by staff and updated.

- *Postcard update campaigns.* But what if you don't have email addresses, or the email address is bad? This is when a postcard update campaign can be used very effectively. A simple double-sided postcard (with return postage) can be created and mailed to the entire database (or a key subset) asking the recipients to update their contact information and return the postcard to the association. Even better, the postcard asks the recipients to go online and update their profiles there (thus saving the association some postage and labor on data updating). Finally, as noted above, if the postcards are mailed first class, the NCOA process will catch address changes and communicate those back to the association. Many associations have used this campaign process with great success.

- *Integrated address verification software.* Address verification software can be integrated to your data management system for updating mailing addresses in real time. Companies such as Melissa Data and the U.S. Postal Service provide services that will check in real time the address being entered by staff or the customer and make suggestions for updating the address to its most accurate and complete form. (Many of us have experienced this on e-commerce websites when the site asks, "Would you like to use this address?") Address verification software does your weeding for you.

- *Data integrity reports.* Data integrity reports are a series of queries or reports that allow the association to identify potential errors or gaps in data. For example, you could build a data integrity report that identifies all members in the database who do not have an email address in the primary email address field (by querying all member records that have a "NULL" value in email address). You could then contact these individuals by phone or search them on the web to determine their email addresses.

Data Integrity Reports

Denise Streszoff of the International Association for Dental Research (IADR) has one of the cleanest databases in the association world. A primary reason is that she has developed, in conjunction with her vendor, a broad array of data integrity reports that she runs on a regular basis. IADR has outsourced the majority of its data entry to a third party, so Denise uses her data integrity reports to perform quality checks on the work done by her outsourcer.

A sampling of her reports includes:

- Checking individual members for organizational membership. Because a membership can be assigned to an individual or an organization, sometimes memberships are assigned incorrectly.
- Checking individuals for more than one current membership.
- Checking individual members to ensure that they've been assigned to a proper division (that is, a chapter). Chapter assignment is based on geography, and sometimes chapters are assigned incorrectly.
- Checking for expiration dates less than join dates. If an expiration date is entered incorrectly, this data integrity report will identify that record.

Using these and many other data integrity reports and executing these reports very frequently (some are run daily, others run weekly), Denise ensures that any data entry errors made are caught and corrected in very short order.

Using the Data to Identify Best Customers

Because the traditional AMS is focused on transactions (membership join and renewal, event registration, product sales, etc.), it is easy to overlook that these databases are collecting a virtual goldmine of behavioral information that associations can use to identify their best customers. And with the addition of CRM functionality that allows associations to capture non-financial interactions (committee and volunteer service; phone calls, emails, and in-person meetings; and web page views and downloads), associations now have a plethora of data that can be used to improve marketing and communication efforts.

With the classic admonition that past behavior does not guarantee future results, every marketing expert knows that, all things being equal, your past best customers are likely to be your future best customers. So identifying who your past best customers are becomes incredibly important. Luckily, with a centralized data management system, you're already collecting the data that will help you identify those best customers.

The key to identifying best customers is to identify the behavior (both transactional and non-transactional) associated with those best customers. In other words, in what activities are your best customers engaged? Here's a sampling that will apply to many associations:

- Membership tenure
- Product purchases

- Event registration, including free and paid, in-person, and online
- Committee and volunteer service
- Donations
- Non-financial interactions, such as in-person meetings, participation in focus groups, surveys, or industry studies

Using the data that you're already capturing can help you identify your best customers and allow you to target them with higher value and more relevant marketing communications.

Sidebar: Using Data to Identify Best Customers

Several years ago, the National Association of College and University Business Officers (NACUBO) embarked on a program to identify their best customers in order to improve their overall marketing effectiveness and decrease direct mail marketing costs.

NACUBO had followed the traditional direct mail approach of mailing conference promotion pieces to all members and a large number of non-members. NACUBO changed their marketing approach by identifying their best customers, based on 12 different areas of activity and participation within NACUBO (for example, attendance at the NACUBO annual meeting, product purchases, listservers, and benchmarking studies) and then marketing most heavily to their best customers.

The marketing mix was changed so that the top 20 percent of best customers received the bulk of the marketing promotions. To illustrate how effective this approach was, consider the data from one of NACUBO's events. Of the 290 attendees who attended the event, 82.5 percent of the attendees were from the top 20 percent of customers. The bottom 50 percent accounted for just 1.7 percent of total attendees.

But more importantly, the cost of attracting these attendees was much *lower* for the top 20 percent than for the bottom 80 percent. For this event, the marketing costs for the top tier was just $7.70 per attendee. Marketing costs for the bottom 50 percent cost nearly $119 each. That's nearly 15 times more expensive to attract the bottom tier versus the top.

And how effective is this over time? Over one year, NACUBO was able to reduce their direct mail expenses by 30 percent and actually increase total event attendance. That's what more effective use of data can do.

Understanding Explicit vs. Implied Interest

Many associations will collect demographic data on their members, asking them, for example, for information on the line of work they are in, the types of products they produce, or the areas of interest they have. All of this data demonstrates explicit interest in something. The association asks, the member answers.

But a lot of the data associations collect demonstrates implied interest that can be used for more effective marketing. For example, when a member or customer attends one of your events focused on a particular subject area (such as healthcare), you now have specific implied interest in this area, which can be used for future marketing and communications with that member or customer. We see this type of implied interest data used in places like Amazon, which will always tell you: "Here's what other customers bought when they bought this product." By virtue of your buying product X, Amazon assumes an implied interest in that product area and suggests other products that may be of interest to you. Associations can do the same thing with their data.

Implied interest can be used for cross-marketing and cross-selling, for serving up website content, and even for identifying future volunteers for interest-specific committees or task forces.

Conclusion

As associations look to their future, one thing is certain: member expectations will continue to rise as competition for their attention increases and they experience innovative organizations—both private sector and associations—that are able to deliver superior user experiences and offer accessible, useful content. To prosper, every association must provide significant value to its customers. To accomplish that, the organization will need the right infrastructure—a well-functioning database—plus the analytic tools and expertise to understand and use the information to its fullest.

Reference

Gammel, David. *Maximum Engagement*. Washington, DC: ASAE, 2011.

About the Authors

Wes Trochlil is the president of Effective Database Management, LLC, in Hamilton, Virginia. He has served as chair of the ASAE Membership Section Council, member of the ASAE Technology Section Council, and is currently a member of the ASAE Executive Management Section Council. Email: wtrochlil@effectivedatabase.com.

Sherry Budziak is CEO of .orgSource. She has more than 20 years of consulting and association leadership experience focused on helping organizations realize the full potential of their technology investments and creating successful strategies to guide their digital future. Email: sherry@orgsource.com.

Organizing and Developing the Membership Function to Deliver Value

9

By Sara Miller, MBA, PMP, CAE

IN THIS CHAPTER
- Membership Department Responsibilities
- Staff Roles and Responsibilities
- Training and Professional Development

At a macro level, membership departments are focused on three key areas: recruiting, engaging, and retaining members. The efforts behind these goals can be classified as marketing or member services. This is fairly consistent across associations. A primary differentiator then is the size of the organization and the corresponding size of the membership department. Other important variables include the type of organization (individual, trade, hybrid) and the number of members.

Membership Department Responsibilities

Regardless of the organization, there are core duties assigned to the membership department. Around the macro level categories of recruitment, engagement, and retention, think broadly about what your association is and could be doing. Try not to become bogged down in staff size or budget restrictions. Within your association's specific constraints, there are always opportunities to move the needle.

Marketing

This area covers the promotional and outreach activities to new and existing members. Through engagement, the section also addresses the actual experience of being a member and opportunities for becoming more involved.

Recruitment Marketing

Recruitment could mean bringing in net new members and/or cultivating existing prospects/leads. In most organizations, regardless of size, the membership department is directly involved in planning and executing the marketing strategy to recruit new members. Membership recruitment tactics may include direct mail, advertising, referral programs, word-of-mouth activities, website, events, public relations, social media, inbound marketing, and telemarketing.

- Review existing marketing efforts for recruiting new members. Understand key drivers for new members (events, campaigns, etc.) and threats to future success (dues increase, competition, workforce changes, etc.).

Renewal Fulfillment

Most membership departments are responsible for the renewal process, including forecasting and reporting renewal rates and successes, sending dues notices, and conducting renewal phone-a-thons or telemarketing campaigns.

- Review existing marketing efforts around retention. Examine your timeline for contacting members (90 days out, 60 days out, etc.). Understand when your members renew. MGI's annual Benchmarking Report is a fantastic resource for comparing your activities to those of other associations.

- At some point, you should stop contacting non-renewing members about renewing or rejoining, but don't set an arbitrary end date. Keep communicating until there is a diminishing return on investment.

Communications

Compared to other departments, the membership team often has the most direct communication with members because it is responsible for changes in records, customer service, order fulfillment, new member orientation, and the distribution of welcome packets.

- Conduct a communications audit to identify all the information your members receive and how often it is delivered. Make sure that members are given correct information, including how to contact the association and who to contact. You must seek permission and allow members to opt out of communications.

Engagement

Membership departments are often involved in the organization's engagement strategy, if not leading the effort. The membership department is continually promoting new opportunities and activities to increase the stickiness between the association and the individual. This work, hopefully, leads to easier renewal decisions and increased retention.

- Review your current outreach strategy. How are you reinforcing the value of the association and membership? In conjunction with the communications audit, map how often you communicate with members and what the messages are. Then identify what is and is not working. It's important to focus on outbound communications, response time, and consistency of message.

- If possible, your team should become members of the association or at least seed their names on the mailing lists. Understanding the current experience of what it's like to be a member will help you be a better membership professional.

- Create your definition of engagement and look at quantifying activities into a single engagement score.

Member Services

This section covers the level of service and customization that you provide. For members, the activities start with joining and continue through renewing. "Member services" also applies to non-members who contact the association for assistance. Every interaction with a member (or prospective member) should be seen as an opportunity to further solidify the relationship and increase the stickiness.

Record Management

Record management includes maintaining accurate and consistent data on members, customers, and prospects. Because all staff may be in contact with members and receive updates, it is essential that you have a systemized approach for changing members' records. This may include permission-based access to the database, which limits certain functions to specific staff. Incorrect information in records could mean that members won't receive all their benefits and, therefore, will be at higher risk of not renewing.

- Once or twice a year, ask your members to update their contact information through the online member portal.

- Run your file against the National Change of Address (NCOA) list and other clean-up files to ensure you have the latest information that meets USPS deliverability standards.

- Develop and maintain standard operating procedures (SOPs) for staff on how to enter data, including what fields are mandatory and what changes are tracked.

Order Entry/Processing

The membership department, in many organizations, is responsible for processing new member applications and renewals. This role is critical to maintaining a good relationship with members, yet it is often an undervalued component of the work performed by the department. If mistakes are made in data entry, the member experience can start negatively with payment issues or a lack of communication to those members.

- Audit your data entry procedures to ensure systems are working properly. Develop regular quality control reports to confirm data integrity.

- Test (or secret shop) your live processes to confirm that activities on the front end and back end are fully functioning. It's surprising how often something just stops working. Don't be caught off-guard.

Surveys and Research

Surveys and research conducted by the membership department will assist the organization in its strategic/tactical planning and benchmarking. Research activities can range from a survey to members about membership to a focus group of non-members regarding educational programs. Regardless, the membership department is usually involved in market research and hosting focus groups.

- Review existing research. This information could be spread throughout the association. Consider creating a central depository of questions and results that is accessible to all staff. Survey fatigue should be a standing concern. People don't like answering the same questions over and over again, especially in rapid succession. Also, the data is interrelated because it's the same set of programs and similar audiences. The entire association can be stronger through shared findings.

Affinity Programs

Because of their close and frequent interaction with members, membership departments should be involved in the selection and monitoring of affinity programs. Many associations use affinity programs to leverage the buying power of their members and secure better pricing on products and services. The revenue streams created by affinity programs can assist an organization in the delivery of its mission. However, such programs should receive continuing oversight for their value as member benefits.

- Review existing programs to ensure quality products, ample promotion, and stable or growing usage.

- Explore new programs that would benefit the members and your association. It's difficult to cold call a company and start an affinity program from scratch. A very large/powerful membership base and/or a specific geographical location will increase your appeal. You can start safe by exploring companies with existing programs.

Mailing Lists

The management and distribution of mailing list rentals is often the responsibility of the membership professional. Many associations have the potential to earn considerable income by renting their mailing lists. Income from mailing list rental is not considered a royalty by the U.S. government and is, therefore, subject to unrelated business income tax.

- Review companies that repeatedly purchase your list. If you aren't doing so already, you may want to purchase their list(s) and/or reach out regarding cross-promotion.

- Some associations are experiencing a decline in revenue from mailing lists as companies are now looking for email addresses. Explore your association's privacy policy and opportunities to refine your list rental program.

Sales

Regardless of size, many organizations rely on the membership department for sales, customer service, and product fulfillment. The data from all transactions should be recorded in the members' files. If you have a sophisticated data program, you can mine the sales information to supplement member personas and quantify member lifetime value.

- Review purchase history to understand who is buying what. Use the information to identify and market to future buyers.

- Understand top purchasers and adjust your marketing efforts to reflect someone's total interactions with the association (instead of solely focusing on membership dues).

- While we're talking specifically about sales, it's also worth noting that volunteerism is a valuable contribution and should be included in communications to members about their commitment to the association and their profession/industry. You now see companies quantify the value of volunteered time as an important "asset" of the association.

Online

Membership functions must participate in leveraging the association's online presence. Associations can increase the value of membership by being responsive to member needs and by engaging members in a two-way dialogue. Blogs and wikis are popular vehicles, as are online chats and social media. By creating such social networks for members, associations can harness their power as the central organizer.

The Member Services area of your website could include membership categories and dues, renewal information, membership application, who should be a member, a self-service portal, etc. Tell-a-friend or "share" features are also popular.

- Review your website with your new/current/lapsed/never member hat on or conduct focus groups to do the same. Identify areas or pages where users get stuck or the content does not meet expectations.

- Review your analytics to understand popular pages and referral sites or search topics. Looking at your online traffic can give you important insight into what people want.

Other Responsibilities

While these are the more common responsibilities of a membership department, there are likely additional projects for your team. Take time to complete the list of responsibilities and identify areas for growth or change.

- Other responsibilities could include event planning, awards programs, or chapters/components.

Right Tasks, Right Time

You now have a master list of your department's current responsibilities. Don't assume that the organization is behind those efforts or that the right tasks have been prioritized. You need to obtain stakeholder input and buy-in.

Board of Directors

The board may be setting the growth goals for membership and/or creating and adjusting the member benefits. Your level of involvement in the decision-making process is as unique as the organization.

Chief Executive Officer

The CEO may have a major role in determining the growth of your organization's constituency and may also determine the distribution of the budget.

Membership Director and Staff

You have an investment in the products and outcomes of your department. From working with members every day, you have expectations of what should be offered and how resources should be allocated.

Other Departments

What are the expectations of your program departments? Is the Meetings group changing how they market the annual event? Is the Public Relations staff increasing media coverage of the organization? How does the work of other departments affect membership?

While these groups are not present in every organization, you may have other stakeholders to consider. Almost everyone affects membership. Your infrastructure must account for these outside influences.

Staff Roles and Responsibilities

Associations are unique. Membership department responsibilities are unique. So it holds true that the infrastructure of membership departments would be unique. From a department of one to units well into the double digits, one size does not fit all. Across organizations, the difference isn't typically whether something either is or is not being done (at least for the core responsibilities), but the degree to which it's being done or the sophistication of the specific function. For example, all membership associations have to send renewal invoices. The difference then isn't whether or not you send invoices, but the number of notices or the degree of personalization.

Association Structures

Before getting into your specifics, it's helpful to take a look at the broader association community. In a recent online search, Association CareerHQ listed 210 jobs with "membership" in the title. Positions included membership associate, membership coordinator, membership manager, director of membership, membership sales associate, and director of membership engagement. In summer 2015, there was a conversation on ASAE Collaborate about the number of members and number of membership staff. The responses varied greatly.

We often classify associations as small, medium, or large. For a small association with perhaps one person working on membership, that person has a very full plate. He or she may receive part-time support from other staff members or rely more on an outside business partner for support. Again, if you accept that the core tasks have to be done in a membership department of any size, then it becomes a matter of prioritization. Recruitment and renewal communications rise to the top of the priority list. Mailing lists may be promoted and sold exclusively by an outside agency. Affinity programs could fall to the bottom of the pile.

Medium and large staff associations have the benefit of additional people who can give more time to these core membership tasks. They also typically have a higher budget. As the association grows, there may be departments dedicated to specific functions like the website. If so, the membership staff will serve as contributors/stakeholders instead of the leader/project manager. With more staff, you may divide marketing efforts between a "recruitment coordinator" and a "retention coordinator." It's worth noting that bigger doesn't guarantee better. Regardless of size, the most successful department is the person/group with clear responsibilities and goals.

Your Membership Department

All of the membership roles are showcased in your department's organizational chart. If you don't already have one, these charts are very easy to create using PowerPoint, Visio, or another tool. Figures 9.1 through 9.4 show a few sample charts.

In setting the best structure for your department, a major decision involves determining what the department should be in three to five years. If membership models need to change, then membership departments should be under the same scrutiny. This means taking a fresh look at the organization of the department. Even if there's no flexibility in adding positions, it's a good practice to routinely evaluate the distribution of work to make sure the department is focused on the right things. As you're going through this process, it's also a good time to review titles and job descriptions.

Figure 9.1   A One-Person Department

Membership
Manager

Figure 9.2   A Small Department

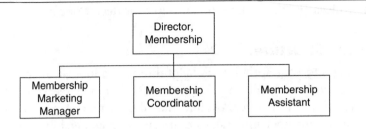

Figure 9.3   A Department Incorporating Customer Service

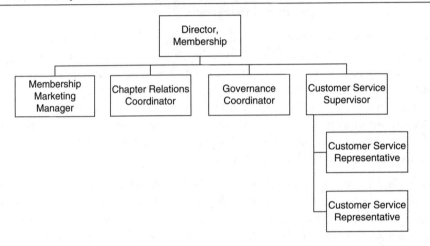

Figure 9.4   A Large Department

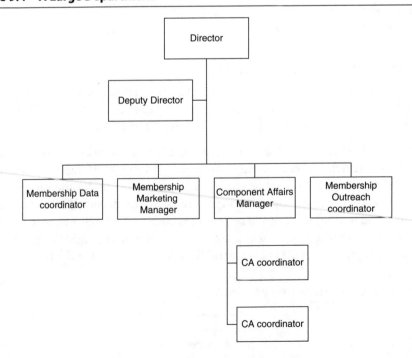

Training and Professional Development

An ongoing training plan is critical to your department's long-term success. There are many forms of training—individual versus team, in-person versus online—and it's good practice to incorporate multiple styles. You most likely have a professional development budget for each employee. If not, you'll have to think more creatively about how to advance your team's competencies.

Individual vs. Team

Depending on the issue, you may decide it's more valuable for the entire team to be trained simultaneously in a specific discipline. For example, you could send each person to a customer service class, but each person would hear a slightly different thing and have a different experience. If you bring in a trainer, then everyone hears the same thing and is able to apply customer service fundamentals in real time to real-world situations.

Team training also works well for organizational efforts like a new product rollout. Again, it's good for everyone to hear the same thing at the same time. If your organization focuses on specific occupations—psychiatrists, lawyers, nurses—your membership team may not have that professional background. Invite your colleagues to share industry trends, workforce development, hot topics, and so on. This makes your team more knowledgeable when talking with members.

Individual training is a solid approach when a person has a specific area he'd like to or needs to develop. Consider the example of public speaking. If someone is improving her presentation skills, she'll likely be more comfortable in front of strangers than with her colleagues.

In Person vs. Online

Similar to the other options, this decision depends on the specific content, available resources, and schedule. Free webinars are fairly common, and providers typically follow up with a recording of the session. Webinar recordings are great for team training because you can stop/start the recording to allow for discussion.

In-person opportunities typically take you away from the office for a few hours or even a few days. Still, it's hard to replicate the power of the experience. If you've been to ASAE's Annual Meeting, you've seen and felt the energy, expertise, and value. It's unique to the environment. This type of expense is more likely an exception than a rule for your staff, but it's an experience people won't soon forget. Again, you have to weigh the costs against the return.

Regardless of the format, you should attempt to extend the learning. Some companies have a practice of requiring reports from anyone who attends a conference. Depending on the event, this structure can work well. I've also had the person lead a team training. Topics like time management work nicely as a presentation because it isn't controversial and the advice benefits everyone. This approach gives the attendees good exposure for their newfound knowledge and further builds their communication skills.

Identifying the Training Topic(s)

If you have a per person budget, start by meeting with each person to understand his or her personal and professional goals. What does the person want to accomplish? There are countless opportunities for specialized training, depending on the person's interest. There are customer service or call center conferences. You could send someone to a project management class if he is a coordinator for your department's activities. There are also opportunities for improving core skills like communicating, writing, and listening. The challenge will be reviewing the options and isolating the one or two opportunities—per person—that will net the greatest return. As a membership department, your staff should have expertise in certain core competencies.

- *Database:* Make sure all staff have a solid understanding of your association management system (AMS), with more specific expertise based on job function. This could include data entry, IQA/reporting, managing batches, processing refunds, and other tasks.

- *Confidentiality:* The membership department deals with confidential information ranging from personal contact details to payments. You should have policies for what information can be shared over the phone/via email, how personal information will be secured, and so on. You should also have checks/balances to review adherence to department/organizational policies. Membership/customer service is a critical entry point for member and customer data, which means it's at a higher risk of being compromised then say your graphics department. You have to make sure your team is properly trained.

- *Customer Service:* If your team talks directly with members, then make sure they're skilled in the art of customer service. Scripts are typically too structured for day-to-day operations, but it's good to provide general guidelines for how to talk to customers. Other proficiencies include active listening and conflict resolution.

- *Membership Basics:* If you have staff who are new to the association world or new to membership, make sure they understand the basics. How is/isn't membership like a traditional product? What do recruitment, engagement, and retention mean? They should also understand membership dues, membership benefits, and the membership lifecycle.

- *Marketing/Sales:* Everyone should understand marketing and sales tactics. For individuals who talk on the phones, these skills will help them sell the organization or up-sell a product. You have to help them feel comfortable on the phone if they're going to stretch from the customer's original request to offering new products and services.

Upselling is about persuading your customers to purchase more advanced products or services than they'd originally planned to buy. For associations, traditional upselling typically includes increasing the amount of a single donation, moving up to the next membership level, or buying an educational product. While upselling to increase revenue is important, it is not the only way to upsell. Associations also consider increasing participation as part of the upselling equation.

Additional Staff Retention Efforts

To keep your members, you maintain a multi-faceted retention strategy. The same should be true for staff. A July 30, 2015, post in Business Insider outlined the "*9 things bosses do that make great employees quit*" (www.businessinsider.com/why-people-quit-their-jobs-2015-7).

1. They overwork people.

2. They don't recognize contributions and reward good work.

3. They don't care about their employees.

4. They don't honor their commitments.

5. They hire and promote the wrong people.

6. They don't let people pursue their passions.

7. They fail to develop people's skills.

8. They fail to engage employees' creativity.

9. They fail to challenge people intellectually.

A robust training program and professional development plan are important components of your staff retention strategy. However, they should not represent the entirety of your efforts. Your human resources team should have a structure in place to support supervisors and staff. Here are a few other ideas to develop your team.

Organization-Wide Staff Values/Culture Team

Does your organization have an employee-led team that is focused on overall retention and workplace satisfaction? Hopefully, the answer is yes so that your department-specific efforts complement organization-wide activities. The Wellness and Recognition Committee at the Association of periOperative Registered Nurses (AORN) plans monthly events from watching TED talks to very competitive cook-offs. The committee also coordinates a popular staff recognition program. ROCK ("Random Occurrence of Co-Worker Kudos") dollars are given to all staff to recognize a co-worker's accomplishment(s). ROCK dollars can be cashed in for gift cards.

Job Descriptions

Make sure your team's job descriptions are correct and current. People should be clear on their priorities. Regardless of the actual size of your department, staff likely wear multiple hats. Staff need to know which hat is most important.

Awards

With or without a financial component, awards are a powerful way to recognize staff. These can take many forms, including individual awards whereby recipients are nominated by staff, team awards nominated by leadership and presented to cross-functional groups, and annual awards voted on by the board of directors.

Informal Staff Recognition

After a successful product launch or following your busy season, recognize the team for their hard work. The recognition could be per person or for the entire team. Examples include taking the team out to lunch or giving each person a gift card to a favorite store/restaurant.

"Likes" Spreadsheet

Keep a running spreadsheet of the team's hobbies and favorites. You can store the document on a shared drive so everyone has access to the information. If you're going to buy gift cards for the team, you want to make sure each person receives what he or she wants. This approach doesn't replace building relationships with your team and you can always supplement the spreadsheet with your own knowledge. This is a quick and easy reference for everyone to use. Fields could include music/artists, movies, hobbies, snack/candy, and restaurants.

If you had $50 to reward your team, what could you do?

- Gift card for each person to a favorite restaurant/store
- Fun gifts for each person to commemorate a large project (tote bag with project name)
- Custom gifts related to the department (personalized Post-its, personalized pens)
- Catered lunch
- Potluck lunch where the team brings the entrees and you supply dessert
- Ice cream party
- Celebrate national days like National Donut Day, National Customer Service Week

---

You've put a lot of energy and resources into building your team. Make sure you're putting the same effort into keeping them.

Summary

By now, you have an updated organizational chart with refreshed titles and job descriptions to match. You have a recognition system in place, and you are committed to ongoing professional development. This doesn't guarantee perfection, but it puts you on the right course.

The membership department is an important part of the association. Your marketing efforts are visible, as the latest membership figures are presented frequently and broadly. Customer service is on the front lines and usually on the receiving end of issues and frustrations that happened upstream. You and the team are going to feel pressured. Don't worry—you're ready. The team has trained for this.

> "The nice thing about teamwork is that you always have others on your side."
>
> *Margaret Carty*

About the Author

Sara Miller, MBA, PMP, CAE, is the director of membership at AORN, the Association of periOperative Registered Nurses. She has more than 15 years of experience working with nonprofits and associations, including management positions at Challenger Center for Space Science Education, the Humane Society of the United States, and the American Public Health Association. Email: hello@saramiller.info.

Membership Categories and Dues Structures

10

By Sheri Jacobs, FASAE, CAE

IN THIS CHAPTER

- A Brief Introduction to Organizational or Enterprise Membership
- New Membership Models Are Emerging in the Association Community
- Membership Categories
- Recruitment of Enterprise or Organizational Membership
- Organization Types

The association community offers an unparalleled breadth of affiliation options, yet all commonly use one of just several dues structures: individual membership, organizational membership, or a hybrid of the two. Although a multitude of environmental and economic factors have made an impact on the decision to join an association, most organizations still utilize a membership dues structure that was established decades ago, when there were fewer alternatives and resources. Who or what *owns* the membership, regardless of who pays the membership dues, defines each type.

We will explore both traditional and new membership dues structures and categories. You will learn the key principles that should be considered prior to undertaking a change to your membership model and be introduced to other organizations that are tackling the external challenges they face when trying to achieve their goals. The chapter concludes with the factors that can impact a successful transition.

One of the most common dues models being used by individual membership societies is a flat fee structure based on factors such as years in practice (experience), title/position, employer type, or country of residence. For example, if you are employed by a trade or professional association, philanthropic organization, or association management company, you may become a member of the Association Forum of Chicagoland. For a flat fee, you will enjoy benefits including discounts on face-to-face and online educational programs; access to online resources; models; samples; a free subscription to its monthly magazine, *FORUM;* and other professional development opportunities. CEOs, consultants, and young professionals may also join the organization for a flat-rate fee, one that is different from the professional staff fee, but includes the same list of benefits and discounts.

This model serves the needs of many associations because it is easy to communicate to individuals who fall into clearly defined categories (for example, student, young professional, academic, government employee, or international member). It does not take into account, however, factors such as interest, behavior, competition, employer support, willingness to pay, and changes in the workforce. Because of this, some organizations are adopting a new membership structure based on how individuals wish to interact with the organization. In addition, many associations offer an online-only option to increase their appeal to individuals who wish to obtain information but have no desire or need to interact with the organization at a deeper level.

A Brief Introduction to Organizational or Enterprise Membership

An organizational membership (also known as an enterprise membership) refers to a structure designed to encourage companies, agencies, firms, institutions (for- and non-profit), and government entities to join an association. With this structure, membership is typically paid by the company and may be based on a variety of factors, including:

- Total revenue
- Total sales
- Percentage of sales
- Number of locations
- Number of employees
- Units of equipment
- Total assets
- Total income

Many organizational membership programs offer a flat dues rate in exchange for membership on an escalating scale based on one of the factors identified above. An alternative to this model is the tiered membership based on the selection of benefits desired and the size of the organization. For example, the California Employers Association offers three types of membership: online, associate, and premier. Each tier begins with a base price and the fee escalates based on the number of employees. With this model, the company chooses the benefits that best fit their needs and the fee is determined by what is considered a "fair share." An organization with five employees will assumedly use fewer benefits than one with 500 employees.

Hybrid membership models tend to have more variations. Some societies offer employers the opportunity to enroll some or all of their employees as individual members at a discounted price. The advantage to the employer is both a cost savings and a consolidated invoice. This type of membership model is most common among medical, CPA, and legal professional associations.

Organizations pay a fee in exchange for a selection of benefits that includes individual memberships for its employees. This structure may attract organizations that wish to consolidate and simplify billing and ensure that all their employees have membership to the professional society. An example of a hybrid membership model is the Massachusetts Medical Society (MMS), which used this concept to build a sustainable model that would allow physicians to join the organization through a group membership program. "Our current membership model was not designed to meet the needs of the new generation of physician employees," said Stephen Phelan, director of membership at the MMS (*The Art of Membership*, p. 150). "We realized that we needed to develop a new program that provided specific benefits to employees but would not cannibalize our current revenue structure. Just like the practice of medicine is changing, our model needed to change."

Groups of five or more physicians are eligible to receive the following discounts:

- 100 percent participation: 30 percent discount
- 90 percent participation: 20 percent discount
- 80 percent participation: 10 percent discount
- 75 percent participation: 5 percent discount

In addition to the savings, group enrollment offers significant practice management benefits:

- Simplified billing with one dues invoice for your entire physician practice
- Accurate membership information with group rosters
- Reduced practice administrative hassles for physicians
- Valuable practice benefit to new-hire prospects by offering free MMS membership

Since this model's inception, the number of members in the group enrollment program has increased by 100 percent, and the organization has saved $10,000 in renewal expenses (*The Art of Membership*, p. 150).

New Membership Models Are Emerging in the Association Community

Based on these considerations, I've outlined a road map on new and exciting membership models that many associations are employing to expand their reach, attract new members, and achieve their strategic goals.

The need to reach *strategic, well-defined goals* should drive any decisions regarding the selection of a membership dues structure for an organization. Before an organization can adopt a new membership structure or change its current one, there should be some consensus regarding the outcomes it wishes to achieve. For example, does the association wish to expand into new markets, increase revenue, increase engagement, attract the next generation of professionals, or support a cause-based mission?

Health Information Management Systems Society (HIMSS) described its motivation in the following statement: "One of the main goals that permeated our strategy documents is to increase audience engagement. We want to increase the audience that has access to our information. Our goal isn't to increase membership. We are a cause-based membership. So we want to have a larger reach first." As a result of this change in its strategy, HIMSS launched an Organizational Affiliate Program to increase engagement within healthcare institutions.

The Association for Operations Management (APICS), on the other hand, wanted to build a membership structure that would encourage membership growth and retention and be more responsive to an episodic need for the benefits APICS offers to members. The change in its structure occurred when the organization saw a dip in membership after the recession that commenced in 2008. It became clear that the traditional membership structure did not provide the flexibility needed to adapt to the changing interests, needs, and economic realities of its audience. The result: a newly designed program that offers individuals more choice—something APICS calls "mass customization"—wherein each person can select what he or she does or does not want in a membership.

The Society of Petroleum Engineers (SPE) built its membership value proposition, including access to a significant amount of information, standards, and a community of peers, around its goals: "Our mission is to collect and disseminate information and be a repository to information. The other is to connect with a network and communicate with others in the industry to share ideas and information."

Other Considerations: e-Memberships

Many organizations allow non-U.S. residents the option to apply for an electronic or digital membership at a lower rate than that of the regular or full membership. An "e-membership," as many groups call it, typically offers members-only access to online content as well as discounts on programs, products, and services. A successful e-membership program often hinges on some level of restriction to an association's intellectual property and other member benefits.

An example of an exception to a restricted e-membership is the one offered by HIMSS. Any individual, regardless of career stage or country of residence, may join the organization through its $30 online membership. However, benefits are limited to increase the likelihood that the HIMSS full membership is preferred. The organization recognizes that not everyone who wishes to access its information and resources has the time, money, or interest in becoming a full member though. Online membership benefits include access to members-only content on www.HIMSS.org, e-newsletters, and event updates. It does *not* include member discount pricing on conferences, webinars, items in its online bookstore, and its eLearning Academy, nor does it include local chapter affiliation or national volunteer opportunities (all highly valued benefits of membership, according to member research studies).

It is also fairly common for organizations to offer a significant dues discount to students and recent graduates. Student or young professional members are given access to all member benefits, but in some instances may be restricted from voting or holding office. To ease the transition from a low student or young professional rate to the full dues rate, many associations offer a gradual dues increase over a period of two to five years, yet this can lead to a low retention rate of new members.

Other Considerations: "Freemium" or Open-Access Membership Model

A "freemium"—a combination of "free" and "premium"—business model provides a core product or service that is always free, but also offers a premium platform of additional products or services that can expand or improve the experience of users of the free platform for a fee.

Freemium models play a key role in business today. They are widely used in a range of industries. A notable example is apps with freemium models, which account for 98 percent of the revenue in Google's app store and 95 percent in Apple's app store. Another well-known example is Skype, which provides free computer-to-computer calling and also sells premium products in the form of voicemail, conference calls, and worldwide connection to landlines and mobile phones. Although these product-driven models may seem unlikely to succeed within the association community, the concept is one worthy of consideration if an association's goal is to expand its reach and membership could be considered a *product* rather than a requirement for affiliation.

Freemium models that target business audiences include MailChimp, an online email contact marketing service with a free tier for low volume users, and MarketingProfs, whose free "basic" tier includes online articles, email newsletters, and discussion forums. The Plano Chamber of Commerce provides a free "Web Marketing Package" to all members, but also offers an "Enhanced Web Marketing Package" for $125 that enhances the member's visibility and information content on the Chamber website and online business directory.

While this disruptive model was initially only used within the software industry, this is no longer the case. Newspapers, music, publishing, telecom, education, and a range of other industries are now facing competition from freemium business models.

CompTIA, a nonprofit trade association with the mission of advancing the global interests of IT professionals and IT channel organizations, created an open-access membership model. The tiered membership structure offers a free membership category to individuals who sign up to become registered users. Within this category of membership, individuals have access to community meetings, select web content, and affinity programs. Premier membership offers the entire organization access to a wealth of exclusive benefits including resources, tools, discounts, and leadership opportunities.

The underlying concept that makes the freemium or open-access model possible is digital production. It is now possible to produce and distribute a wide variety of value propositions using digital distribution channels and the Internet. Because of the decreasing cost of computers, storage, and Internet bandwidth, the marginal cost of distributing this Internet-accessible value proposition is virtually zero. Music is a prime example; once a musician has produced an album, it costs him practically the same to have either 10 people or 1 million people download the album.

This creates a situation in which you can give away a core product for free and create a profitable business model from just up-selling or selling exclusive access to a smaller audience. This trend will only continue, as digital costs steadily decline and an ever-increasing array of value propositions can be delivered through the Internet.

Other Considerations: Multi-Tier Membership Model

The multi-tier membership model is based on the idea of offering a choice of membership categories based on benefits and price. A multi-tier model offers potential members increased flexibility because they can select the category based on what they need and value. The multi-tier model also takes into account ability to pay and willingness to pay. Within the multi-tier model there can be two, three, or more options:

In the *basic-premium (low/high) membership model*, the association would set up a large price differential between the two categories (e.g., $199/$399). Before prices are set, the organization would need to determine which benefits would be offered in each category, the percentage of current members who are likely to select the low and high rate, and the break-even and growth potential of each. The lower level would be used to attract and retain customers, information seekers, and reluctant members. It may also attract young professionals who may not have their employer support at this point in their careers. The difference in price between the two categories should reflect an amount greater than the savings offered by using a key member benefit. If it's priced at or below the lower threshold, the association will have a greater chance of attracting individuals who already hold a membership in another organization, are new to the industry, or are at the beginning of their careers, as well as those who must pay for membership out of their own pockets. If the value the association delivers exceeds the price, it should also experience higher retention rates.

The goal of the *full-premium (medium/high) membership approach* is to minimize the difference between the two membership categories in order to encourage the majority of members to select the higher priced membership option and feel good about the value they receive for that price. A premium membership priced higher than the current dues may require the association to invest additional resources into creating exclusive events and opportunities and to offer a higher level of customer service (concierge level).

A *two-tier pricing model* could help the association meet the needs of all members: those who wish to have some level of affiliation with the organization and those who see the advantages of utilizing more of the organization's resources. By paying a minimal fee, members will have the opportunity to upgrade their membership to the premium category. Although it is more common to offer three options, a two-tier pricing program can be used when an organization wishes to offer a simplified membership program, with the option of upgrading when additional benefits are desired. This structure is relatively easy to manage and could result in higher revenue for the organization. If the association does not experience as high a level of interest in the premium membership category, the organization is not projected to realize a loss in revenue if the full price is similar to the current price of membership.

In terms of the *good-better-best (low/medium/high) membership model,* individuals appreciate choice but do not want to be overloaded with options. A three-tier model provides them with a basis for comparison and shows how the price changes when different features are added or subtracted. This model allows individuals to select the membership category based on needs, interests, and willingness or ability to pay. It offers the greatest amount of flexibility, yet is still easy to communicate and understand. The *good* price is a budget-friendly option that provides an entry-level fee in exchange for membership in the association. The *good* price will attract price-sensitive individuals who may not receive financial support from their employers or are unfamiliar with the benefits of being a member of the organization. The *better* level should be very close to what the association currently offers, both in features and price. The *best* level of membership offers prestige and exclusive opportunities in exchange for a higher level of support. Individuals who select the *best* option will be the least price-sensitive.

Research and experience tell us that the majority of members and prospects will select the middle tier when given the choice of three price points. This model can provide additional revenue for an organization and help it grow if it is able to add real value to each tier. With a small price differential between the tiers, the association can minimize the risk of implementing this model and having the vast majority of members select the bottom two tiers.

Tiered Membership Design Overview

- A tiered membership structure is designed to increase the number of options that will appeal to prospective and current members. Too many options, however, can create paralysis or indecision among potential members.

- Each year, some individuals allow their memberships to lapse. Although "the cost of dues" is frequently cited as the reason they allowed their membership to drop, a dues structure with just one membership option does not provide an alternative way to engage with the organization based on willingness and ability to pay.

- The lowest tier of a membership model should eliminate a barrier for new members and/or younger members to affiliate with the organization, but not jeopardize the financial stability of the organization. If the prospective member audience is large enough to provide sufficient revenue at the lower price, and the organization has the resources to actively promote and market the entry-level membership, the organization may have more flexibility with the lowest tier of membership. On the other hand, if an organization offers individuals the opportunity to join the organization for a low price, the appeal of saving money may outweigh the value received at the full membership level.

- An enhanced membership category should create new opportunities for members who are already serving as ambassadors to the industry to increase their commitment to the organization and provide exclusive access and benefits.

Membership Categories

An association's bylaws establish the legal parameters for membership in the organization by defining qualifications of who may be members. These definitions of membership are often written broadly to allow the association flexibility in determining which types of members to recruit.

For example, many associations create a category of membership that includes individuals or organizations that are affiliated with or interested in the profession that the association represents. Similarly, organizations that serve a diverse population of members may create different rights and privileges for various categories of membership, including:

- Eligibility to vote in elections
- The right to hold office
- Participation in committees
- Different dues amounts and/or benefits

Membership Term and Billing Cycle

The basic term of membership in most associations is one year, but that year is measured—and dues may be assessed—in different ways. Some calendar years begin in January, while others pursue renewals at the anniversary date of joining.

- **Calendar Year Billing Cycle:** Associations that renew all members at the same time of year conduct the dues cycle on a calendar year. When an individual or company joins an association, their first-year dues are either prorated based on the number of months remaining in the calendar year or they receive a prorated invoice for the second year of membership. This format may be easier for small-staff associations to manage, yet it could deter some first-year members from renewing their membership because they will receive an invoice before the end of 12 months.

- **Anniversary Billing Cycle:** Some associations invoice members on the anniversary of the date when they first joined the organization. While this format offers a steady cash flow throughout the year, it requires ongoing staff dedication to the renewal process. A primary advantage to an anniversary billing cycle is that members will enjoy a full 12 months of membership before being required to renew.

What Is the Basis for Dues Billing?	Organization Type		Staff Size			
Total	**Trade**	**IMO**	**Small (1–10 FTEs)**	**Medium (11–29 FTEs)**	**Large (30+ FTEs)**	
Number of respondents	262	110	152	104	74	84
Anniversary	38%	30%	45%	31%	37%	49%
Calendar year	50%	53%	47%	55%	53%	40%
Other	12%	17%	8%	14%	10%	11%

Source: Benchmarking in Association Management: Membership and Components Policies and Procedures. ASAE. 2012.

Recruitment of Enterprise or Organizational Members

One of the crucial steps in building a successful enterprise program is being able to identify the right contact for the sales process. For many associations, this has meant learning more about the key decision-makers within an organization, past purchasing behavior, and the needs of the employer. The decision-maker and the key account person are often two different individuals with varying levels of awareness, value, and loyalty to the association. This dynamic often presents a challenge for organizations trying to increase engagement and participation or build a prospect list. In some instances, organizations have found success by leveraging existing relationships to help build greater awareness within the company.

For example, when HIMSS recruits organizations to join their affiliate program, they begin by researching the current spend rate based on memberships and conference registrations and then show the recruits how much they could save by transitioning into their enterprise membership program.

Internal acceptance and collaboration are essential to the success of an enterprise model that bundles programs, products, and membership. A successful program may result in an overall increase in revenue, memberships, and purchases; however, profit margins per sale may decrease significantly.

A potential challenge to creating an enterprise membership program could be the shift within the association that focuses on meeting the needs of the employer before the needs of the individual member. In addition, individuals who join the organization through an enterprise program may be less inclined to feel a strong affiliation or loyalty to the organization.

Successful organizational membership programs adhere to the following key principles:

- *Affordable.* A membership program must be realistic and affordable regardless of the value delivered. Understanding an organization's general price threshold is essential.

- *Equitable.* The dues program should take into consideration all types and sizes of organizations. For example, a program should be designed so that a small, medium, or large company or organization will find value in the price point and the offerings.

- *Simple.* The dues program must be easy to comprehend so that it can be clearly communicated to members and prospects. Too many options may confuse potential member recruits.

- *Well Aligned.* A membership program should support the strategic goals of the association; it should be aligned with the organization's mission and vision.

- *Scalable.* The program should provide room for growth and be sustainable until it reaches its full potential.

The following factors must be considered before a new membership model is selected:

- *Competition (Next Best Alternatives):* What do members receive from your organization that cannot be obtained from another organization? Competition goes beyond membership. If an individual can access information, build or enhance her network, obtain continuing education, and maintain the certification without belonging to any organization, she may not see the need to join yours.

- *Value:* If current and potential members could customize their membership, what benefits provide the most value and garner the highest levels of interest? Can your association offer a membership model that appeals to the interests, needs, and motivations of each market segment you serve?

- *Challenges:* What are some of the major challenges or obstacles to maintaining a membership in your association? How does this differ by category, income, career stage, employer support, and other factors? If employers will no longer pay for membership dues, will members renew?

- *Bundling Benefits:* How many individuals prefer a membership model whereby benefits are included in one annual base price versus an "a la carte" membership? What should be bundled with membership?

- *Anchor Price:* The first perception of a price lingers in the minds of prospective and current members. The perceived value of membership will be strongly influenced by the new price in comparison to the original amount paid. For example, if a member paid $395 to join the organization and received member discounts on education, access to research and information, and a subscription to the association's magazine, any changes to the membership proposition will be compared in price and benefits to the first price paid.

Before creating a new membership structure, consider the following questions:

- Has your organization examined the financial implications and value proposition for the organizational membership program? Although a tiered structure may attract more organizations, it typically requires a significant investment of staff time and resources. Before selecting either a flat fee or a tiered pricing structure, organizations must consider the following:
  - In a tiered structure where larger organizations pay higher dues, how can the total value of membership (benefits, networking opportunities, recognition) equal that of increased dues for larger organizations without creating unfair inequities?
  - Are there opportunities to "up-sell" to a member once a relationship has been established to generate additional revenues?

- Has your association identified the organizations and individuals who should be members but are currently not? It is important for associations to identify organizations and industries that are aligned with their goals, and in some cases even deny membership to those that did not meet criteria. For example, the Student Youth Travel Association (SYTA) has clear standards that its members must meet and undergo a board approval process. An organization must consider who should be a member and why it is important for that entity or audience segment to be part of the organization.

- What changes will need to occur to manage the logistics, mechanics, delivery, and expectations of an organizational membership program? Most of the challenges associations experience when launching (or relaunching) an organizational membership program can be traced back to a lack of internal resources needed to manage membership. Smaller organizations often struggle with an ongoing membership renewal process based on the anniversary of when the member joined. In fact, every organization we have interviewed for benchmarking studies on this topic cited the need to staff up membership departments to meet needs of an organizational membership program. Some of the possible issues your association should consider include:
  - Can the database track organizations as well as individual designators within the organization?
  - Is flexible billing—such as monthly or quarterly—an option?
  - Who will be the primary member contact and who should sign off on the application form?
  - Which communications should extend beyond the primary point of contact? Can your organization customize this decision based on the needs of the organizational member?
  - What is the value proposition for the individual participant in the program? What is the value proposition for the organization? Which one will be the primary driver of the program?
  - How will success be measured? What if success is intangible?
  - How will nonmembers within member organizations be treated? Should they receive member discounts?
  - What are the price points to ensure dues and program/event fees are set appropriately before the program is launched?

Best Practices

When launching an enterprise membership program, it is important to be patient. It may be a long sales cycle. Organizations need to identify and build relationships with key decision-makers. Many organizations found that it took months, and in some cases over a year, to close a sale.

- Dedicate sufficient resources to support a customized program. It is essential that organizations include staff from membership, customer service, and professional development in the management of the program.

- Pilot the program before a full-scale launch. Be prepared to adjust and make changes based on feedback from early participants. Every organization that offers an enterprise membership program has made some modifications to the program based on interest, need, participation, and feedback from members.

- Enterprise membership programs usually require some level of customization. Participation in an enterprise program can be a significant line item expense. Participants may evaluate the return on the investment on an annual basis. To ensure high levels of retention, it is important that the program be customized to meet the needs of the member.

Organization Types

Individual Membership Organization (IMO)

Membership is tied to an individual's name. Professional societies, unions, and donor-based organizations are commonly structured as IMOs. Most associations allow membership to be portable, in that the individual member remains a member regardless of changes in employment setting or location. With more than 143,000 individual members in 147 countries, the Society of Petroleum Engineers is the world's largest individual member organization serving managers, engineers, scientists, and other professionals worldwide in the upstream segment of the oil and gas industry.

Trade Association

Voluntary associations of businesses organized on a geographic or industrial basis to promote and develop commercial opportunities within its sphere of operation and/or to voice publicly the views of members on matters of common interest are considered trade associations. The U.S. Chamber of Commerce is the world's largest trade association business organization, representing the interests of more than 3 million businesses of all sizes, sectors, and regions. Members include state and local chambers, associations, and small businesses.

Federation Associations

Membership organizations whose members are other associations operate in a federated structure in which each party shares a percentage of membership dues. In many cases, a federated structure includes relationships at the national, regional, state, or local level. The National Association of Home Builders (NAHB) is a federation of more than 800 state and local associations and represents more than 140,000 members.

Components (Chapters, Sections)

Components, according to ASAE's definition, are an affiliated or independent society, chapter, branch, special-interest group, or division of an international, national, state, regional, or local organization. Some associations require all members to join the component and the national or international organization. For example, the American Dental Association requires individuals to belong to the local, state, and national organization. Other organizations, such as the Society for Human Resource Management (SHRM), allow individuals to join an affiliate chapter, the national organization, or both. SHRM has more than 575 affiliate chapters in the United States and abroad. SHRM chapters are autonomous organizations.

Reference

Jacobs, Sheri. *The Art of Membership: How to Attract, Retain, and Cement Member Loyalty.* Hoboken, NJ: John Wiley & Sons, 2014.

About the Author

Sheri Jacobs, FASAE, CAE, a best-selling author, keynote speaker, and association management veteran with nearly 20 years of experience, serves as the CEO and president of Avenue M Group, one of the nation's leading market research firms focused exclusively on the association community.

Jacobs started her nonprofit career in the development office of the Chicago Children's Museum and moved into marketing after becoming a founding officer of Picture This Projects, a nonprofit organization that empowers underserved children in Chicago. She transitioned from the philanthropic community to the association community in 1994 when she became the director of membership and marketing at the American Academy of Implant Dentistry and joined the American Bar Association Law Practice Management Division in 1999. In 2002, Jacobs joined the Association Forum of Chicagoland as the chief marketing officer and director of membership. During her tenure at the Association Forum, she built award-winning campaigns that resulted in double-digit membership and meeting attendance growth.

Over the years, Jacobs has served in numerous leadership and volunteer roles, including as chair of the ASAE Foundation Development Committee, member of the Professional Development Council, chair of the ASAE Membership Council, and a member of the Marketing Council. Jacobs' success in the field has led her to become an accomplished author. She is the co-editor and a contributor to ASAE's best-selling membership book, *The Art of Membership: How to Attract, Retain, and Cement Member Loyalty* (2014), *Membership Essentials* (2007), and *199 Ideas: Powerful Marketing Tactics That Sell* (ASAE, 2010).

In 2015, the Association Forum of Chicagoland awarded the John C. Thiel Distinguished Service Award to Jacobs in recognition for her outstanding service to the association community. Contact Jacobs at Jacobs@avenuemgroup.com.

The Role of Volunteers in Membership/ Volunteer Management

11

By Miriam Wolk, CAE

"When members suddenly make a connection between what the association does and what is critically important to them, they are converted from participants to loyal members, donors, and champions."

(Anna Caraveli, *Associations Now,* March/April 2015)

Why Volunteers Matter

Almost every association mandates some sort of volunteer leadership in its bylaws, and these boards and committees are critical to ensuring that the association functions legally and successfully. However, volunteers play a role well beyond an association's process and procedures. Certainly, they accomplish work that staff cannot accomplish alone, such as the development of expert resources for the field. However, a volunteer's contribution to the association should go well beyond just work product.

According to the Bureau of Labor Statistics, Americans over the age of 16 continue to volunteer at extremely high numbers, with 62.8 million giving their time to help others in 2014 (www.bls.gov/news.release/volun.nr0.htm). Associations are perfectly poised to maximize this interest in volunteerism by engaging individuals who have already made the choice to affiliate through membership, and more and more of these are making the choice to volunteer. According to The Power of A (2015), associations are seeing an increase in the number of their members who serve as volunteer leaders, with rates rising from 31.9 percent to 44.8 percent from 2014 to 2015.

Association members who serve as volunteer leaders and have a meaningful experience are more likely to renew their individual memberships or recommend their companies renew trade association memberships. They are more likely to participate in face-to-face educational programs, purchase publications, encourage their companies or vendor partners to exhibit at trade shows or expos, and support the association through sponsorships, donations, or other financial activities. Most importantly, engaged volunteers serve as member ambassadors, demonstrating to their peers the value of being involved in the association, which ultimately becomes the backbone of association recruitment, retention, and engagement activities. The foundation for this success starts with creating a volunteer environment in which individuals feel they are making meaningful contributions to the association, are acknowledged for their efforts, and are supporting the broader mission of their association, their profession, and the industry.

In this chapter, we will look at how this is accomplished by reviewing:

- Different types of volunteer opportunities
- How to create a meaningful volunteer experience
- The role of the volunteer versus the role of staff
- Volunteers as association ambassadors

Different Types of Volunteer Opportunities

While the exact structure of your volunteer leadership will be determined by your association's bylaws, all associations should create opportunities for volunteer leadership that will drive activities that help the association meet the goals articulated in its strategic plan, as well as identify leaders within the association who are future candidates for executive leadership, including members of the board of directors and executive officers. Depending on how your association's bylaws are written, your association will have various opportunities for volunteer engagement.

Board of Directors

The board of directors serves as the managing body of the association. Board members are elected by members of the association, either by popular vote or as a slate approved by the membership. The board will be led by executive officers—typically a chairman and chairman-elect. Some association bylaws have a longer "ladder" for leadership, including first or second vice presidents or vice chairmen. Boards can also include a secretary, who is responsible for the recorded minutes of a meeting, as well as a treasurer, who is responsible for the fiduciary duties of the association. It is a best practice for officers to have served as at-large board members prior to assuming board leadership. This will allow the board members to gain experience with the association's mission, bylaws, and process, and thus give them the experience needed to act on issues and motions.

Board member candidates can be identified either through a formal "Call for Volunteers," where members self-identify their interest through a written application or interview, or through a nominating committee, which meets and recommends a slate of candidates. Your association's bylaws will ultimately determine how board members are selected. A crucial factor to keep in mind when identifying board members is reflecting the diversity of your association's membership: Because the board is acting on behalf of the membership, members of the board should reflect the make-up of your association's membership as much as possible, while still conforming to the association's bylaws. These diverse board members will be able to share a variety of perspectives and experiences that will allow them to act on behalf of the broader membership, rather than one discrete member type or sector.

Types of diversity to keep in mind would include:

1. *Geographic Diversity:* Does your board have members from across various geographic regions? If your membership is international, do you have representatives from the countries and continents reflected in the membership?

2. *Professional Diversity:* If there are different position types included in your association, are those position types reflected in the members of your board? For example, at a higher-education legal association, you might include general counsel, as well as specialists in employment law, tax law, and intellectual property law.

3. *Company Diversity:* Trade associations will often include member companies of various sizes and types. The board of directors of a trade association with a diverse company membership should include representatives from both small and large companies.

4. *Personal Diversity:* Types of personal diversity to include on a board might be gender, age, and ethnic background.

Committees

Committees can serve as an excellent opportunity to develop programs, resources, and other activities for the members of the association, as well as to help the association with policy and procedural activities. For example, a Food Safety Committee might consist of experts in that field who develop resources related to that subject, such as educational sessions or white papers, while a Membership Committee might consist of individual members who interview potential new members and make recommendations to the board of directors regarding the approval of their association membership, or who are responsible for identifying and recruiting potential new members. Regardless of the scope of work of the committee, individual members should reflect the same diversity taken into account above for the formation of the association's board of directors.

Your association's bylaws may set a maximum number of individuals who can serve on a committee at any given time. If your bylaws limit the number of individuals who may sit on a committee, it may be helpful to establish term limits so that more members have the opportunity to serve, bringing a fresh perspective to the committee's activities. In this case, consider staggering terms so that new committee members will have the opportunity to learn from committee members with more experience.

If your bylaws do not set a maximum number of volunteers on a board or committee, consider "How many is too many?" While a "the more, the merrier" approach may seem to allow a larger number of individuals to be involved, having too many people on a committee may dilute the experience, not allow individuals to contribute meaningfully, and cause meetings to be unorganized. With a large group, dividing the group into formal subcommittees that work on individual projects on the work plan will allow more members to contribute in a meaningful way. In addition, subcommittees create opportunities for more individual leaders and contributors, which creates the opportunity to identify future committee leaders and board members.

Additionally, whether mandated by bylaws or not, each committee should have a chairman. The chairman should work with association staff to preside over the committee's meetings and ensure that the committee's work plan is completed. Adding a vice chairman, who will ultimately ascend to chairman, also provides continuity of leadership for the committee. The chairman and vice chairman should work closely with association staff to develop committee agendas, monitor the progress of the work plan, and manage all committee activities. In many associations, the chairman and/or the vice chairman might also serve as a member of the board of directors. This ensures clear communication between the committee and board of directors on the committee's activities and how they fit into your association's broader strategic plan.

For trade associations in particular, committee service can provide an opportunity to expand your roster of individual champions within a member company. Rather than having contact with only one company representative, you can work with your member companies to identify additional contacts who can serve on expert or procedural committees. Should your primary contact depart the company or choose not to advocate for continued member engagement, other volunteer leaders within the company, especially those who have had a meaningful volunteer experience, can help ensure company retention, as well as increased engagement and financial support.

Committee service can also serve as a strong opportunity for member recruitment, especially if your bylaws do not limit the membership categories eligible to serve on committees. For companies that aren't yet members of the association, provide an overview of the committee opportunities available and the process for joining the committees. You can also encourage current committee volunteers to speak directly with interested members on the value of the committee's work. Some associations elect to have a committee specifically focused on membership. Depending on your association's bylaws, this committee will have various responsibilities, including:

- If your association requires that certain members apply for admission to the association, your membership committee might have responsibility for interviewing members, reviewing applications, and making recommendations on admission.

- Responsibility for recruiting new members through personal campaigns and outreach. Peer-to-peer recommendation is often a major driver for membership recruitment, so having dedicated members who are enthusiastic about your association can help with member outreach.

- Reaching out to members who are considering dropping their membership.

- Meeting with new members to help orient them to the association.

- Representing the association at meetings and programs, including trade shows, town hall meetings, and other industry events.

If your association does not have a formal membership committee, consider how you might engage your current volunteer leadership to serve some of the peer recruitment, retention, and engagement functions typically performed by a member committee. Ideas for engaging volunteer leaders in membership activities will be discussed later in this chapter.

Ad Hoc Opportunities

Ad hoc volunteers may not formally serve on a board or committee, but the services they can provide to the association are truly valuable. Ad hoc volunteers may serve on a project that is limited in time or scope, without a formal commitment to regular meetings or committee duties. For example, they may serve as judges for an awards program or contribute an article to your association newsletter. Ad hoc volunteer opportunities provide an environment for individuals who are not ready for a more formal time commitment to the association, but want to contribute in some manner. If you are hearing from your members that their primary objection to volunteer service is "lack of time," ad hoc opportunities can provide an avenue to contribute to the association without the pressure of required travel, meetings, or other time commitments that may be a barrier to their participation. A positive ad hoc experience may then encourage these individuals to invest more time in the association in the future through committee membership or board service. Likewise, individuals who have less career or professional experience can use ad hoc volunteer opportunities to develop their leadership experience to better prepare them for more formal future service.

> "Joel Dolci, CAE, president and CEO of the New York Society of Association Executives (NYSAE), has long espoused task-based volunteerism, particularly for NYSAE's annual professional recognition awards. 'Reviewing nominations for NYSAE's Synergy Awards represents an opportunity for members to utilize their expertise,' says Dolci. 'But they can do so without the level of time commitment required for some other committees, such as membership or education.'"
>
> *(Michael Cummings, 2014)*

Creating a Meaningful Volunteer Experience

Turning member volunteers into association champions starts with a meaningful volunteer experience, which is more than having a name listed on a committee roster. Volunteers should understand their role in the association, as well as how their activities relate to the association's strategic plan and serve the broader membership. Through structured orientation of new volunteers, clear direction, organized meetings, recognition, and evaluation and feedback, your association will create an environment in which volunteers are engaged and eager to further support the association.

Volunteer Recruitment

The process to volunteer for a board or committee should be transparent and welcoming. Caryl Garais Tynan, director of membership services at the American College of Phlebology, suggests: "Have an easy-to-understand form that outlines skills, time, and expertise needed. Respond and complete the appointment quickly to provide instant gratification." Create an area on your association website and member orientation kit that explains the various volunteer opportunities available, the activities and time commitments required, and the process for applying or volunteering. You can also consider offering an education session or webinar that will allow interested volunteers to ask questions of association leaders or staff about the volunteer experience. Follow up as quickly as possible with all interested volunteers with information about their appointments. If for some reason a member representative isn't selected to volunteer, provide him with additional feedback on how he might gain additional experience, such as observing meetings or participating more in association activities, or provide additional available options, such as available ad hoc activities. This will prevent these individuals from becoming discouraged about the volunteer process, as well as encourage them to stay engaged with the association until they're able to join their desired board or committee.

> ### *Some Questions to Ask That Can Reveal a Volunteer's Passion*
>
> - What would you like to do to support our cause?
> - Why are you interested in our cause?
> - What has been your most enjoyable volunteer experience to date?
> - In your opinion, what is the most meaningful or gratifying part of our organization?
> - What is the one thing you would like to see our organization do that we are not doing today?
>
> From there, provide opportunities for volunteers to participate beyond their initial roles. Invite them to provide input on programs and projects.
>
> *Source:* Anthony Sudler, *Better Volunteering Structure, More Engaged Volunteers*, May 8, 2012. www.asaecenter.org/Resources/articledetailnew.cfm?ItemNumber=170100

To gauge a volunteer's potential, ask the following questions:

- What are the possible contributions?
- What are the strengths?
- Is he or she connected in the community?
- What can he or she bring to your organization?

To gauge volunteer commitment, answer the following questions:

- Does the volunteer connect to any aspect of our cause?
- Is the person volunteering for a valid reason?
- Does the volunteer connect to the individuals of our organization?
- Does the volunteer appear proud and satisfied with the contribution?

To gauge volunteer performance, answer the following questions:

- How is the volunteer benefiting the organization?
- Is the volunteer consistent?
- Is the volunteer flexible to the needs of the organization?
- Does the volunteer perform agreed-on activities with a level of consistency?

Orientation

Associations traditionally provide a formal orientation process for incoming members of an association's board of directors. However, all incoming association volunteers could benefit from a formal orientation to the association and their role as volunteer leaders. The orientation should include the association's structure and governance, the association's mission and strategic plan, the charge of the committee, and their work plan. Volunteers who understand how they and their activities fit into the broader association mission and strategic plan are more likely to be focused, engaged, and feel that they have meaningfully contributed to the association. Orientations can take place in person at the volunteer's first meeting, or by webinar or conference call. Rather than just providing orientation materials in a static environment, a successful orientation will provide an opportunity for new volunteers to engage with the orientation leaders, ask questions, and provide direct feedback on their experience. After an interactive orientation, new volunteer leaders should feel energized and engaged to participate in their committee's activities and support the association.

Board/Committee Charge

A successful committee will have a "charge" from the board of directors. The charge provides direction to the committee and will serve as a guide for the committee's activities. For example, the charge to a "Committee on Education" might be "To recommend and develop professional development programs for the association's members that will assist them with enhancing their knowledge in the field and furthering their careers." A strong charge will help keep a committee focused on projects and activities that tie directly back to an association's strategic plan.

Committee Work Plan

A successful committee will also have a work plan, with activities that tie back to the charge. The activities on the work plan should be prioritized, with a goal for completion. The committee should regularly review the work plan to ensure activities are being completed in a timely manner. For example, a committee on supply chain management with a charge to develop programs and services for supply chain professionals might have a work plan that includes developing workshop topics and the creation of a designated number of pamphlets or white papers on supply chain topics. The membership committee might have a work plan that charges them to meet certain recruitment, retention, and engagement metrics. For example, the committee could be charged with recruiting a certain number of members or hosting a certain number of industry outreach events.

Volunteer Interaction and Communication

Your boards and committees may be mandated by your association's bylaws to meet in person a certain number of times a year. Committee members who attend in-person meetings, but see no interaction between meetings, are less likely to be engaged. Therefore, staff and association leadership should communicate frequently with committee members in between meetings. Communication can occur by conference call or email, as well as by interim subcommittee or work group discussions. Communication should also go beyond "asks" for registration or financial support. Staff liaisons and volunteer leaders can share articles and other information of interest to the volunteer leaders. This information adds value to the individual's participation in the volunteer group and creates incentives for increased participation.

While some associations choose to hold committee meetings as standalone events, consider scheduling your committee meetings adjacent to regular association programs and events. This will minimize additional travel costs for your volunteer leaders, especially if your association does not cover travel costs. This will also encourage them to register for these events. Creating "volunteer leader"–only functions at association events, such as meal functions or receptions, provides an additional avenue for networking and adds value to volunteer engagement. In addition to these activities, your association might also consider creating an annual forum only for volunteer leaders during which they can not only conduct their committee business, but also network with other volunteer leaders and participate in group education sessions.

Should it be appropriate to the committee's agenda and discussion and allowed in the association's bylaws, your association might also consider allowing members to observe committee meetings to achieve an increased understanding of the committee's work. Allowing for observation creates an inclusive environment for members that encourages them to increase their personal engagement. Staff liaisons should coordinate with their committee leadership on the appropriate role of these observers, including how and whether they can participate in the meeting directly.

Tip: Stewarding

We should steward volunteers the same way we do our donors: It's the little things that count. Try these stewardship activities and observe how your volunteers react:

1. Write handwritten thank-you notes.
2. Make thank-you phone calls; ask to speak with the volunteer's spouse and sing your volunteer's praises.
3. Have a small ($5) gift waiting for the person at a meeting.
4. Invite people to tell their stories and the reasons they volunteer in your news-letter.
5. Introduce them to the CEO for a brief chat.
6. Send birthday and holiday cards.

www.asaecenter.org/Resources/articledetailnew.cfm?ItemNumber=170100)

Volunteer Recognition

While some associations reimburse board and committee members for their travel expenses, many volunteer leaders use their company or association funds for travel related to volunteer activities. In addition, they are using both professional and personal time to serve the association. Given this, it is important to recognize your association's volunteer leaders frequently and meaningfully. For example, according to Weaver (2008): "The International Society for Pharmaceutical Engineering celebrates an annual Volunteer Appreciation Week, during which the organization sends a personal letter out to all of its volunteers worldwide. ISPE also gives committee members a 50 percent discount off all education fees, and the organization recognizes their efforts at an annual leadership dinner at the main conference."

Your association should consider what recognition activities will be valued by your volunteers, including, but not limited to:

- Visual designations at in-person events, such as ribbons or pins, that allow members to identify themselves and be recognized as volunteer leaders. For example, according to a June 2006 article in *Associations Now*: "The top member-to-member recruiters of the National Home Builders Association, Washington, D.C., are easy to identify by the spike-shaped lapel pins that they wear to show their levels of recruiting success. They are members of the NAHB Spike Club Program. Those who participate in the member-to-member recruitment campaign are called 'Spikes' because they are among the most valued members of the association."

- Special networking or social events exclusively for volunteer leaders, such as private meal functions at association events at your annual conference.

- Recognition in association publications, such as in your annual conference's on-site program, and on signage or slides at association events, such as a walk-in slide loop at your annual conference general session.

- Personal correspondence, such as a letter from the chairman of the board or chief staff officer.

- Discounts or complimentary access to association events or publications.

While more time-consuming, consider personalizing your recognition activities as much as possible. Idea Architects says: "Yes, sending out the mail-merged thank-you note is better than sending nothing. But the underlying message is 'we care enough about your generosity that we mail-merged you this letter.' Contrast the likely value of that effort with a short handwritten note in which you personally comment on the specific contributions the volunteer made. Which would engage you more?" (www.ideaarthitects.com).

Regardless of what your association does to acknowledge your volunteers, volunteers should be acknowledged and thanked often and sincerely, and reminded that their service creates meaningful value for the association. As Anthony Sudler (2012) says, "A committed, passionate, and high-performing volunteer can advance your cause, become a true advocate for your organization, and simply brighten your day. Volunteers may start in one place within your organization, but you are responsible for guiding them. As you execute this process, be genuine, respectful, and thoughtful. You will find that many volunteers will become part of your organization's fiber and family."

Evaluation

All associations should seek regular feedback from volunteer leaders on their volunteer experience. While exit interviews for retiring board or committee members can be helpful, your association should also ask volunteer leaders for frequent feedback during their service to assess any areas that can be enhanced or corrected.

Feedback can be collected through surveys and personal interviews with leaders and then shared with staff liaisons, committee leadership, and the board of directors for further action. For example, on its Board Performance Evaluation Form, the American Coal Council asks its volunteers to assess their understanding of the association's mission and vision, their knowledge of association programs, their communication with staff, their focus on priorities, strategies and outcomes, and other metrics relevant to successful board performance (www.asaecenter.org/Resources/modelsdetailamh.cfm?itemNumber=203916).

The Role of the Volunteer vs. the Role of Staff

Volunteer leaders are often leaders in their company or field, and thus used to playing a management role in their daily professional lives. This can sometimes create confusion or conflict in their role in dealing with association activities and management. A clear orientation process on the role of board and committee members will help educate volunteer leaders on their role within the association. However, times may arise when a volunteer leader may act beyond the scope of his or her role. When these situations occur, it is important to manage them in a professional and consistent manner.

The Role of the Staff Liaison

A successful board or committee will have strong relationships between a dedicated staff liaison or liaisons, committee leadership, and committee members. The staff liaison is responsible for supporting the work of the committee, preparing the committee for its meetings, and facilitating communication between the committee and the association. Depending on the size of your association, a membership manager may only have interaction with the membership committee, or may also serve as the liaison to additional committees that drive content and oversee awards programs and other association functions. Since vibrant, engaged committees are an essential part of a strong membership experience, membership managers supporting activities outside of the traditional membership function should see their role as helping to contribute to a positive membership culture that will ultimately lead to strong member loyalty.

Prior to in-person meetings or conference calls, staff liaisons should meet with the committee leadership to formalize the committee agenda, as well as the flow of the meeting. The staff liaison will also work with committee leaders to develop committee materials and disseminate information to committee members in advance of the meeting. Committee members should receive organized meeting documents well in advance of their scheduled meeting so that they have time to review the information and be prepared for discussion. Committee members who do not have the opportunity to review meeting materials in advance of a meeting are less likely to be engaged in discussions, and thus will not have as positive a volunteer experience.

An engaged member volunteer, Shep Hyken (2015) says it best when asked about the most critical aspects of volunteer relations: "Two words come to mind: communication and trust. As with any good business relationship, communication is paramount. From there, trust and confidence are earned (on both sides). Updates are crucial to inform the board of progress. Board members must respect and trust the staff to do their job. My personal goal is to trust the staff and the process we have in place, and to avoid the temptation to micromanage. It really is amazing how great results are achieved when you don't get in the way of excellent people doing their job.

When Conflicts Occur

While a thorough orientation process and ongoing communication between volunteer leaders and staff should set the stage for a successful volunteer experience, situations may arise in which conflicts occur between volunteer leaders and staff, as well as between individual volunteers or groups of volunteer leaders. In these types of situations, the best practice is "member to member, staff to staff." Since this may be an unfamiliar concept for your volunteer leaders, your association can help clearly define the differences between member and staff responsibilities by providing written guidelines during your volunteer orientation. For example, the Medical Group Management Association includes specific information and job descriptions in its orientation materials titled "Role of Committee vs. Role of Staff: Who Does What and When" (https://www.asaecenter.org/files/secure/index.cfm?FileID=143469)

Volunteer leaders are not responsible for directly disciplining association staff. If a volunteer leader has a conflict with an individual staff member, the volunteer leader should not approach the staff member directly. Instead, the issue should be brought to the attention of the chief staff executive, who will address the situation directly with the staff member. For example, if a staff member is not meeting promised deadlines for deliverables, or if the chairman is attempting to communicate with the staff member and not getting a response, the chairman should reach out to the chief staff executive to make him or her aware of the situation and work directly with the staff member to resolve the issue.

If a board or committee member is acting beyond the scope of his role or in a manner that is disruptive to the committee charge, work plan, or dynamic, it is a best practice to have a chairman or executive leader, rather than an association staff member, address this issue. For example, you may have a situation in which an individual volunteer might dominate the conversation during a meeting, which is frustrating to the other members of the group. In this instance, the chairman should approach the individual committee member privately and share that, although his contributions and ideas are valuable, it's important to allow all committee members to have the opportunity to contribute to the discussion. In some cases, if the board or committee member's actions threaten the legal or financial status of the association, it is important that the association consult with counsel on next steps.

In all cases, ensure that any conflicts or disagreements are handled quickly, professionally, and consistently. Ongoing conflicts or conflicts that aren't handled in a consistent manner will create a less than positive experience for volunteer leaders that can dissuade them from future participation and also give them a less than positive view of the association that might affect their future engagement.

Volunteers as Association Ambassadors

Now that you have successfully laid the foundation for engaged volunteer leadership, you should have individual member representatives who are eager to serve as champions for your association. While your association may have a formal membership committee with responsibility for recruiting, retaining, engaging, and/or approving new members, all volunteer leaders should be encouraged to serve as ambassadors for the association and encourage individuals and companies in their network to engage with the association.

Since the board of directors is directly responsible for the fiduciary success of the association, the board should be regularly engaged in the success of association membership activities. All board meetings should include an overview of membership, including the status of the association's recruitment and retention efforts, as well as benchmarking data against prior year performance and budgets. Board members should also be familiar with the association programs and services that contribute to member recruitment and retention.

Your association might require members of its board of directors to recruit a certain number of members a year. If not, consider engaging your board members in recruitment and retention activities. With their positions as professional and industry leaders, the message of membership value coming from a peer in the field, rather than staff, can carry even stronger relevance. To add a spirit of competition or reward programs, associations can create board competitions with incentives such as an enhanced travel and lodging experience at an association program.

Beyond presenting data to the board, consider sharing key membership metrics with all of your volunteer leaders so that they understand how the association's success in membership contributes to the overall success of the association. An article in *Associations Now* by Joe Rominiecki (2013) states: "A major emerging tool, however, is data, and a lot of it. Once a month, the Institute of Electrical and Electronics Engineers (IEEE) staff send a detailed, 12- to 15-page report with updates on membership numbers across the organization, all of which is connected to the key goals and directives for IEEE's membership development efforts. John Day, director of member products and programs, says the report has become a key driver of volunteers' contributions to membership development, particularly in recruitment, where Day says that about 50 percent of IEEE's new members every year can be attributed to volunteer outreach.

In addition to data, provide your individual volunteer leaders with resources and talking points on how to engage their professional peers. For example, United Fresh's market segment boards each review lists of companies in their industry sector not currently engaged in the association and encourage these board members to reach out to them and encourage their involvement. Staff liaisons provide talking points and assist with crafting letters that volunteer leaders can send directly or that the association can send on their behalf.

If you have volunteer leaders who have successfully assisted the association with member recruitment, retention, and engagement, ensure that these volunteers are recognized for their efforts. For example, on formal member recruitment reports to the board, include the names of the members who successfully referred the candidates. You can also recognize these members through thank-you correspondence, incentives related to association participation, including meeting and membership discounts, and more personal incentives such as gift cards or sweepstakes entries. For example, the Society of Petroleum Engineers (SPE) "local affiliates recruit members and are tracked from September 1 through August 31 of the following year. SPE assesses how many new members the section gains as well as how many it retains and groups them according to size. Winning sections receive $1,000, recognition at SPE's annual meeting, and a mention in its monthly journal" (*Associations Now*, April 2011).

Conclusion

While association membership is quantitative and transactional on the surface, ultimately, for both professional and trade associations, it is a personal, qualitative decision to affiliate. A positive, well-organized volunteer experience where members feel they are contributing meaningfully to association activities and are rewarded for their efforts creates an ideal membership environment where members are happy to support the association through their time, money, and energy. This will lead to a vibrant association environment with enriched resources and programs, as well as a community where individual member representatives are actively engaged with championing the association for many years to come.

References

A Little Recognition Can Go a Long Way. *Associations Now,* April 2011.

American Coal Council. Board Performance Evaluation Form.
   www.asaecenter.org/Resources/modelsdetailamh.cfm?itemNumber=203916.

Cummings, Michael. *The Power of Short-Term Projects for Volunteer Engagement.*
   www.asaecenter.org. December 1. 2014.

Hyken, Shep. Leader to Leader: Motivation and Staff Relations. *Associations Now*, January/
   February 2015.

ModelWorks: Pin Recognition on Your Associations. *Associations Now Plus,* June 2006.

Rominiecki, Joe. Empower Volunteers with Membership Data. *Associations Now*, August 17,
   2013.

Sudler, Anthony. Better Volunteering Structure, More Engaged Volunteers.
   www.asaecenter.org/Resources/articledetailnew.cfm?ItemNumber=170100. May 8, 2012.

Tynan, Caryl Garais. 8 Easy Volunteer Victories, ASAE Component Relations Section
   Council newsletter, n.d.

Weaver, Elizabeth. Thanks to You: Increase Member Engagement with Volunteer
   Recognition Programs. *Associations Now Plus,* September 2008.

About the Author

Miriam Wolk, CAE, joined United Fresh Produce Association as director of membership in July 2008 and was promoted to senior director of membership in August 2010 and to vice president of membership and marketing in January 2013. In October 2014, she transitioned to the role of vice president of member services. Her responsibilities include oversight and organization of association business development activities, formulating and executing recruitment campaigns and retention activities, overseeing new member orientation, and managing the association membership database. She frequently travels to regional events to promote the value of United Fresh membership and programs. Wolk serves as the staff liaison to United Fresh's Wholesaler-Distributor Board, Member Relations Task Force, Floral Advisory Committee, and Produce Excellence in Foodservice Awards. Prior to joining the United Fresh staff, Wolk served as manager of membership and outreach services for the National Association of College and University Attorneys (NACUA), as well as at The Advisory Board Company, where she held several positions in business development, marketing strategy, and member services. Wolk is a 1999 Phi Beta Kappa graduate of American University with a B.A. degree in literature. Email: mwolk@unitedfresh.org.

Recruitment and Renewal Strategies

12

By Tony Rossell

T he two transactional milestones in the membership experience are recruitment— when someone joins the association—and renewal—when someone continues his or her membership.

Because of the importance of these milestones in the member relationship, associations have invested heavily to develop best practices in these areas. This chapter will highlight many of these best practices for building effective recruitment and renewal strategies.

Recruitment Strategies

Let's start out by looking at membership recruitment strategies in five key areas:

1. The Target Market—Who you want to reach
2. The Membership Offer—What a member will receive
3. The Marketing Message—Why a member should join
4. The Promotional Tactics—How a member will be reached
5. The Testing and Tracking—Where to take future efforts

Without recruiting new members, it is impossible for an association to grow. Every association leaks members. Members of professional associations retire or pass away; companies in trade associations merge or close; and members of avocational associations change their interests. These members need to be replaced and more added to result in membership growth.

Associations that have had great success in recruiting new members have systematically applied strategies in the five disciplines listed above—target markets, membership offers, marketing messages, promotional tactics, and testing and tracking—to grow their membership.

Target Market—Who

Successful membership marketers will agree that the people whom you target with your promotion is the single biggest factor in the success or failure of your efforts. Whether you are using direct mail, telemarketing, email, or any other media to recruit members, the *who* you are reaching is defined by the lists—and the selections you make within those lists—that you create or choose to use in your recruitment efforts. Here are three strategies to find the best member targets for your organization.

Harvest Your Database

Without realizing it, many associations are sitting on a goldmine of potential members hidden away in various spreadsheets and databases across the association. All list research should start with your internal databases. Conduct a census of names stored in your association to identify prospective members for whom you may already have a record and a relationship. These will include lapsed members, nonmember conference attendees, volunteers, chapter members, nonmember buyers of products (books, professional development), and inquirers. Without a doubt, these are some of the best prospects to contact for membership because they are already aware of your organization.

Build Your Own List

Potential members are often seeking a solution to a problem or looking for information. So in order to build your own prospect list, help potential members find you as they search online for the solution to their problem. This can be accomplished through search engine optimization (SEO) of your website and through your social media channels. Additionally, paid inbound marketing and content marketing techniques are effective in highlighting your solutions. These options include keyword search engine marketing (SEM) ads, and placing targeted ads on Facebook, LinkedIn, Twitter, and other websites.

Your goal when a prospect searches for your information and finds material provided by you is to gain an opt-in and contact information in exchange for the information being shared. This process of trading content for contact builds your database of potential members with those who have a demonstrated interest and a need for the resources that you provide—essentially connecting you with a perfect prospective member.

Do Outside List Research

When you begin to look for lists outside your organization, ask your members what other organizations they are members of and what professional magazines they read. The lists that best match the behavior of your current members are likely to work for recruiting new members.

You will also want to take a look at where organizations like yours advertise and exhibit. Chances are the subscribers or members of these organizations also will be good prospects.

Another source of prospects is compiled lists. These are databases combined from many sources, such as professional licensure lists. They are highly selectable and can be rented for one-time use or in some cases leased for a year or more of usage.

Finally, help from list professionals can be very valuable. A good list broker will help you find the lists that have worked successfully for other associations. Brokers also have subscriptions to the major list databases to help them locate the most appropriate lists. Because the list owner pays the sales commission to the broker, working with a list broker does not add any more costs to renting outside lists.

The Offer—What

Many prospective members are aware of your association. They have thought from time to time of joining. However, year after year, they remain on the sidelines. Special offers or incentives to join can be effective in moving people from window shoppers to buyers. Everyone loves a sale. A special offer can be effective with any promotion used to acquire members, from mail to radio to a website.

Offer strategy comes into play by matching your special incentive to the sales objective that you are trying to accomplish. For example, if an association has a strong product offering, but low market awareness, a free trial offer may be the best method to persuade a member to sample and then ultimately join.

Here are some examples of special offers used in recruitment to help acquire new members:

- *A discount off the regular first-year dues rate.* The amount of the discount must be appropriate to the product/situation. Generally, a discount should be 10 to 25 percent. Too small a discount does little to increase response; too much can cheapen the product and dampen response. In membership recruitment, a properly targeted discount will produce both more new members and more revenue than a full-price offer.

- *An appropriate price point to impact the perception of cost.* Discounting is most effective when it lowers the dues amount to what pricing strategists call a "price point." Price points, like those that end in a 7 or a 9, typically receive higher response rates than other dollar denominations. That's why store items sell for $7.99. A $39 membership dues offer typically will be more successful than a $41 offer in total dollars and in the number of responses.

- *A no-risk or free trial offer allows for trying before buying.* Prospective members may be reticent to commit to a full year of membership. However, allowing them to sample membership for a limited time—often including an agreement to receive an invoice that may be used to either pay for the membership or to cancel the trial—reduces the risk to a potential member. This offer is a favorite in magazine circulation development and will almost always outperform a hard, or up-front, payment offer. A tightly managed fulfillment and billing system is required to administer this offer effectively.

- *A complimentary membership when attending a convention at the non-member rate.* Some associations bundle membership into attendance or major purchases by a non-member. Since the prospect receives this membership for "free," a requirement for the association is to demonstrate the value of membership over the course of the year before renewal efforts begin.

- *A sweepstakes to win a trip or prize.* A sweepstakes can get the attention of a potential member sitting on the fence considering joining. Sweepstakes work best for impulse memberships like a magazine-based membership or a contribution/donation membership. For many years, the Aircraft Owners and Pilots Association (AOPA) has run a membership sweepstakes offering a beautifully refurbished vintage aircraft. Sweepstakes offers must meet specific regulations and legal requirements established by the United States Postal Service and the Federal Trade Commission.

- *A premium or gift awarded for joining.* The best premiums appeal to the self-interest of the prospective member (e.g., salary surveys, special reports, white papers, and survey data). A dental association, for example, offers graduating students a white paper titled "Keys to a Successful Career in Dentistry" if they join. If fulfilled through a PDF or existing inventory previously produced by the association, then the cost to fulfill the offer comes at very little added expense.

- *An extended membership.* Offering more of the product can sometimes increase response (e.g., 15 months of membership for the price of 12). This is especially appropriate when an association operates on a calendar year membership. It avoids prorated dues confusion. Extra months of membership work best in markets where the product is already well known to the prospective member. An extended membership is less appealing to someone trying out membership with an unfamiliar organization.

- *An installment payment option.* This increases response, especially on a high-ticket membership. This offer would typically require a credit card that can be debited at regular intervals (monthly, quarterly, annually) and a system to manage credit card rejections.

Whatever offer you try to help move prospects to take action, it is best to make it available with a defined response deadline. A deadline will often heighten response rates and brings closure to fulfilling the incentive. Offers with deadlines outperform offers without them. Generally, use a deadline of 60 to 90 days from your launch date. The offer also must be accessible on the website when someone wants to join. Allowing the prospective member to enter a special offer code from the promotion on the join page of the website is the most common method to fulfill an offer.

The Marketing Message—Why

Once you have decided whom to direct your promotion to and what special incentive you are making available, you need to decide what you want to say to prospective members.

Addressing Needs

Developing your marketing message begins with gleaning information about your prospective members from market research. A wide variety of research tools are available to gain quantitative and qualitative data related to recruiting new members. It is outside the scope of this chapter to present a full list of research opportunities.

However, it is important to note that useful information can be gathered inexpensively and in a relatively short time period through the use of focus groups and simple phone interviews. These tools effectively provide qualitative information that can help in understanding what is going on in a prospective member's mind when it comes time to join. Excellent questions to ask members and potential members in research might be:

- "Can you tell me the thought process or evaluation that you go through when choosing to join an association?"

- "What would prevent you from becoming a member?"

- "How would you convince a colleague or friend to become a member in this association?"

Another source of insight for developing your marketing message comes from ASAE's 2007 study, *The Decision to Join* (DTJ). This survey recorded feedback from 16,944 members, former members, and prospective members of eighteen professional associations.

DTJ reported that the three most important personal benefits in the decision to join were:

- Opportunities to network with other professionals in the field

- Access to the most up-to-date information available in the field

- Professional development or education program offerings (p. 29)

DTJ highlighted that "the decision to join an association reflects an expanded understanding of what constitutes a benefit." Members do not simply make calculated self-interest decisions, but also join based on benefits the association provides to the field or profession, including:

- Promoting a greater appreciation of the role and value of the field among practitioners.

- Providing standards or guidelines that support quality.

- Maintaining a code of ethics for practice. (p. 1)

To recruit members, you need to take the information the market research has provided and craft it into what marketers call *the value proposition* or the unique selling proposition.

The membership proposition succinctly answers the question: "Why should I join your organization?" Think in terms of the very real and practical needs that are met by your organization.

Crafting Benefits Copy

Once you have determined the major reason that someone would want to join your organization, it is critical to translate all the key selling points or features for your organization into benefits. For example, a feature-based message related to an association newsletter might read: "As a member, you receive 12 monthly issues of our *Alert* newsletter." A benefit copy approach might read: "Our *Alert* newsletter gives you instant access to job-critical reports." Similarly, feature-based copy about your magazine might say: "Receive the flagship magazine of the ABC association." But translating this into benefit copy may result in: "ABC's magazine tells you the real story you won't find anywhere else about our industry." Benefit-based copy includes a promise to your member.

Finally, remember these copywriting tips as you write your promotion:

- Think of your membership promotion as a conversation between a salesperson and a prospective member. Ask and answer, the questions any prospective member would ask. And be sure to deal directly with typical sales objections (e.g., "It seems too expensive" or "I'm not sure it will be useful to me").

- Specifics are what make copy effective. Use real examples, numbers, product data, and testimonials.

- Often the best lead is buried somewhere deep in your promotion. Pull the buried lead to the beginning to help the reader get to the point quickly.

- Always include a call to action in your copy that clearly directs the reader to do something specific like "Take advantage of this limited-time special offer to join now by going to our website."

Promotional Tactics—How

Now it is time to determine what marketing tool(s) or channels should be used to reach your target audience with the offer and message that you have developed. Your selection of channels is chiefly driven by which best provides the ability to reach your market segment and the expected return on investment.

Reaching Prospects

You will need to obtain email addresses to send emails and phone numbers to do telemarketing. These may or may not be available in your database or from outside lists for your particular market.

Your prospective members also must have the ability to respond to your promotion. For example, if your prospective members are classroom teachers, their names, addresses, emails, and school phone numbers are available in commercial databases, but since they are in classrooms, they are not easily reachable during the day for telemarketing.

Inbound Marketing: An Emerging and Powerful Marketing Channel

A rapidly emerging and evolving tool in the marketing mix available to recruit new members is *inbound marketing*. This channel helps reach new prospects who may not have interacted with your association before and allows them to raise their hands in search of the very information and products that your membership provides.

Typically, inbound marketing is driven by two powerful elements—great content and broad-based online reach. As a tool it is most effective when integrated with outbound marketing channels like email, direct mail, telemarketing, and personal sales calls.

Inbound marketing works by offering a prospective member access to free content provided on an offer-specific microsite or landing page within an organization's website. To access the content, the prospect provides contact information and his or her opt-in to receiving additional communications from your organization that you use to nurture the relationship through additional relevant content and invitations to join. Lead capture and relationship building are the core of inbound marketing.

Inbound marketing can start with your owned media by optimizing your website's SEO, blogging, and offering content through your social media channels.

However, to reach out beyond your current audience, there are four paid sources where you can share your content offers to bring someone to your microsite and start a relationship.

1. *Paid Search Engine Marketing (SEM)*—Search ads appear when a prospective member enters a word or phrase into a search engine that matches one of your keywords. The ad is then presented to the person seeking the information with a link to your microsite providing the very content that the person is searching to find.

2. *Content Ads*—Whereas search ads are driven by keywords, content ads are shown on other websites offering information that relates to your products and services. When the prospective member's reading interests are a match to what you have to offer, your ad is displayed with a link to your microsite.

3. *Social Media Advertising*—Many social media sites offer millions more impressions than any association site will achieve. So placing ads on these sites ensures great exposure and also offers great targeting. For example, LinkedIn allows you to target ads to very specific job classifications, titles, and associations, and Facebook allows you to match your current members to potential prospects who have the same characteristics and display ads to these look-alike audiences.

4. *Google and Facebook Remarketing*—After all of your efforts to drive a prospective member to your website, you may be shocked at how many abandon your site before completing the transaction. Remarketing efforts—following your visitors around the Internet and Facebook with ads—encourages those visitors to return to your site to gain more information and perhaps complete their transaction.

All of these paid inbound online marketing sources come with these additional benefits:

- *Awareness*—Many more prospects will see your content offers than will click on them, but you typically pay just for clicks.
- *Coverage*—Online advertising gives you access to every corner of the world where there is an Internet connection.
- *Flexibility*—With these online efforts, you can adjust and allocate funds on a daily basis to maximize response.
- *Speed*—You can literally have a digital advertising program up and running and producing responses in a day.
- *Measurement*—You can know impressions, clicks, and, with good tracking, the number of members joining.

Because inbound marketing is a developing marketing technology, new opportunities become available almost daily. But even as the tactics change, the strategy will remain relevant. Inbound marketing helps you initiate a contact with a prospective member; nurture the relationship by demonstrating value, and encouraging the prospect to join your organization.

Return on Investment

Return on investment (ROI) may drive your selection of marketing channels. Some ways of going to market, such as face-to-face sales, are very expensive and are used chiefly for high-dollar, low-volume membership sales. For example, a personal sales call to a prospective trade association member may be worthwhile because the dues payment would be very high, but a personal sales visit may not be economical to recruit an individual member paying a low dues rate. Likewise, use of email is generally more cost-effective when recruiting members globally, compared to direct mail.

Table 12.1 lists the marketing channels regularly used for membership recruitment and some of the advantages and disadvantages of each. They are listed in relative cost order from most expensive to least expensive per impression.

Table 12.1. Marketing Channels Compared

Channel Type	Advantages	Disadvantages
Face-to Face-Sales	Allows for true one-to-one communication. Each sales presentation is customized for the prospect.	One of the most costly marketing options available, ranging from $100 to $300 per sales call. It requires higher dues and a high close rate to be an economical option.
Telephone Sales and Telemarketing	An excellent medium to reach former members and higher dues prospects.	Costs can range from $5 to $15 per prospect contact. Legal "do not call" requirements apply to some associations.
Direct Mail	The historical work horse of membership recruitment. Highly selectable direct mail lists are available to help reach specific targets.	Costs can range from $.50 to $1.50 per piece mailed. This will be lower for associations that can take advantage of USPS nonprofit postage rates.
Email	Very economical, especially if the email address is held by the association. Outside email lists are increasingly available for rental with targeted selects. Recipients' behavior can be monitored for open and click through rates.	Low delivery and open rates can mean your message will not be read. Legal requirements for CAN-SPAM along with Canada's Anti-Spam Law (CASL) for opt-in and opt-out apply.
Print Advertising	Effective tool to build awareness about the benefits of membership.	Usually does not generate enough tracked new members to cover the cost.
Search Engine Marketing (SEM) and Content Ads	Ads are presented to those seeking specific information or interested in compatible content, and costs are based on those who click through to your landing page, not on ad impressions.	To be effective, ads require ongoing staff time to monitor and optimize keywords and bids. Tracking effectiveness depends on the code placement on landing sites.
Member-Get-a-Member (MGM)	Classic recruitment option that can build excitement and take advantage of dedicated volunteers to share the benefits of membership. (See Chapter 13 for a full discussion of MGM programs.)	Requires building a system to capture new members and recognize recruiters and ongoing staff involvement to maintain enthusiasm.

(continued)

Table 12.1. Marketing Channels Compared (*continued*)

Channel Type	Advantages	Disadvantages
Online Inbound Marketing	Offers broad worldwide exposure and allows prospects to initiate a relationship in order to access content through online ads and social media. Offers precise tracking opportunities (see sidebar for more information).	Requires the production of engaging content, like blog posts, podcasts, video, and white papers, and the establishment of distribution channels where this content can be featured.
Word of Mouth	Creatively intense, but very low cost. Builds awareness by producing a buzz about your association.	Unpredictable. You may get people talking about your organization, but this may not translate into paid memberships.

Testing, Tracking, and Analysis—Where to Go in the Future

Perhaps the most important discipline in membership recruitment is testing, tracking the results, and analyzing returns. Effective testing and tracking practices point you to where you can deploy your resources most effectively and economically.

The renowned marketing professor Philip Kotler (1999) said, "Successful companies are learning companies. They collect feedback from the marketplace, audit and evaluate results, and take corrections designed to improve their performance. Good marketing works by constantly monitoring its position in relation to its destination" (p. 34).

This recommendation was affirmed in the research undertaken for *7 Measures of Success* (2006, 2012): "If there's one phrase that sets remarkable associations apart from their counterparts, it's 'Data, data, data.' They gather information, analyze it, and then use it to become even better" (p. 38).

A successful membership recruitment test can double or even triple the ROI of a marketing campaign. In fact, without testing, over time a marketing program is likely to see diminished returns and substantially under-achieve its potential. If testing is so important, then how should it be done?

Many associations are challenged in this area. For example, as Table 12.2 highlights, only 30 percent of individual membership associations and 15 percent of trade associations do A/B split marketing testing, and only 16 percent and 10 percent, respectively, do lifetime value analysis on their membership campaigns.

The Art of Testing

There are two aspects of testing, the art and the science. The art of testing involves thinking outside the box and creating a new way to do things. Each membership recruitment project should start with a brainstorming session that asks "What if?" or "How about?"

Table 12.2. Membership Analysis Used by Individual and Trade Associations

Types of Analysis Used to Measure Campaign Effectiveness		
	Individual (n = 302)	Trade (n = 174)
Response rate analysis	56%	47%
Return on investment (ROI)	39%	17%
Source code or keycode capture analysis	31%	11%
A/B split marketing tests	30%	15%
Cost of acquisition	23%	9%
Lifetime value analysis	16%	10%
Data mining/modeling	13%	7%
Computer match-back to prospect database	12%	5%
Net return after servicing costs	9%	6%
None	25%	33%
Other	2%	3%

Source: 2015 *MGI Membership Marketing Benchmarking Report.*

Bob Stone (2007, p. 468), in the landmark book, *Successful Direct Marketing Methods*, suggests asking the following questions to start the creative thought process:

- Can we combine?
- Can we add?
- Can we eliminate?
- Can we make an association?
- Can we simplify?
- Can we substitute?
- Can we reverse?

In addition to brainstorming, there are some specific high-leverage areas to consider testing, including:

- *Lists.* One of the easiest and most productive tests is trying new lists. Trying a new file you identified hidden away in your database or a third-party list offers the greatest potential to improve results. Some organizations find a new qualified list of prospects will perform at more than double the response of a regularly used tried-and-true list. Since list selection is the single biggest factor in the effectiveness of a promotion, it makes sense to test the lists that you are using.

- *Frequency.* Instead of launching one or two recruitment campaigns, try marketing more frequently to top prospects and customers. This is a test that almost always produces a profitable outcome because you may maintain the same number of total contacts, but you are allocating more resources to the very best prospects.

- *Special Offers.* Try an A/B split of two different new member offers, like a dues discount against a gift for joining. A good incentive can double the response rate and increase ROI, even taking the cost of the offer into consideration.

- *Creative.* Test different copy platforms focusing on a different reason for joining. Try new graphics and colors. Often a new message or look to a promotion will encourage a prospect to take a second look.

- *Channels.* Many marketing channels are available today and, with planning, each one can be tested and tracked. Split your list two ways and try a stand-alone email compared to a combination of direct mail with an accompanying email or follow-up phone call and see which generates more members at an acceptable ROI. Combining multiple channels to targeted prospects can often produce the best overall results.

The Science of Testing

Equally important to the art of testing is the science of testing. The science of testing starts with creating proper test structures. Good testing requires establishing a control group and testing against it. This is done by drawing a portion of names from a control group of the marketing effort and using them for the test. Then structure the test by holding everything else constant except the variable that is to be tested. For example, if the test is for a special discount offer, then, on the test segment, maintain the same graphics and approach as the control package and send the test promotion to a subset of the control names in the promotion.

A test obviously does not always produce better returns than the existing control. That's why tests should go to small segments of a larger promotion. However, in each test cell statisticians tell us that, ideally, you want a minimum of 40 paid responses to have a statistically valid test. Therefore, the number of anticipated responses will dictate the size of each test segment. For instance, if a 0.5 percent response rate is expected, then the test cell should include a minimum of 8,000 names $(40/0.005 = 8,000)$.

Tracking

The other challenging yet critical component of the science of testing is tracking. Despite the difficulty of tracking, the potential returns of testing are so great that an organization needs to build a mechanism to track returns. Membership professionals will have to work with the organization's IT staff and order-processing staff to find the best way to track returns from a test. Source coding options include personalizing a mailed membership reply form with a promotion code for each list and test version and having the code entered from mailed-in responses. The first digit in the code might represent the effort, the second digit might represent the version (test or control offer), and the third might represent the list.

To capture the code for web orders, entering the promotion code can be required for the prospective member in order to receive the special offer or discount. And finally, a match-back process is used by many associations comparing the new member returns each month against the prospect files used for recent promotions and adding the source code to the responder record.

Testing and tracking are ongoing processes. Over time, they become part of the culture of an organization. A focus on testing ensures the flow of new ideas and approaches to keep an organization's membership efforts vibrant and effective.

Analysis

The analysis process translates the data accumulated from tracking into actionable information. At its fundamental level, analysis compares the responses in the control group against the test group to determine which generated a higher return on investment.

Membership recruitment analysis should include the following basic information for each effort, list, and offer:

- Response rate
- Cost to obtain a member
- Revenue per member
- Return on investment

Additionally, more sophisticated analysis will highlight the long-term financial outcomes from a campaign, including the anticipated lifetime value of a member based on renewals and non-dues revenue. A full explanation of the critical calculations involved in lifetime value is provided in Chapter 16.

Renewal Strategies

With an effective recruitment strategy in place, the next important step in the membership transactional milestone is establishing an effective renewal strategy. (See Exhibit 12.1 for a calculation of the steady state.)

Membership renewals for an association have a profound impact on what direction the total membership number is headed. If an association, for example, adds 10,000 new members a year, the steady state of the association's membership count will vary greatly depending on the renewal rate achieved by the association. For example, with 10,000 new members a year:

- At a 65 percent renewal rate, an association has a steady state membership of 28,571 members.
- At a 75 percent renewal rate, an association has a steady state membership of 40,000 members.
- At a 90 percent renewal rate, an association has a steady state membership of 100,000 members.

Exhibit 12.1. Calculating Membership Steady State

A *steady state analysis* provides a projection of the destination or equilibrium for the total membership of an association based on the current level of new member input and lapsed rate. In the same way that a person's weight will ultimately reach a steady state if the amount of calories consumed remains stable with the number of calories burned, a membership will ultimately come to an equilibrium based on a constant number of members joining and lapsing.

To calculate this steady state, start with how many total new members you have added to your association in the past year. Next, take the reciprocal of your current membership renewal rate for the association (the percentage of non-renewing members) presented as a decimal (.30 for 30%). Plug each number into the following formula.

New Member Input/Reciprocal of Renewal Rate (or Lapse Rate) Shown as a Decimal = Membership Steady State

For example, 10,000 New Member Input/.20 Lapse Rate = 50,000 Membership Steady State

---

If renewal rates are so important, what strategies drive renewal rates, and how can an association increase them?

Any discussion of renewing members must begin with the understanding that the association needs to deliver value to members in order to keep them. Membership renewals represent a member's chance to vote on how well the organization has served the member's needs over the previous year. Positive or negative responses are measured through membership renewals. The 2015 *Membership Marketing Benchmarking Report* highlights that outside of employment and company issues the top reasons for members not renewing are lack of engagement, return on investment for the dues rate, and lack of value.

Once an association has built a valuable membership product, the next step required for retaining members is to benchmark and track renewals to understand how best to communicate the value of the membership product to members.

But before looking at benchmarking renewals, understand that definitions vary widely in the association field for the terms "membership renewal" and "membership retention." The terms are used synonymously in this chapter to mean members who continue with the organization for an additional year. Based on this definition, the number of members eligible to renew is *not* how many renewal notices will be sent out. Instead, the renewal rate includes the total number of paid members continuing in the association, including multi-year members (who may not receive a renewal notice this year) and life members. However, it is acceptable to calculate both a retention rate and a renewal rate. The retention rate would represent all continuing members (including life and multi-year members) while the renewal rate would be based only on those members up for renewal in a given year. If both retention and renewal rates are calculated, then the retention rate should be used when calculating the associations' membership steady state.

Benchmarking

Because of the impact of various business and environmental factors, there is no such thing as a "good" or "bad" renewal rate. Although you may be able to do some limited benchmarking of renewals against associations similar to yours, the purpose of calculating the renewal rate is to help your association focus on improving the level of members you retain.

Factors Influencing Retention

As a general rule of thumb, associations will see renewal rates vary between 60 percent and 90 percent.

This wide variance in membership retention is influenced in part by the type of business model in which an association functions and by economic and sociological factors. Some of the factors that influence renewal rates both positively and negatively include:

- *Individual membership organization versus trade association membership.* Associations that offer an individual membership as opposed to associations with institutional or company memberships typically will see lower renewal rates. The 2015 *Membership Marketing Benchmarking Report* shows that the mean renewal rate is 79 percent for an individual membership association and 87 percent for a trade association.

- *Consumer-paid dues versus company-reimbursed dues.* Associations that serve a market where dues are reimbursed or paid for by an employer will see better renewal rates than those where dues are paid out-of-pocket by individuals.

- *Growing versus declining memberships.* Associations with a rapidly growing membership tend to have lower renewal rates than groups with a steady or declining membership. This occurs because growing associations have a larger proportion of first-year members, and first-year members typically renew at a much lower rate than longer-term members do.

- *Incentive-generated members versus full-price members.* The stronger the incentive used to get members to join an association, the lower the renewal rate will be when compared to members who joined with no incentive. Members who receive a complimentary membership when they attend the annual meeting, for example, will not renew as well as members who join at full price.

- *Transient industry versus stable industry.* Associations that serve highly transient markets, where job turnover is high or members are moving out of the industry, will see lower renewal rates than a steady marketplace. A job change for an individual association member or a merger for a trade association member raises the likelihood of not renewing membership.

- *Short membership grace period versus longer grace period.* Business rules on when a member is considered lapsed vary between associations. Some associations count members as renewing if they receive payment within 90 days of expiration. Other associations lapse a member on expiration and consider a payment 90 days after expiration to be a membership reinstatement.

So while comparing or benchmarking renewal rates from one association to another is a challenge, evaluating how members are "voting" for your particular association is critical in measuring the health of your organization. This measurement is accomplished through membership tracking and reporting.

Exhibit 12.2. Calculating Membership Renewal Rates

Renewal rate measures the number of members kept over a given period of time—usually during a fiscal or calendar year. To calculate the renewal rate, subtract from the current membership the new members who have joined over the past 12 months (this determines the net renewed members still with the organization), then divide this number into the total membership from the same time in the previous year (those eligible to renew). Convert this to a percentage and you have the renewal rate.

The formula is:

(Total Number of Members Today minus 12 months of new members)/Total Number of Members in Previous Year = Renewal Rate

(105,000 – 15,000))/100,000 = .90 (or 90 percent) Renewal Rate

---

Tracking

Three levels of tracking can be applied when looking at membership renewals. The first level is the macro or "big picture" view. Exhibit 12.2 shows the formula to calculate the overall annual membership renewal rate for an association.

But macro tracking for renewals should go beyond the aggregate renewal rate and look at the membership segments that may be supporting growth or pulling down membership numbers. For example, one important area to measure is the renewal rate for first-year or "conversion" members. New members tend to renew at lower levels than other membership segments. The macro look at membership shows how much or how little these members are affecting the overall membership.

The macro level of tracking is important because, unless you identify where your membership bucket is leaking, it becomes much more challenging to fix it.

These key macro measurements will vary from association to association based on what demographics and characteristics have the biggest impact on the organization. However, for most associations, the best indicators to track for an overview of membership include:

- Total Membership
  - Current membership
  - Membership the same month in the previous year
  - Percentage increase or decrease in year-to-year membership

- New Members by Month
  - Current new members
  - New members the same month in the previous year

- Membership Conversion (First-Year Member Renewals) by Month
  - First-year members eligible to renew (renewal cohort)
  - First-year members who actually do renew
  - Conversion renewal rates (renewing new members/eligible to renew new members)

- Year Two and Subsequent Renewals (Y2+) by Month
  - Y2+ members eligible to renew (renewal cohort)
  - Y2+ members who actually do renew
  - Y2+ renewal rates (renewing members/members eligible to renew)

- Total Renewals by Month
  - Total members eligible to renew (renewal cohort)
  - Total members who actually do renew
  - Total renewal rates (renewing members/members eligible to renew)

Separate tabs can also be set up for tracking these same key variables by membership type (student, regular, associate, corporate, etc.).

The second level of tracking helps to measure the performance of each cohort within the membership renewal efforts. It highlights at what point in the communication process members are prompted to respond.

This is a helpful method to track renewals because members may use the initial mailing notice to renew their memberships, but they may have been prompted to take action by the third notice. So tracking a code can be misleading. To measure the action that produces the renewal response, renewals can be tracked through a filtering process. Let's say the renewal cohort for a given month starts out at 1,000 members who receive the first renewal notification. If, in the next month, the remaining members of the cohort who receive a notice are 750, then it can be inferred that the first notice generated a 25 percent return. This calculation is done through each step of the renewal program.

To fully track using this method, a final "phantom" renewal count needs to be run to show how many members have not paid to renew after all the renewal activities have been completed.

Finally, the micro level of renewal tracking uses source codes to measure the response of specific head-to-head renewal tests that you are incorporating in the renewal series. As noted earlier, tracking renewal codes has the potential to produce misleading information. So this method is best used when tracking very specific tests or changes to the renewal program.

Micro tracking is accomplished by adding a key code or source code to the renewal form. When the form is returned through the mail, this code is added to the member's record. To capture response on the web and through email, unique URLs can be established that incorporate the source code.

Ultimately, the reason to track is so that an association has information available to take concrete actions and use the tools available in the marketing arsenal to address specific renewal challenges. Once a system is in place to monitor the renewal program, a wealth of information will be available on each month's reports. For example, it may become evident that certain membership categories have weaker or stronger renewal rates, or there may be a difference in renewal rates between conversions (new members) and multi-year members (longer-term members). Tracking provides the data to make informed marketing decisions and allocate resources to address weaker renewing segments.

Optimizing Renewals

Once tracking information is in place, the renewal system can be updated and monitored. Optimizing an association's renewal program can be broken down into four key areas.

Frequency and Timing

Perhaps one of the simplest and often one of the most effective ways to improve renewals is simply to increase the frequency of notices by initiating contact sooner and continuing efforts longer. Increasing the number of notices sent to a member should be considered if tracking reveals that the final notices of the renewal program are generating a positive response rate. Also, if subsequent reinstatement efforts to bring back former members produce a strong response, this indicates that renewal efforts are likely inadequate.

Research results have consistently shown that individual membership associations that begin renewal efforts more than three months prior to expiration and those that conclude renewal efforts more than three months after expiration are more likely to realize comparatively higher renewal rates. The messages in early renewal notifications can emphasize helping the association save money through an early response. Later renewal messages may increase urgency and highlight the upcoming cutoff of member benefits.

Channels

We live in a world with many marketing messages that can distract us. So getting your renewal request to rise above the static of other marketing efforts and be noticed by a member can be a challenge. As a way to gain more attention, consider including a variety of channels in your marketing mix. Some of the most frequently used marketing channels for renewal efforts are noted in Table 12.3.

And because an association has an existing relationship with a member, some of the constraints that might apply to new member recruitment under CAN SPAM, the FCC Telephone Consumer Protection Act, and the Junk Fax Prevention Act do not apply to renewal efforts. For example, fax advertisements and text messages may be sent to U.S. members with whom the association has an established business relationship (EBR), as long as the fax number was provided voluntarily by the member and consent was given to receive text messages.

Additionally, adding a last issue renewal notice as a tip-on or cover wrap to the final magazine a member will receive can be cost-effective, as the publication will already be printed and mailed as part of the normal fulfillment of benefits.

Table 12.3. Top Marketing Channels for Renewals

	Individual (n = 340)	Trade (n = 196)
Email marketing	78%	66%
Mail	61%	51%
Staff phone calls	21%	58%
Peer member contacts	16%	19%
Telemarketing	11%	8%
Chapter phone calls	8%	5%
Magazine cover wraps	6%	1%
Board phone calls	5%	10%
Social media contacts	5%	1%
Employer contacts	4%	4%
Fax	1%	3%
Texting	1%	1%
Renewal app for mobile devices	0%	–
Other	6%	7%

Source: 2015 *MGI Membership Marketing Benchmarking Report.*

A sample plan for frequency, timing, and channels for a renewal series is provided in Table 12.4.

Table 12.4. Sample Membership Renewal Contact Schedule

Month	Activity
1	Email New Member or Renewal Acknowledgment
2	Email Orientation Series and Benefits Review
3	No Renewal Contact
4	No Renewal Contact
5	NCOA (Address Correction for Membership File)
6	No Renewal Contact
7	No Renewal Contact
8	Pre-Renewal Email Advisory w/Benefits Review
9	Mail and Email Notice 1
10	Email Notice 2
11	Mail and Email Notice 3
12	Expiration Email Notice and Text Alert 4
13	Mail and Email with "Last Issue" Tip-On Notice 5
14	Email and Telephone (Paid Firm, Staff, Chapter, or Board) Notice 6
15	Email Notice 7

Payment Options

It is not uncommon to find out that members did not renew simply because they did not get around to it. In fact, many associations find that members actually lapse more from omission than commission. They do not make an active decision not to renew; they just forget about renewing. To overcome this challenge, look at offering different options to simply eliminate the need for a member to have to make a renewal decision each year. Table 12.5 highlights some of the renewal payment options that associations offer.

Automatic credit card renewals and installment renewal payments have proven very effective for many associations. For example, the American Occupational Therapy Association instituted a monthly payment option, with auto-renewal, for member dues a number of years ago. Results continue to be very positive, with renewals up 15 percent among participants, equating to about $350,000 in annual dues revenue.

Some of these payment options change the renewal dynamic from asking the member to act proactively to continue a membership, to requiring the member to act proactively to *end* a membership.

Budgeting

As you read about higher frequency of contact, new marketing channels, and adding payment options, the question of paying for these added activities will certainly come up. However, keep in mind that it is very hard to lose money on membership renewal efforts because you are reaching out to an audience that is aware of you and has some level of relationship established with your organization. And the 60 percent to 90 percent typical renewal rate means the cost to send out one more renewal notice, an additional email, or even to make a phone call, is minor compared to the ROI you will receive trying to recruit new members.

Table 12.5. Membership Renewal Payment Options

Top Renewal Options		
	Individual (n = 247)	Trade (n = 116)
Multi-year renewals	38%	16%
Installment renewal payments (monthly, quarterly)	37%	66%
Automatic annual credit card renewal	32%	19%
Lifetime membership	32%	3%
Early-renewal discounts	18%	19%
Gift or premiums for renewal	16%	8%
Renewal bill-me	10%	24%
Automatic annual electronic funds transfer (EFT) renewals	11%	20%

Source: 2015 MGI Membership Marketing Benchmarking Report.

Nevertheless, most associations under-invest in keeping their members. As a rule of thumb, the budget to keep members should be increased until the response rate drops to a point at which the investment of staff time is not productive in trying to renew members, or the cost of generating a renewing member equals or exceeds the cost of acquiring the least expensive brand new member. In the rare event that tracking reveals the cost of renewing a member is higher than acquiring a new member, then decreasing the level of expenditure would be appropriate.

Conclusion

Thousands of impressions and interactions go into the relationship between a potential member becoming aware of an association, deciding to join, and then making the decision to renew. Some of these interactions are under the control of the association and some are not. But research and experience have demonstrated over time that well-planned and executed recruitment and renewal programs have helped many associations achieve exponential growth rates. Focus on the two transactional milestones of a member's relationship with your association, and membership growth will follow.

References

ASAE. *7 Measures of Success: What Remarkable Associations Do That Others Don't.* Washington, DC: ASAE, 2006, 2012.

Bluhm, Chris. Can a Monthly Payment Option Work at Your Association? *Associations Now,* October 10, 2013.

Dalton, James, & Dignam, Monica. *The Decision to Join: How Individuals Determine Value and Why They Choose to Belong.* Perfect Paperback, 2015.

Kotler, Philip. *Kotler on Marketing.* New York: Simon and Schuster, 1999.

Marketing General. *Membership Marketing Benchmarking Report.* Alexandria, VA: Marketing General, Inc., 2014.

Marketing General. *Membership Marketing Benchmarking Report.* Alexandria, VA: Marketing General, Inc., 2015.

Stone, Bob, & Jacobs, Ron. *Successful Direct Marketing Methods* (7th ed.). New York: McGraw-Hill, 2001.

About the Author

Tony Rossell serves as the senior vice president of Marketing General Incorporated in Alexandria, Virginia. A frequent writer and speaker on association marketing topics, he writes The Membership Marketing Blog. Send email to Tony@MarketingGeneral.com.

Member-Get-a-Member Campaigns

13

By Melanie J. Penoyar, CAE

"People influence people. Nothing influences people more than a recommendation from a trusted friend. A trusted referral influences people more than the best broadcast message. A trusted referral is the Holy Grail of advertising."

Mark Zuckerberg, Facebook CEO

A sking members to help you help others through a simple referral process can have more impact than any membership brochure, direct mail or advertising campaign and can cost comparably less. In short, give your members something to talk about and harness that energy to get them to ask others to join or get involved. The 2015 Marketing General (MGI) *Membership Marketing Benchmarking Report* (p. 23) lists word-of-mouth marketing as one of the most effective marketing channels for acquiring new members.

One of the best sources for finding new members are current members who have experienced the value of your organization firsthand. Consider the following statistics regarding the power of social recommendations:

- ASAE's landmark study *The Decision to Join* (2007) estimates that 77.7 percent of members first hear about an association through a personal or professional referral (p. 83).

- According to Nielsen, 84 percent of consumers say they either completely or somewhat trust recommendations from family and friends about products—making these recommendations the information source ranked highest for trustworthiness.

- According to Ed Keller and Brad Fay (2012), Americans engage in many conversations about brands every day and "more than two-thirds of those conversations involve a recommendation to buy, consider, or avoid the brand."

- Word-of-mouth communication is a critical part of the brand choice process. The data for this finding comes from large, representative, continuous tracking surveys that ask people to record their recent brand-related conversations. The startling finding is that only 8 percent of the conversations take place through social media, instant and text messages, and email, while 90 percent of conversations are offline. https://www.ama.org/publications/MarketingNews/Pages/The-Power-of-Word-of-Mouth.aspx.

The power of word-of-mouth marketing can be illustrated through the use of a Member-Get-a-Member Campaign (MGAM). When integrated into the mix of other outreach activities, a well-orchestrated MGAM campaign can provide measureable return to aid in reaching your annual membership recruitment goals. In addition, a MGAM campaign is a great way to engage members and reward current advocates simply for talking about you.

Members are consumers and, as consumers, share their thoughts and opinions about your organization with others. Creating positive buzz by exceeding the expectations of your member community is not only a good strategy to feed your engagement and retention efforts, but it also helps you to recruit new members. When members talk about your association, it comes with a passion and authenticity that cannot be duplicated with traditional media. MGAM campaigns leverage word-of-mouth marketing with the purpose and intent of recruiting new members. While some members will help you naturally and tell others how great your cause or content might be, others need to be asked and or provided with an incentive to act. Frequently, these efforts are coupled with rewards and recognition for those who recruit new members, creating a win-win scenario for all involved.

The success of any recruitment effort is based on a great list. Many current members have the ability to readily identify eligible prospects through work and other life interactions. Jamie Moesch, senior director, member experience at IEEE, the world's largest association dedicated to the advancement of technology, believes in member-to-member recruitment efforts. "Members are best equipped to fill in gaps, to identify whom they want to see included in the community, and to have real, relevant, and personal conversations with potential members," stated Moesch in an interview.

Elements of a MGAM Campaign

MGAM campaigns can target individual or organizational membership types and be episodic or run for an extended time period. Key considerations for any effort consist of:

- Goals and strategy
- Marketing tactics and budget

- Rewards and rules
- Tracking and reporting
- Guidance

Developing Your Campaign Goals and Strategy

First, you must decide whom you want to target. When we interviewed Lori Hatcher, senior vice president of membership and marketing at the Urban Land Institute, she stated: "In our program we were not just looking to increase the quantity of new members, but our MGAM efforts focus on the quality of new members. We asked current leaders to identify decision-makers and key companies in their areas and ask them to join. We segmented our approach and rewards system to strategically attract members who are most likely to find value in the organization and actively participate." Consider whom you want to approach and then determine the best way to further develop your effort.

How will you know whether your effort has been successful? While the development of a campaign might represent an activity, goals and key performance indicators for this specific type of campaign consist of:

- Goals
  - Total new members by member type and by specific demographics
  - Revenue from efforts

- Key performance indicators
  - Number of recruiters
  - Number of referrals
  - Number of new members by recruiter
  - Net promoter score

Determine the measurable goals for your MGAM campaign up-front. MGAM campaigns can be used to target all or specific membership segments and range in scope from small and informal to large and heavily engineered. The American Water Works Association is dedicated to creating a better world through better water. With a hybrid membership structure, AWWA annually runs a campaign targeting professionals and organizations who work in the water sector. A recruitment goal is set each year. The effort is targeted to bring in approximately 2,000 new members or 28 percent of its annual recruitment goal. While the goals are more heavily weighted toward individual memberships, organizational memberships represent 3 percent of the target goal. A revenue total is associated with this membership mix.

IEEE's MGAM campaign brings in approximately 19,000 new members or 22 percent of new members annually. In an interview Moesch stated: "If you are questioning your need for a MGAM campaign, know that, while not a panacea for all your membership growth needs, when incorporated into the mix of other activities, MGAM campaigns can produce significant results." Moesch added that the MGAM campaign has been successful in recruiting both students and international members, particularly in Asia and the Middle East.

"There is only one thing in the world worse than being talked about, and that is not being talked about."

Oscar Wilde, The Picture of Dorian Grey

Another key performance indicator is the number of recruiters participating in the effort. Moesch adds that "If we could just get every member of IEEE to recruit one colleague, we could double in size!" Following this logic, AWWA has put more emphasis on increasing the number of recruiters participating in its program in recent years. AWWA has approximately 800 recruiters. Based on past trends, for each new recruiter added, AWWA acquires 2.5 new members.

While it might not be possible to predict the exact number of recruiters you can acquire, it is helpful to know and improve your net promoter score (NPS). Created by Fred Reicheld, NPS is one way to see how your association is doing in the eyes of members. The score determines how likely your members are to say good things about your association and refer others to your ranks, using a simple measurement. This can be determined by asking: "How likely is it that you would recommend XYZ association to a friend or a colleague?" accompanied by a 10-point scale where 10 is extremely likely. Consider adding this question to membership, event, product, or other surveys. Working to increase this number over time may not only increase your MGAM results, but help you to identify your universe of potential advocates.

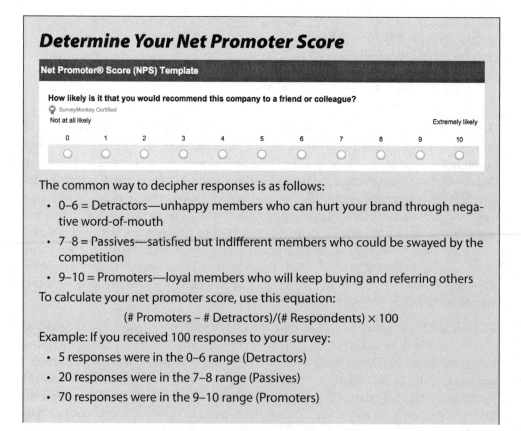

Determine Your Net Promoter Score

Net Promoter® Score (NPS) Template

How likely is it that you would recommend this company to a friend or colleague?

SurveyMonkey Certified

Not at all likely   Extremely likely

0	1	2	3	4	5	6	7	8	9	10
○	○	○	○	○	○	○	○	○	○	○

The common way to decipher responses is as follows:

- 0–6 = Detractors—unhappy members who can hurt your brand through negative word-of-mouth
- 7 8 = Passives—satisfied but indifferent members who could be swayed by the competition
- 9–10 = Promoters—loyal members who will keep buying and referring others

To calculate your net promoter score, use this equation:

$$(\text{# Promoters} - \text{# Detractors})/(\text{# Respondents}) \times 100$$

Example: If you received 100 responses to your survey:

- 5 responses were in the 0–6 range (Detractors)
- 20 responses were in the 7–8 range (Passives)
- 70 responses were in the 9–10 range (Promoters)

The percentages for each group is 5 percent, 20 percent, and 70 percent, respectively. Subtract 5 percent (Detractors) from 70 percent (Promoters), which equals 65 percent. The NPS should always be shown as an integer, making the NPS in this example 65 (per the SurveyMonkey website).

Tracking and Reporting

The key to any good MGAM effort is a good tracking and reporting system. Determining your tracking method will be important. What piece/s of information will serve as the unique identifier for recruiters? Is keeping track of the relationship between the recruiter and the new member important to your plan? If a reward system will be part of the campaign, how will the rules and data be integrated to complete the fulfillment of the effort? Answer these questions and only collect the data you need to complete the campaign successfully.

While perhaps there are more, two types of approaches have been identified during this investigation, described below:

- *Passive Approach.* Using this approach a recruiter asks a prospect to join and provides the prospect with a member number or unique identifier to be submitted with the purchase of membership. Recognition of the recruiter relationship is dependent on the prospect supplying the recruiter's information to the association. Frequently, the recruiter's member number, email address, name, or a combination of these three may be used to identify the recruiter relationship.

- *Active Approach.* Recruiters provide the association with the contact information for prospects for follow-up. Sometimes this follow-up is facilitated by the recruiter using tools provided by the association, and in other instances the association follows up with the prospect on behalf of the recruiter, but regardless, the list of prospects provided can be tracked back to the recruiter.

AWWA's MGAM campaign takes a passive approach. The recruiter's member number or email address is requested to help connect the recruiter relationship. While the recruiter's name can be used, common names like Bob Smith frequently cause confusion, and the wrong recruiter may be assigned by mistake. Recruiter information may be returned on a physical application, electronically, or over the phone. In addition, new members are given opportunities to tell AWWA by whom they were referred. On-boarding communications push new members to a landing page that further asks or confirms an individual's recruiter relationship. Online, new members can search for their recruiter. In addition, should a recruiter visit the landing page, he is able to see the names of individuals he has referred who have joined AWWA. Whatever method you choose, your tracking system needs to be easy to decipher and reliable. Figures 13.1 shows an example of a thank-you sent to new recruits.

ULI took an active approach when developing their member-to-member recruitment effort. Recruiters use an online portal to input referrals and send emails to prospective members. A simple interface makes it easy for recruiters to participate. The group's "Membership Pays" campaign materials state: "It's as easy as one, two, three."

Figure 13.1. AWWA Thank-You Page Graphic as an Example

When a recruiter invites a prospect to join, she arrives at a landing page where she can search whether a prospect is already a member. If not, the recruiter proceeds to invite the prospect to join via a customizable email invitation and link. Recruiters are able to see online whom they have referred and who has joined.

Either of these methods can be made simple and easy to use; however, an active approach provides the association with the ability to grow prospect lists that can be qualified and remarketed to over time. Try to collect a mailing address and make sure to follow CAN-SPAM protocol when contacting leads. Regardless, don't let technology hold you back. Dream big, start small, and scale to your current level of technological sophistication.

Rewards and Rules

Frequently, MGAM campaigns utilize an awards and/or rewards system to incentivize participation. Many systems have a base level of recognition that acknowledges recruitment for a member, such as a thank-you note, a recruiter lapel pin, a small promotional item, or credit for purchase of goods and services. Often, rewards build with added and defined levels of recruiting success. Some programs allow the recruiter to pick from a set of prizes or ask the association to make a charitable donation in the recruiter's name. Others define specific prizes to be given when recruiters reach defined levels of activity, but the basic concept is that the rewards grow with the number of recruits. Higher success leads to bigger, cooler prizes and additional recognition opportunities. To spur activity in longer MGAM campaigns, prize drawings for cash or other items may be used to push recruiters to action in a specific time period.

In 2012, AWWA switched from providing promotional items to AMEX gift cards and experienced a measurable increase in participation. In addition, expenses decreased, as closets full of not-so-great water clocks, shower timers, tool kits, and flashlights were no longer needed. While a surge of new recruiters surfaced in the two years following the change, the growth rate has slowed in subsequent years. Feedback from recruiters tells us that this incentive is more enticing than previous offerings. While finding a better incentive was a great step forward, this also helped the planning team see that switching things up over time created renewed interest in the program.

All recruiters in the AWWA program are eligible for a grand prize drawing each year that consists of travel and registration to the AWWA annual conference or $1,000 cash. A separate drawing is also held for new members who come in through the MGAM program. While the registration and travel have a higher overall value, the $1,000 cash prize is picked most frequently.

In addition, AWWA offers an extensive awards program that utilizes a point system based on cumulative year-over-year recruitment. These awards are given to both members and AWWA sections. A VIP awards celebration is hosted during the association's annual conference, and both the volunteer and staff person who has recruited the most new members are recognized on stage at the opening general session in front of thousands of attendees.

While you need to know your members to understand what meaningful recognition to provide, everyone likes to be thanked and recognized. If you have not changed your campaign in many years, take the opportunity to look at it through your members' eyes. You should also take into consideration other limitations or industry norms that your members might practice in regard to gifts or prize drawings. Ask your members what rewards and incentives might spur them to action. Fresh thinking and tweaking could revitalize recruiters and engage more members.

As part of the campaign development process, establish clear rules of participation that include how incentives are obtained, what member types qualify for incentives, who is eligible to participate, and when awards and prizes will be distributed. Last, think about how you will aggregate your data to determine the winners.

Marketing Tactics and Budget

How do you promote your MGAM campaign? Just like other membership marketing activities, MGAM campaigns utilize a variety of marketing tactics to spread the word and encourage members to recruit others. Depending on your budget, your effort may include email, direct mail, campaign landing pages, flyers, ads and other marketing collateral, social media elements, testimonial videos, in-person and phone outreach to support the effort. The key is to place your message where members go most frequently.

One tactic IEEE takes advantage of is placing information in the "Acknowledgment Kit" they mail to members after they renew. "We include tear off referral cards, shown in Figure 13.2. While the cards are also available online for download, the tactic serves as a great reminder to participate in the program," adds Moesch.

Carolyn Brennan, director, membership and marketing, at ULI states: "Just like other marketing campaigns at ULI, tactics are mapped and planned throughout the year, then measured for effectiveness and adjusted accordingly." ULI has used email messages, house magazine ads, web ads, social media, flyers, and postcards (see Figure 13.3) to promote the program. In addition, ULI uses its field staff to carry and market the program locally, including participation by local membership committee members, and further incentivizes the program by executing a competition for the most membership conversions.

Design your marketing campaign using the mix of media to which your members respond best; however, support materials frequently include an online toolkit of resources. While you will need resources to support and motivate recruiters, don't forget that the recruiter needs to be able to represent your organization well and communicate clearly with potential new members.

Figure 13.2. IEEE Referral Card

Figure 13.3. ULI Flyer and Postcard

1025 Thomas Jefferson Street, N.W.
Suite 500 West
Washington, D.C. 20007

Your recruiter toolkit might include the following resources:

- Landing page with clear call to action for recruiters
- Simple instructions that communicate the ease of participation
- Encouragement to help the recruiter tell his or her member story to others
- Conversation starters
- Talking points
- Social media posts
- Recruiter cards that can be handed to prospects that include instructions to join
- Form letters or suggested email text
- Overview of key products and services
- Factsheets
- FAQs
- Tutorial webinar

Support materials for prospects might include:

- Landing page for prospects referred to the association with simple instructions to join
- Campaign flyer outlining key benefits of membership
- Membership application/links to join
- Any necessary promotional codes
- Video content of members talking about the value of membership

In addition, if you are a chapter-based organization, expand your reach by pushing out additional materials to be used in the field. Consider adding chapter resources like these:

- Webinar on how to execute the campaign best
- Graphics
- Banner ads (see Figure 13.4)
- Print ads
- Campaign flyer outlining key benefits of the program to potential recruiters

If your program is new, you might start with a simple approach by asking members to just recruit one new member in a calendar year. If you are re-launching a program, pay attention to how you segment your members and messages. Craft appropriate messages for each audience segment. In addition to member segments you might typically use, consider the following segments:

- Current recruiters
- Past recruiters

Figure 13.4. ULI Banner Ad

Membership Pays
Invite new members, earn points, and redeem them for rewards!
You must be a member to participate - Login required.

- Current and past volunteers
- Members who were recruited
- Members with specific demographic profile to acquire more of the same
- New members

How much will a MGMA campaign cost? No matter the scale of the campaign, start by making a list of all the communication vehicles your organization uses today. Next break down the list into free and paid options. Many MGMA campaigns can simply be marketed by piggy-backing on current marketing efforts. Consider placing messages in the following places:

- Newsletter
- Magazine
- New member kit
- On-boarding communications
- Web banner ads
- Conference program
- Social media platforms
- Online communities

Consider a direct mail component if your budget will allow. MGMA campaigns can be affordable and scaled to meet your organization's budget constraints.

Mapping Your Campaign Process

Your MGAM campaign may involve multiple communication touch points and tasks, data reports and calculations, and even other staff resources to make the effort run seamlessly. While it is recommended that your process be as simple as possible for the end-user, the campaign itself may be complex and require dedicated time and resources. If well planned, MGAM can work effectively using a manual procedure, but attempt to automate as much as possible. If fulfillment requires multiple individuals, make sure they are briefed on the process and expectations in advance.

Regardless of your technology, it is recommend that you map the recruiter and new recruit experience out from start to finish in detail, as missed steps can affect the perception of members, recruiters, and both new and prospective members. Aim to create a great recruiting experience and encourage fun along the way.

Case Study

Members of the Urban Land Institute encompass the entire spectrum of land use and real estate development disciplines. In reaction to the economic difficulties experienced in the United Sates in 2008, ULI's membership declined from an all-time high of 41,000 to 25,500. Lori Hatcher, ULI senior vice president, membership and marketing, explained: "It was the worst recession for real estate since the Great Depression."

"Our members still believed in us, but where companies had 10 members previously, after the market crash they had only 5," recalled Carolyn Brennan, director of membership and marketing in our interview.

ULI had built a successful MGAM program in the early 2000s. At that time the goal was to get anyone and everyone to join the organization. Membership growth expectations were high as the real estate market soared. Multiple audiences were targeted: young professionals, students, international members, and employees of government, nonprofits, and universities. The program successfully recruited from 1,500 to 1,800 new members in its best years. The campaign was simple, and new members just told ULI who referred them on paper forms.

In 2010, ULI was in membership-rebuilding mode and decided to revitalize its MGAM campaign. The team made a strategic decision to tailor its "Membership Pays" initiative to attract decision-makers. "Ultimately, decision-makers make decisions about membership. Our thought process was to target the top executives in our most exclusive membership category and expand from there," said Hatcher. In addition, this particular membership type had high retention rates, and the team was interested in members who would stick with them for the long run.

Recruiters were lured with a points system based closely on a system used by American Express. For every membership dollar acquired, recruiters were given one point. Points could be spent to purchase meeting registration and other desired content.

Brennan was the architect of the overall campaign. She envisioned a web-based referral platform based on a for-profit referral shopping site like Gilt Groupe. Brennan stated: "We met with the IT department to talk about future possibilities and mapped out a new customer relationship process. The combination of the IT brains and marketing brains created the scope and mechanics of the concept." In addition,

Brennan collaborated with the ULI Online communications team to create the outwardly facing web elements and the user interface. The draft concept was then put through usability testing before releasing the campaign to primetime. The project took 18 months to create from start to finish.

The finished product provided recruiters with a simple interface to input referral information about prospective members and email them an invitation to join. The ULI team would poke recruiters to follow up with prospects who had not joined and push incentives. The invitation and recruiter message are shown in Figures 13.5 and 13.6.

The results of the effort included:

- 1,814 leads acquired

- 414 new members joined, representing a 22.8 percent conversion rate
  - 112 full members or members representing the targeted senior-executive membership category joined at $1,200 each, representing $134,400 in revenue

Figure 13.5. ULI Invite

From: Membership Pays <membershippays@uli.org>
Subject: **Carolyn Spaw would like to invite you to join ULI**
Date: May 22, 2014 2:09:10 AM GMT+05:30
To: Carolyn Brennan <Carolyn.Brennan@ULI.org>

Urban Land Institute

Dear Carolyn,

Please accept this personal invitation to join the Urban Land Institute, a nonprofit research and education organization supported by its members who represent the entire spectrum of land use and real estate development disciplines, working in private enterprise and public service.

Being a member of ULI allows you to make connections with the right people, gain access to a wealth of information and resources you won't find anywhere else, get the tools for future success, and improve your community. As a member myself, I know it is an excellent value, and that is why I wanted to invite you to join.

Please contact me if you would like to learn more about why I joined ULI.

What Should You Do Next?

- Read more about ULI membership by visiting www.uli.org/join

Thank You,
Carolyn Spaw

This message was sent to you by the Membership Pays Automated System on behalf of the above individual. Please do not reply directly to this message. If you are not interested in joining ULI, you may decline my invitation. If you have any questions, please contact MembershipPays@uli.org.

1025 Thomas Jefferson Street   202.624.7000   Manage My Email: MyULI.org
Suite 500 W   202.624.7140   Unsubscribe: Do Not Disturb
Washington, DC 20007   www.uli.org

Figure 13.6. ULI Recruiter Message

Having trouble viewing this message?, <u>click here.</u>

Dear Matt,

I noticed that you have invited someone to join ULI using our Membership Pays program, and I wanted to give you an update. Below you will find a list of those people you invited who have not yet joined and the e-mail address you used to invite them. I thought you might like to know so you can follow up with another message or meet them for coffee, tell them why you are a member of ULI, and encourage them to join.

Placeholder Name#1	PlaceholderEmail1@Test.com
Placeholder Name#2	PlaceholderEmail2@Test.com
Placeholder Name#3	PlaceholderEmail3@Test.com
Placeholder Name#4	PlaceholderEmail4@Test.com
Placeholder Name#5	PlaceholderEmail5@Test.com

Now is a good time to check in with them again because if they make the decision to join by October 5, you will be entered into a drawing for your choice of a free registration to the ULI Fall Meeting in Denver, October 16–19, 2012, or the ULI Spring Meeting in San Diego, May 15–17, 2013. Also, of course, when they join, you earn points that can be exchanged for prizes.

Thank you for supporting ULI as a member and for helping strengthen our network.

Best regards,
Carolyn Spaw
ULI Membership

ULI-the Urban Land Institute 1025
Thomas Jefferson St., N.W.
Suite 500 West
Washington, D.C. 20007-5201

Manage My Email: <u>MyULI.org</u>
Unsubscribe: <u>Do Not Disturb</u>

The mission of the Urban Land Institute is to provide leadership in the responsible use of land and in creating and sustaining thriving communities worldwide.

- 302 associate members or members representing the industry at a lower level joined at $430 each, representing $129,860

- $264,260 was generated in total revenue

Hatcher relayed that the best decision they made was to focus on decision-makers; however, if there was a lesson learned during the project, it was that good data matters. In the future, they will pay more attention to cleaning the data provided by recruiters.

When asked whether she would recommend a MGAM program to other associations, Hatcher responded with: "Absolutely! Members are your best opportunity to get the best next member."

About ULI

ULI, the Urban Land Institute, is a 501(c) (3) nonprofit research and education organization supported by its members. Founded in 1936, ULI has more than 35,000 members worldwide, representing the entire spectrum of land use and real estate development disciplines working in private enterprise and public service.

References

Dalton, James. *The Decision to Join: What Association Boards Should Know and Do About Membership and Affiliation*. Washington, DC: ASAE, 2009.

Dalton, James, & Dignam, Monica. *The Decision to Join: How Individuals Determine Value and Why They Choose to Belong*. Perfect Paperback, 2007.

Keller, Ed, & Fay, Brad. *The Face-to-Face Book: Why Real Relationships Rule in a Digital Marketplace*. New York: Free Press, 2012.

Mark Zuckerberg Quote: http://techcrunch.com/2007/11/06/liveblogging-facebook-advertising-announcement/

Marketing General. *Membership Marketing Benchmarking Report*. Alexandria, VA: Marketing General, Inc., 2014.

Marketing General. *Membership Marketing Benchmarking Report*. Alexandria, VA: Marketing General, Inc., 2015.

Survey Monkey. http://help.surveymonkey.com/articles/en_US/kb/Using-a-SurveyMonkey-Survey-to-Measure-Net-Promoter-Score

About the Author

Melanie J. Penoyar, CAE, senior manager of membership at the American Water Works Association, has been championing strategic planning, membership, marketing, and business development efforts for nonprofits for more than 18 years. A frequent industry speaker and self-proclaimed association junkie, Penoyar resides in Denver, Colorado. Contact Melanie at mpenoyar@awwa.org.

Digital Engagement

Online Communities, Web Delivery of Benefits, and Social Networking and Media

14

By Benjamin Martin, CAE

IN THIS CHAPTER

- Online Communities and Social Networks
- Social Media
- Web Delivery of Benefits

It's no secret that a more engaged member is a more valuable member. They're more likely to renew, volunteer, evangelize for the association, and contribute to a foundation or PAC. In the past, members could only engage with their associations by attending events, serving on committees, and reading publications. Today's technology gives members the opportunity to engage with your association and their fellow members every day of the year, from virtually anywhere.

It should come as no surprise to the reader that today's members have very different expectations of their associations than their forbearers had, due to profound changes in web technology that we've witnessed over the past decades. Today's members are accustomed to placing orders with Amazon anytime, anywhere from their mobile devices and having their orders appear on their doorsteps in two days (or less); asking Siri for driving directions with a push of a button and having those directions played moments later over their car stereos; tapping into their social networks for answers to their questions and getting responses in real time; and watching movies or sending text messages to their friends and family from 35,000 feet aboard a transcontinental flight.

By the time this book's third edition is printed, there will be some new technological wizardry that will have pushed expectations of our associations to a new extreme. Associations that embrace their members' higher technological expectations by making products, networking, and services available to their members in convenient online form will increase their chances of keeping pace in the race for relevance.

In this chapter, we will discuss five key issues that impact the success of an online engagement strategy:

1. Pros and cons of owning versus renting your online presence

2. How to engage in the social media conversation for maximum impact

3. What you need to know about the stages of private community development

4. How to motivate your members to participate in your community

5. How to effectively enable members to consume association services online.

Online Communities and Social Networks

Broadly speaking, there are two kinds of online communities. There are private (gated, white-label) communities that are run on websites powered by licensed or owned community software. The other kind is a public online community hosted on a public social network such as LinkedIn or Facebook. However, it should be noted that it's not as if communities on public social networks are completely open and public—access can be controlled by the community's creator.

What kind of community should your organization use?

At the time of this writing, private communities are gaining in popularity among associations. The major online community vendors serving the association sector are all experiencing rapid growth. New community products are joining the market with increasing frequency. Why?

More and more organizations are realizing that it's more beneficial to own their online presence than to rent it.

When you build your organization's social presence on public social networking sites you're beholden to their rules. The rules are not written in your favor, and they're constantly changing. Ultimately, it's the shareholders of the public social networks who benefit when your members engage on their websites. In short, when you use public social media sites to support your organization's goals, you're not the customer. You're the product.

Public social networks, particularly Facebook, have also been steadily decreasing the organic reach that organizations formerly enjoyed. The average organic reach of a Facebook page post to a page with fewer than 500,000 "likes" is less than 2 percent. This means that Facebook posts are unlikely to ever be seen by the people who have "liked" your page.

Many associations have grown wise to this state of affairs and have elected to invest in a private online community to take control of their digital presence. Private online communities enable organizations to better control their online destiny by:

- Deepening engagement beyond simple likes and favorites

- Gaining the ability to view engagement data that public social media sites will never reveal

- Increasing the likelihood that their messages will be seen

- Setting community rules that favor their stakeholders

- Combining members' online and traditional engagement in reports to help them gain a fuller understanding of their activities

- Monetizing their communities through advertising, sponsorship, and pay-for-access

Running your own online community may require a more significant investment of time and money than leveraging public social sites, but the ROI is both higher and more predictable.

Case Study

TCEA (formerly the Texas Computer Education Association) launched a private online community in 2011. Since then, TCEA has experienced rapid membership growth from outside the state of Texas, even internationally. This diversification of the membership compelled the association to officially change its name, removing the word Texas, to TCEA.

Lori Gracey, their CEO, says, "In July 2011 when we launched the community, we had 386 out of state and international members. As of April 2015, we have 834, a 54 percent increase. That's an additional $20,160 in dues revenue."

The number of in-state members added since the community launched has also increased by 26 percent. In 2015, that represents an additional $176,150. In 2015 alone, the ROI of TCEA's community initiative—measured only by a single year's increased dues revenue—is $196,875.

TCEA has also seen increased attendance from these out-of-state and international members at their annual convention. In 2011, they had 28 international and 350 from outside Texas. In 2015, they had 102 international attendees and 597 from beyond Texas.

Gracey says, "The growth in membership is attributable to the specialized content available only to members in the community and the networking with peers that they can do there."

What if you've built a significant following on public social media sites? Should you just dump them? No! As long as you understand how to leverage the public social networks to your advantage, you can benefit from their reach and relevance in your members' lives.

The key is to never make the public social networks the ultimate destination for any content your organization publishes. Your content belongs on your own websites. Think of social media sites as places to post invitations to your party.

However, you can't just post announcements and invitations and expect to be successful. You must participate in the conversation. Invitations are received best when they've been requested, so monitor the conversation happening in your organization's social networks, and when topics surface that your organization can help with, invite people to your site to read, watch, or discuss whatever your association has to offer.

If you don't already have a presence on public social media sites, you should, as they present a significant opportunity to extend your reach. LinkedIn groups, for example, can grow rapidly and provide your organization a steady stream of prospective members and vendors. Try joining some existing LinkedIn groups for your profession or industry.

> Visit http://bit.ly/1PHhklc to read about a 2015 Gold Circle Award winning organization that turned a $25,000 investment in LinkedIn advertising into $465,255 in first year dues.

As discussed above, participate—don't advertise—in the groups. Be helpful. Answer questions. Point members to your organization's resources and events when a relevant topic is being discussed. Invite users to check out discussions or resources in your private online community.

We'll leave the social networking topic, having barely scratched the surface, as there's a wide selection of resources available on the topic. Private communities haven't received as much treatment, especially within the association profession, so let's turn our attention to that topic.

There are five phases to launching a private online community benefit for your members:

1. Set a Community Strategy Aligned with Your Strategic Plan

Everything your association does needs to be guided by your strategic plan, and your community is no exception. If you don't document a focused strategy, your community is likely to become a dumping ground for all kinds of unrelated stuff. As you'll learn throughout this chapter, having a clear, easy to understand community is essential to engaging your members. Presenting members with too many options will scatter whatever engagement you do receive.

To develop a community strategy, start with understanding your members' wants, needs, and motivations. When your members get together, do they enjoy talking shop, chit-chatting, or listening attentively to experts? Are they motivated by advancing their careers, achieving mastery in their field, or giving back and paying it forward? To what extent do members want to elevate their status among their peers?

Then consider how their motivations align with mandates in your strategic plan. Does your strategic plan call for your association to provide a means for your members to network and collaborate? Do you need to organize members around an important program in your organization's strategic plan? You can build a community strategy around these.

Having a focused strategy will require saying no to other potential uses for the community, at least to begin with. Once you gain traction with your initial strategy, you can potentially branch out to others.

Also, identify the staff who will oversee and manage the community during this phase. When they have had a say in decision making in this early phase, they will be more invested in the process.

Resources

- Download a worksheet to help your organization zero in on the right community strategy for you at http://bit.ly/cofactor.

- Download a sample community strategy template at http://bit.ly/costrategy.

2. Select an Online Community Platform

Based on your community strategy, create a list of your most important community technology requirements and prioritize it. Not all of your requirements are equal; force yourself to make these hard choices. Distribute the prioritized requirements list to community software vendors and ask them to submit a proposal if their features meet the requirements.

Don't let the community vendor's account executive just do a standard product demonstration. Take control of your demos by using your requirements list as the agenda, and ask the vendors to show you how their software satisfies the requirements.

These are the top 10 features to look for in a community platform.

1. *Data synchronization between your association management system (AMS or equivalent) database and the community platform.* At a minimum, it should support a one-way transfer of member data from the database to the community platform. Two-way data synchronizations are also available. These allow the users to update their information within the community and have it write back to your AMS, as well as writing community engagement data into members' activity records, which lets you factor community activity into engagement reports. Database integration projects will extend your implementation project more than anything else, so give preference to platforms that have "standard integrations" with your database.

2. *Single sign-on to the organization's main website*, because nothing stifles engagement quite like being logged into a members-only section of the website and being asked again for your username and password when clicking over to the online community. Logging in is the single biggest barrier to engagement. You *must* help your members bypass the login screen.

3. *Email notifications sent on a schedule determined by the end-user.* The community manager may have the ability to set the defaults for their frequency, but the end-users should be able to set notifications to arrive on a schedule they prefer. Give preference to platforms offering visually appealing email notifications with obvious calls to action (reply, view this thread, forward) and the ability to customize the notifications with your branding and advertising.

4. *Resource directory, file upload/download, or document sharing.* The simpler the resources feature, the better off you'll be. It's difficult enough to convince members to share their samples, and the more complicated it is to add them to the community, the less inclined they'll be to suffer through the process.

5. *Discussion forums or groups.* The primary way that you will obtain engagement from your community members is through discussion groups. Look for a simple discussion interface that makes it not just easy, but enticing, to reply to posts and start new discussions. Interfaces that can aggregate all of "my recent discussions" or "most recent discussions" in a single screen are best-of-breed.

6. *Reply-by-email or auto-login email notification links.* From experience, we know that most users interact with online communities when they receive email notifications. Login failure crushes engagement metrics, but you can virtually eliminate this challenge by choosing an online community platform that offers the ability to start or reply to a discussion by email. Some platforms offer an email notification auto-login feature that allow users to bypass the login screen by way of a "link tokening" or "gatekeeper" procedure.

7. *Mobile experience.* There is now more mobile Internet traffic than desktop Internet traffic. Some vendors tout native apps, but mobile-friendly pages are far more effective in reaching the broadest possible swath of your users. However, as of this writing, online communities delivered exclusively through a mobile app are starting to crop up. These present opportunities for micro-engagement (I have 3 minutes until my Uber car arrives, let me glance at my phone and see what's happening in my network) and location-aware networking. (I'm traveling in Seattle today; are any of my contacts in town, too?)

8. *Messaging engine.* There are two cases in which a more sophisticated feature is the better choice, and this is one of them. Look for products that allow community administrators to send messages to certain segments of users, merge in member or community data, and have messages sent automatically when triggered by a member's activity or at certain time-based intervals.

9. *Reports.* This is the second instance in which you want to give preference to sophisticated features. Virtually all vendors have some level of reporting, but some of the best out there can tell you things like which users (not just how many, but the specific people) who have taken a specific action during a timeframe you define. Precious few online community platforms offer a query tool, but if you find one that also satisfies your other requirements, give it serious consideration. Also look for web analytics (either native or Google Analytics–compatible) and report automation (e.g., having a daily report of everyone who logged in for the first time e-mailed to you).

10. *Design flexibility.* Look for platforms that allow the community manager to configure the layout of the home page, interior pages, menus, banner advertising, and other content. More advanced users may want the ability to override the cascading style sheet, embed custom code into widgets or blocks, and configure the content of error pages (access denied, page not found, etc.).

Resource

- Download the annual Online Community Software Selection Guide at bit.ly/SelectionGuide15.

3. Implement the Community Software

Most community implementations take between 2 and 4 months, but some can last longer. There are typically two major projects in an online community implementation: visual design and data integration. Your implementation will likely consist of weekly phone calls covering assignments and decisions for both your team and the community software vendor.

The best advice I can give about implementation is to keep it simple. Think MVP: minimum viable platform. Resist the temptation to stand up every feature that the community software offers. This extends and complicates your implementation and also tends to blur your laser-focused community strategy. What is the minimum feature set that will support your community strategy? Deploy only these features. You can always activate other features later.

When evaluating proposals during the selection process, pay close attention to the implementation fees and services. The old adage, "you get what you pay for" applies to implementations. Some vendors offer white-glove implementation services, while others offer more of a self-service approach. If details about implementation are lacking in the proposal, ask the vendor if you can speak to the implementation manager your account would be assigned to, and find out what their process is.

Expect to fill out a bunch of forms at the beginning of your implementation. You'll be asked for things like:

- Community name
- Web address where the community will live
- Default time zone
- Application programming interface (API) key and password for your database
- Style guide, including brand colors, logos, and fonts
- Key association staff and contact information
- Anticipated go-live date

Once your community is designed, configured, and integrated, conduct alpha testing with your staff and make adjustments as lessons are learned. Then do a round of beta testing with your members and make more adjustments as needed. You must validate that users are able to easily complete common community tasks such as:

- Logging in
- Completing their profiles
- Joining a group
- Starting a discussion
- Replying to a discussion
- Adjusting their email notification settings

Do not "sign-off" on implementation until you have completed alpha and beta testing and all requested adjustments have been completed.

4. Release the Community to Your Members

You never get a second chance to make a first impression. We encourage our clients to introduce members into the community in phases. This allows your community manager to resolve issues with a smaller number of users in the community.

Let's use a metaphor. Do you remember college move-in day? Me neither. But I just Googled it, and here's what I learned. College students are assigned a specific date and time at which they are permitted to pull their cars up, unload, and move into their dorm rooms. Can you imagine what would happen if they weren't phased in and were given free license to just show up and move in whenever? It would be a disaster! Parents of college students reading this are thinking: "It's a disaster even with this level of coordination!"

The metaphor breaks down a bit, because most campus dormitories have been lived in before and there's a level of confidence that things will work as expected based on experience. But your community is brand new, and you can't know for sure that everything will work as expected, because you have no experience running this community before.

Before going live, you'll want to seed content (discussion posts, replies to posts, resources, blog posts, etc.) so that members have something to engage with right away. Solicit the help of 200 volunteers to help seed this content. If your experience is like ours, only 25 to 50 percent will follow through on the request, giving you 50 to 100 active users at launch, which is—conveniently—the number of active members you need to hit critical mass (more on that in a minute).

When you go live with your new community, avoid flashy launch campaigns and don't make a big deal about your community until it's actually a big deal. Your community should go live on an average day, not on the first day of a major event. A slow, steady build is more effective than a noisy launch.

Also, temper expectations with management and the board. Some communities need up to two years to reach critical mass, which is the point at which more activity is generated by the members without help from the community manager.

5. Commit to a Scientific Community Management Process

"If you build it, they will come" only works in the movies. Effective community management is a process. To keep your community vibrant, there are daily, weekly, monthly, quarterly, and yearly community management routines that should be followed. If you don't have a dedicated community manager to do them, add the tasks as recurring appointments in your calendar, and set reminders so you remember to do them. It's critical to make the process part of your daily routine.

Sample Community Management Tasks

Daily: welcome newcomers

Weekly: seed new discussion posts

Monthly: send community newsletter

Quarterly: remind users of the terms of use

Yearly: evaluate community strategy

Can these tasks be divided among multiple staff or assigned to volunteers? Yes, in theory. In practice, however, we've found that communities that are managed "by committee" do poorly compared to those that have an accountable and responsible owner. If you must spread community management tasks over multiple staff or volunteers, ensure that the responsibilities are clear, understood, and that you have processes in place to ensure compliance with the procedure—including redundancies so that there's no single point of failure.

When you apply principles gleaned from sociology and psychology to the routine process, you're virtually guaranteed to ensure a vibrant online community. So much of what drives our members' participation in communities (or lack thereof) has nothing to do with technology, and everything to do with motivation.

In 1986, psychologists D.M. McMillan and D.W. Chavis theorized a "Sense of Community," which determines the extent to which people are motivated to be active and productive members in their community. While the theories put forth by Chavis and McMillan were intended to help neighborhoods increase a sense of community in a physical location, they are applicable to online communities. Community management is the process of increasing motivation to contribute to the group by increasing its members sense of community.

According to McMillan and Chavis (https://www.dropbox.com/s/tjzqcgdsrty9fw1/Sense-of-Community.pdf?dl=0), sense of community is driven by four attributes:

1. Membership

Five factors contribute to people's belief that they are accepted members of their community:

- *Boundaries.* Not just anyone can belong to the community. There are standards or criteria for joining.

- *Emotional safety.* Members need to feel that they will not be ridiculed for their beliefs or opinions in their community.

- *Sense of belonging and identification.* A feeling that they truly belong, and are accepted by their fellow members.

- *Personal investment.* Members are willing to contribute their resources to the betterment of the community and the other members.

- *Common symbol system.* Members associate a word, phrase, logo, or other totem as being representative of their community. Members of a strong community will often have inside jokes or a unique shared vocabulary.

Practical things that community managers can do to reinforce the feeling of membership are:

- Welcome newcomers quickly and engage them right away.

- Enforce a policy that prohibits personal attacks on members' beliefs or opinions.

- Invite members into specific discussion topics where you think their voices should be heard.

- Give your community a name and logo that resonate with the association's members.

- Print stickers or swag with the community logo, give them to active members, and ask them to post "selfies" with them in your community.

2. Influence

Community members feel they can affect what their community represents and does. If members feel they have no influence over their fellow members or the community itself, they will be less motivated to engage.

Practical things that community managers can do to reinforce the feeling of influence are:

- Solicit and publish stories of members who have changed how they work based on advice received in the community.

- Allow for "likes" in your community and publish a list of members whose posts have had the most likes over a period of time.

- Give members the ability to identify the accepted solution to a question asked in discussion threads.

- Propose a small project for the community to complete (or allow them to come up with one of their own), such as an e-book, webinar, or conference session.

- Periodically provide members an opportunity to participate in a process to propose revisions to the community guidelines.

- Hold an annual vote to induct a member into a community hall of fame.

3. Integration and Fulfillment of Needs

Members feel that their needs and wants are being met, and that the things they value are congruent with those of the community. Practical things that community managers can do to reinforce the feeling that members' needs are being met and that their values are similar to the community's are:

- Create a page containing recent posts with no responses and encourage community members to reply.

- Deploy a feature in discussion threads that allows users to state that they have the same question or issue.

- Give members the opportunity to participate in a process to create (and later, revise) a page that embodies the community's shared values.

4. Shared Emotional Connection

Considered the highest sense of community attainable, people feel emotionally invested in the well-being of—and even spiritually connected to—their fellow members. Practical things that community managers can do to help members develop a shared emotional connection are:

- Hold regularly scheduled events, both live and virtual.

- Photograph or video members at events shaking hands, with arms around each other, laughing, or even embracing, and post them in your community.

- Reward video posts, selfies, and disclosure of challenges and successes.

- Solicit and publish stories of members who have entered into mentoring relationships, have become friends on a personal level, or even have become romantically involved.

- Encourage "field reports" from members who have organized their own in-person gatherings.

- Don't prohibit off-topic discussions.

Social Media

There is no shortage of advice and books on social media. For the purpose of this chapter, we have distinguished between social networking communities, like Facebook and LinkedIn, and social media. In-depth reading on the finer points of social media for associations is recommended in the sidebar above. The following is a cursory list of social media and their most effective uses for associations. Given the short relevance cycle of many social media sites, keep in mind that the following are up-to-date as of 2015 and may be outdated before the third edition of this book is published.

Blogs

- Blogging platforms have evolved to the point that they resemble full-fledged content management systems (CMSs), and simple websites can now run on them.

- Content marketing continues to gain in popularity, and blogging platforms are widely used to distribute it.

- Search engine optimization continues to be an effective way to raise awareness online, and blogging has long been considered one of the best ways to increase an organization's SEO.

- Some organizations use blogs to provide a steady stream of original thought leadership content within their industry or profession.

- Blogs can be used as a "house organ" to publish association news that may not be appropriate for a newsletter or magazine.

Twitter

- Comprised of no more than 140 characters, tweets are quickly consumed and easily shared, so they are among the most viral of all forms of social media.

- Hashtags allow Twitter users to categorize their tweets, making them ideal for aggregating, publishing, and monitoring topics relevant to an industry, profession, or event.

- Tweet Chats are generally 60-minute periods of time in which people discuss niche topics in real time on Twitter—there's even one for the association profession called #assnchat.

- Twitter is often used by users to air grievances about customer service. Organizations should monitor Twitter to act on any tweets directed at them.

Image Sharing Sites

- In 2015, image sharing sites, such as Pinterest, Instagram, and Snapchat, were among the most trafficked social media platforms. With the content primarily consumed on mobile apps, image sharing sites are effective for reaching audiences with at-a-glance content while they're on the go.

- Some organizations use image sharing sites as a way to distribute infographics and visually compelling examples of their members' work (e.g., architects, artists, photographers, and chefs).

Forums

- Reddit allows users to engage in forum discussions in a wide variety of topics—there's probably one for your industry or profession—on a publicly available platform. Its users, called Redditors, are highly engaged and numerous, capable of mobilizing thousands of users in a short period of time.

- We discussed private online communities at the beginning of this chapter, and associations aren't the only ones creating them. There are specialized online communities—unaffiliated with any association—for engineers, human resource professionals, doctors, and athletic trainers. Associations should keep watch for specialized communities cropping up in their sphere of influence and consider ways to partner with them. Some leading organizations have gone so far as to acquire specialty communities and fold them into their association's pool of member benefits.

Table 14.1. Social Media Used by Association

	Individual (n = 341)	Trade (n = 196)	Combination (n = 214)
Facebook	91%	81%	94%
Twitter	87%	82%	86%
LinkedIn (Public)	60%	68%	61%
YouTube	56%	58%	52%
LinkedIn (Association Members Only)	36%	35%	34%
Association Blog	24%	26%	32%
Google +	22%	13%	20%
Private Association Social Network	17%	11%	13%
Pinterest	15%	10%	18%
Association Listserv	13%	13%	15%
Flickr	11%	13%	14%
Wikis	3%	3%	2%
Ning/Groupsite	0%	2%	2%
None—we don't use social media	2%	2%	0%
Other	8%	6%	7%

Source: 2015 *Membership Marketing Benchmarking Report.*

Video Sharing Services

- Video sharing services such as YouTube continue to gain in popularity. In 2015, there were more searches executed on YouTube than on Bing, Microsoft's search engine.

- Short-format video sharing tools are also surging. Vine, a sharing service for 5-second video clips, was recently acquired by Twitter.

- In 2015, interest in live streaming mobile apps was rekindled with the increasing popularity of Meerkat and Periscope. These apps allow users to stream video over the web in real time from their mobile devices.

See Table 14.1 for a breakout of social media being used by associations.

Web Delivery of Benefits

Your members expect to be able to access all association services over the web. After all, they've never had to call Amazon or visit their warehouse to get what they need, and these expectations are applied to their associations: member directory, education, samples and templates, networking, registering for meetings, renewing their membership, and anything else they need from your organization.

But an increasing number of your members now expect to access association services on their mobile devices. In fact, some members—especially those working in third-world countries—interact almost exclusively with their organizations by mobile devices. According to comScore, as of June 2014, the ratio of time spent on desktops and mobile devices among U.S. adults was 60 percent on mobile to 40 percent on desktop computer. It won't be long before members expect a mobile delivery of benefits in the same way they expect it over the web.

There are two general approaches to delivering benefits to mobile devices:

Mobile Web

Many content management systems (CMSs) are now mobile *responsive*. This means that, as the screen size is reduced, the content scales and moves around to accommodate the narrower space, requiring less pinching and zooming to read and engage with the content. A quick and easy solution to making your association's content mobile-accessible, this approach is not necessarily optimal.

When using a mobile device, the vast majority of users will not want to use every feature that your website offers. For this reason, some organizations choose to deploy mobile *adaptive* websites that strip out features that go mostly unused on mobile devices, concentrating on the most-used features and content, and putting them front and center on the mobile browser. You can identify these content pages and features by examining your web analytics and segmenting the traffic to show only pages visited by users who used mobile devices. Creating an adaptive design requires more planning and time to deploy, so it is generally more costly than a responsive design.

Native Mobile Apps

In the same comScore study mentioned above, it was found that 87 percent of time using a mobile device was spent inside of a mobile app. In general, mobile apps are capable of delivering a richer user experience than can be achieved through a mobile browser. Compare YouTube's user experience in the browser and in its mobile app and notice the difference.

Mobile apps, however, do require the user to download and install the app (which is a barrier to engagement), whereas a browser is standard equipment on every smartphone. A 2014 study from Localytics found that 20 percent of mobile apps are only opened once.

The emerging best practice among associations is a "both-and" approach. Offering a mobile responsive or adaptive website to accommodate the browser experience, plus a native mobile app for certain content or services that demand a more elegant user experience.

Conclusion

Your members' expectations for the way they engage digitally with your association are shaped by the experiences they have with other companies' and organizations' technologies. Those expectations are continually evolving; so, too, should your organization's digital engagement capabilities.

Remember that this book was published in 2016, and this text will stand still while technology continues to advance. This book's publishing partner, ASAE, can help you stay abreast of changes in engagement technology for associations. Become a member, or take advantage of free resources at www.asaecenter.org.

About the Author

Benjamin Martin, CAE, was recognized as one of "Five to Watch" by ASAE's *Associations Now* magazine, and is a winner of the National Association of REALTORS®, Technology Spotlight Award. Martin is an association executive with more than a dozen years of experience in trade and individual membership organizations. He is the chief engagement officer at Online Community Results, providing outsourced online community management, consulting, coaching, and strategy services. Email: ben@onlinecommunityresults.com.

Membership Communication

15

By Christy Jones, CAE

The art of communicating reinvents itself as surroundings change. First we had to learn to understand change is a constant, then came the rapidity of change, and now it has almost come full circle: What message to which audience and which method of communication is needed for recruitment, engagement, and retention of members? Traditional competition (time, other organizations, and for-profits), combined with technological advances, continue to force associations to think beyond simply reviewing how they do business and delve into how they meet the necessities of change, messaging, and engagement on all levels of business. As a membership professional, your challenge is to make sure your communications enhance the value proposition to both current and future members and customers. The expectations you set for a prospect need to be fulfilled or they simply won't renew. Keeping current members engaged is crucial. As with most things, successful communication begins with research. This chapter will help you use communications in your recruitment, engagement, and retention outreach and help you build a communications strategy for your association.

Understanding Your Members' World

If your organization hasn't conducted a recent member survey, see Chapters 7 (An Overview of Membership Research) and 8 (Mission ~~Im~~possible: Using Data to Drive Organizational Excellence), particularly the sections focusing on segmenting around need rather than demographics, then realize it's time. No matter what type or size of an association, implementing regular primary research (direct surveys, focus groups, online polls, etc.) is crucial to the building of any communication plan. Make sure to include a mix of demographics, lapsed members, and prospective members whenever possible. Understanding the interests of your target audience, knowing what messages they want to hear and by what method, can be accomplished only when the right research has been done.

In addition to—not in place of—conducting regular member research, it is also prudent to conduct periodic 360-degree environmental scans of your industry and to examine secondary market research produced by outside organizations, such as government agencies or academic institutions, to gain insights about positioning your organization and to check trends in your industry and in the association community. Members and customers want to know you are thinking ahead and are preparing for their future needs. Such research provides insight into how your marketplace is changing, where you may find new prospective members, and what new technologies will reach them.

The following three sections list resources for both conducting environmental scans (what/how do your members or potential members want to hear from you), as well as resources that help use communication for the key essentials of membership, recruitment, engagement, and retention. Knowing that different types and sizes of associations have different needs, sizes, and budgets to work from, these sources encompass a variety of helpful information from which to pick and choose—again, what is important for your audience? Also included is a list of sources referred to throughout this chapter.

Excellent resources for associations can be found through ASAE (www.asaecenter .org) and your local allied societies. A good resource, *Environmental Scanning for Associations: The Everyday Guide to Capturing, Analyzing, and Interpreting Strategic Information*,[1] provides guidance on conducting environmental scans, another research tool in getting to know your potential and current target audience.

In addition to resources you have found that highlight what is important to your specific trade, profession, or community, the following resources will help guide you in your efforts to create a two-way street between your association and its members:

- *7 Measures of Success: What Remarkable Associations Do That Others Don't: Revised and Updated Edition.*[2] Original and objective research tailored to the association community's needs, *7 Measures of Success* provides empirical data and 7 success factors common among visionary nonprofits.

- *The Art of Membership: How to Attract, Retain, and Cement Member Loyalty.*[3] In the book, author Sheri Jacobs raises a key challenge associations face when they wish to communicate with members. According to Jacobs, "We live in a time during which people are skeptical of statements or claims that promise to solve their problems, make life better, or offer to improve a current situation. They are bombarded with so many messages and sales pitches that an internal defense mechanism is usually advising them to question advertising claims, marketing messages, or sales pitches. With that in mind, you need to build trust by addressing prospective members' concerns up front and proactively overcome objections. Unless they are moved to join, or become active within your association due to a desire to advance a mission or influence legislative actions, most people will try to determine if what you offer meets their needs, for the right price. Remember, it isn't always that the price is so high that they can't afford it; it could be that (1) the value does not equal the cost or (2) the value is there but a number of factors may exist that prevent the individual from using or taking advantage of the membership."

Emerging Demographic Trends Impacting Membership Communications

Another crucial area of research for any communicator focuses on emerging trends. In 2014, the ASAE Foundation published a new report, *Exploring the Future of Membership*.[4] This report is comprised of four white papers by different sources that include qualitative and quantitative research, case studies, and recommended approaches. The white paper, *The Future of Association Engagement*[5] by Association Laboratory provides key findings relevant to those of us developing communication strategies in associations. Potential and current members have different expectations of communication methods/messages today, more varied than in the past, which is an important trend to keep top-of-mind. Understanding the differences in demographics today is important to understanding which communication strategy/tactic may work best for that audience. Examples include:

- "Two substantial generational audiences important to the association (Baby Boomers and Millennials) have very different expectations of what engagement means and how engagement manifests itself in behavior." (p. 15)

- "Individuals have less time to engage and choose different paths of engagement because organizations are running leaner and meaner due to their ROI awareness." (p. 20)

- "Almost 8 in 10 association executives say their members are concerned about managing the volume of incoming information; no other concern approaches that level of universality." (p. 25)

- "Association members now operate in an environment characterized by a decentralized web of access points for information and content that is no longer specific to an organization or location." (p. 26)

- "Development of relevant content, customization of content for distinct audiences, and the delivery of this content; all in a way that meets member expectation is essential to successful member strategy." (p. 27)

This white paper, as well as the three others included in the report, do give recommendations and case studies that are very helpful to use for your own communication possibilities.

Another general resource is *The Next America*,[6] by Paul Taylor and the Pew Research Center. Focusing on emerging changes in demographics; this report is an invaluable resource for any organization wanting to know the impact these are making today as well as tomorrow. Boomers versus Millennials, economic divides, cultural impacts—this book provides so much critical information. I would share it with your top executives after you finish reading it.

A word of caution—be careful not to divide your members simply by demographics. You need to know as much about them as possible, but don't classify them into groups only because they are in a certain segment. Sheri Jacobs, in an article based on her book, *The Art of Membership*,[7] says it well: "Classifying individuals based only on demographic factors such as birth year (or generation), gender, work setting, or title, may be of little use, because members of these groups sometimes have little more in common than those characteristics."

More and more associations are either going global or are looking to do so. Are you part of this trend? Do you know what the global impacts on associations are and how they affect communication strategies? There is a more in-depth overview in Chapter 6: Managing a Global Membership.

Communicating in a Global World

Here are some tips for Communicating in a Global World from Bonnie Koenig, president of Going International.[8]

- Take time zones into consideration when planning anything that will happen in real time (webinars, live streaming, etc.). Make sure all communications you send out have a time, including which time zone that time is in.

- Acronyms tend to be very local—the more diverse the group you are communicating with is, the more you should minimize the use of acronyms or make sure you clarify what any acronym stands for.

- Clarify your communication channels and loops—who needs to be part of the decision making, who needs to be consulted, and who will just be kept apprised? This is important for any association (and may vary by types of decision), but the more geographically spread or culturally diverse your association or its work becomes, the greater the chance that people will be left out of the communication channels. Clarifying them in advance can minimize this and align expectations.

- Recognize that band-width (the capacity to download from the Internet) can vary dramatically around the world. This will be important, for example, if you are on a web-based group call or webinar. Some participants may regularly lose the connection or have a harder time hearing.

- Be careful of humor on social media. It does not always translate in short phrases without more context.
- Personal relationships matter—despite an increasingly virtual world, taking the time to build and nurture personal relationships is appreciated by those of all cultures.
- Practice a "global mindset" (it is a practice) so that remembering these things become routine to your staff. There is a spectrum of how people engage globally— starting with those who don't think about these differences at all (although they are not intending to disparage anyone). These little things can make a big difference to members, partners, and others in your international network.

Harnessing Today's Communication Tools

Positioning

Market research and environmental scans provide the background knowledge needed to understand where you stand compared to similar organizations. Positioning your organization is the natural next step. Membership communicators know the importance of flexibility, transparency, and inclusion. How do we present ourselves to members, non-members, and potential members? Where are we compared to our competitors?

Your association's mission statement should guide the communications and public relations efforts that attempt to define what your organization does and who it represents. Succinctly articulate these ideas in a couple of sentences, and those statements should guide the appeals you draft to whatever audience segments you address (see Chapter 3, Defining Value). Whatever vehicles you use to initially position your organization—whether brochures, website, conferences, or lobbying efforts—they should address the needs of the new audiences as well as your established members.

To that point, what are you doing to engage new members as well as current ones? Meeting expectations created before they join (whether through reading your direct mail appeals, website, emails, magazine, even listening to face-to-face descriptions of membership) is just as crucial to retention as are those techniques you use to engage new and current members. It's surprising how much focus is put on after the individual/company has joined, when meeting initial expectations (which you have created) goes a long way toward not just joining, but staying with your association.

Strategic Ideas and New Tactical Examples

The following are some useful ideas and methods of communicating that are just the tip of the iceberg. In addition to a plethora of books on the subject, there are thousands of articles focusing on the "best" ways to communicate to your target audience. Those listed below focus on the association community. Choose methods that would resonate with you and your members and consider giving them a try:

- Member Engagement: From Participation to Relationships[9] by Anna Caraveli is a great resource. Using several associations as examples, Caraveli showcases the synergy between communication and engagement by members/volunteers. "When members suddenly make a connection between what the association does and what is critically important to them, they are converted from participants to loyal members/donors and champions."

- The American Association of University Women (AAUW) uses numerous ways to engage members. They are subscribed (with permission) to the online Action Alert newsletter, which updates them on actions about women's issues on Capitol Hill, as well as providing them opportunities to take action; introduce new members to branches (aka chapters) in their area; alert them of events of interest; use social media extensively; and ultimately provide leadership seminars for branches so that they develop engagement opportunities locally.

- Carrie Kolar posts membership communication blogs on Webbright Services. Her blog, *Successful Communication Strategies for Associations*,[10] compiles a variety of blogs with many tips and tools for effective communication strategies. Another quick resource by Kolar, *Most Common Methods to Communicate with Association Members*,[11] gives some down and dirty "How-To"s for today's audiences.

- I stumbled on Rad's Blog and noticed they were having a Nonprofit Blog Carnival. The results from numerous contributors resulted in Top 5 Tips for Standing Out from the Crowd: Are your nonprofit communications emotional, empowering, authentic, challenging, or newsworthy?[12] This is a very useful read.

- We've all been told storytelling is an effective way to communicate. This article, The Science of Storytelling: Why Telling a Story Is the Most Powerful Way to Activate Our Brains,[13] popped up on Facebook recently, and I had to share it, as it really shows how to make use of storytelling properly.

- A good overall review can be found in *Making an Impact with Your Membership Materials: What Works, What Doesn't, Part 1*.[14] Part 2 wasn't published when this went to print, so check back under ASAE Resources.

- AAUW's Younger Women Task Force Chapters serve our aged 20 to 40 group. Younger members want to give their time for a cause, but they want to do so in a fashion that suits their busy lifestyles. Virtually connecting through online webinars, such as "I hate networking but it landed me my dream job" helps recruit and retain this audience. Two items of interest for this audience are Making Membership Relevant[15] (Gen Y) and *A Guide to Recruiting and Retaining Next-Gen Association Professionals*.[16]

Better Member Communications (Feb. 16, 2015)

1. Members like instant gratification. Contact new members immediately upon receipt of their dues payments. This is critical, as it lets the new member know that his or her payment was received while also showing that the member is important enough to deserve a quick response.

2. Members are not important just because of their checkbooks. Over time, many associations become comfortable with primarily communicating with their

members when they want them to purchase something. We all want members to pay to attend our big conferences and meetings. We all want members to purchase our publications and research studies. Associations cannot communicate with members only when they offer them something for purchase or they will become immune to our marketing messages. Even more important, they may start to question whether we value them as individuals or just for the money they can put in our pockets.

3. Not every member responds to the same method of communication. We all have different preferences as to how we want to receive information. Use multiple methods of communication to share information about the same topic, issue, or promotion.

4. Members like to interact with volunteers as well as staff members. Members like knowing they are being heard by staff and key volunteers. By varying who communicates with members, your association will increase the likelihood of having members open and read your communications.

Association Website: From "Static" to Engagement of Prospects and Members

Traditional ways of using your website to enhance member interaction include providing free members-only access to publications or discounted prices on them, email lists, discussion boards, newsgroups, podcasts, online training and certification programs, online directories, e-commerce opportunities, online registrations, and webinars. However, technology's pace is fast, and these items, while expected today, are not necessarily what will drive new members or keep members and non-members visiting your website tomorrow. The number of people using the web interactively—actually contributing content rather than just using it as a knowledge/information resource—continues to grow daily. The more your members use the Internet interactively, the more they will look to their association's website to do the same.

Since an organization's website is a primary communications tool, reaching both members and potential members with ongoing communications, it's essential to examine the quality of the communications offered on your website.

- Is your website used by both members and non-members, with advantages to both audiences?

- Or is it a public information website that members would rather see the public attracted to than have as a "member-only" benefit?

- How is your organization's website primarily used by members? Do members perceive your site as "member-only benefits" locked behind a firewall of sorts? Is it key to member recruitment and retention?

AAUW completed the redesign of its national website following an 18-month development process. This extended period of time allowed for a complete user interface facelift (including a member survey, shown in Appendix I), migration of existing content and functionality to a new open source platform (WordPress) and programming language (PHP), and a future-proofed information architecture. Prior to the redesign, the website consisted mainly of content created for print and repurposed to the online channel. Now, AAUW's web properties are a central channel in our communications objectives. All marketing content—emails, ads, advocacy alerts, newsletters, social media, print collateral—direct constituents to the website. New content types were introduced—events, articles, resources—in addition to static pages and blogs. Each piece of content is further tagged and categorized to relate to other content. This strategy strengthens internal linking strategies and improves content marketing search engine optimization (SEO).

Whether your website should be for members only, the public, or both depends on the nature of your organization. Is yours a trade association whose members would benefit from giving the public access to information such as safety standards or general industry insights? What are the legal issues of posting member information online? Is yours a professional society that doesn't need to reach beyond a potential member base? The key is conducting the necessary research to determine what would be best for your organization, its members, and its customers. Then you can understand how to tailor this important communications tool to best serve your members and attract prospects.

Developing Member Engagement

"Traditional" communication methods are no longer traditional and are continually changing every aspect based on one common thread: What do members want to know, which methods do they prefer, how do they want it delivered, how do they want to engage, and in what time frame? What can be made adaptable to your needs? (See the survey in Appendix I.)

Segment Your Audience

You simply cannot market to your membership in one voice unless you are one of the fortunate few with a very concise purpose. Even professional associations will attract members for different reasons. Between social, new, and traditional media, the average member is bombarded with messages from a variety of organizations. AAUW used the following criteria when planning our latest conference. What do you need to review for future planning?

- Local members—minimal travel expense and home state pride.
- Attendees of the prior two conventions—they've come before and loved it.
- Former leaders—they are passionately dedicated to the organization.
- Recently joined and never attended—they need to know what they are missing.
- Everyone else!

You cannot communicate to any one audience in the same manner without losing opportunity. Questions to ask as you are developing messaging include:

- What exactly do you want from the attendee or reader?
- What is the primary motivator for that attendee or reader?
- What is the hook you will use to achieve the desired results?

Changes in Print Pieces

A well-loved and award-winning member benefit, AAUW's flagship magazine *Outlook*, was getting a little long in the tooth. It was redesigned to create a magazine that let us show off good content and appeal to a huge age range. AAUW just won two Excel Awards from Association Media and Publishing for single-topic issues. In order to engage members, it grew to include member stories. Before this focus changed, very few member comments were received. Now questions, comments, and notes of praise from members are regular.

AAUW has also been doing some deliberate experimentation with how to make *Outlook* more accessible and to repurpose some of the content online. There is now a digital version—a PDF that goes out to members who opt in—provided by a vendor, that has some live links and fun interactivity and is considered well worth the investment. Current issues live behind the member wall, but when the next issue is released, past issues are opened up. "Browsers" are also engaging in AAUW's goal—persuading them to join.

A more seamless new member experience has been the result. Print and online stories are coordinated. Emails are sent pre-post publication and include questions whose answers are only found in the publications. A new member's guide was developed and organized like the website for ease of reference by the reader. The same issues and similar language are used so that new members can toggle easily between the two formats and find out more information online.

Channels

The impact of social and new media on member communications strategy is beyond comprehension. Conduct an audit of your current e-newsletters to determine:

- What is its purpose? Or what do you want to achieve?
- Who is your audience?
- What is the best channel to reach them?
- How will you measure effectiveness?

You also must conduct an email analytics review simultaneously. If your open rate is low and your click-through rate lower, then you'll need to dive deeper into the questions above, as was done with AAUW's e-communications piece, *Mission & Action*.[17] *Mission & Action* is the only e-newsletter received by every member. Because of that, every department wanted to include important dates and reminders, which resulted in a newsletter not indicative of its name. It became a dumping ground for the promotion of individual departments' projects, rather than for AAUW's programs overall. A quick audit of the open rate (under 10 percent) and the click-through rate (anywhere from 2 to 4.5 percent, on average) indicated that, while everyone was receiving *Mission & Action*, no one was reading it. See Exhibit 15.1.

AAUW determined that the best way to gather pertinent information was through our online content "Quad" process (Appendix II). In reviewing submitted quads, it became a quick determination which submissions were best suited for inclusion

Exhibit 15.1. AAUW's Mission and Action Newsletter Before

Mission &Action
AAUW's e-newsletter

CONVENTION

Your Best Convention Rate Expires in a Week!

Check out the just-released workshop offerings for our do-not-miss event in San Diego, June 18–21. And register before the rates go up on January 16.

READ MORE »

PROGRAMS

Find Out How You Can Get Women's History into Local Classrooms

Join our January 22 webinar to learn how you can connect with schools and teach students about the fight for women's suffrage.

READ MORE »

MEMBERSHIP

Submit Your Magnum Opus: The AAUW Art Contest Is Open!

AAUW artists, now is the time to submit your work — any medium on any theme. The deadline for submissions is January 28.

READ MORE »

ADVOCACY

Your New Resource on Human Trafficking

Use the latest data and AAUW talking points to fight this horrific crime.

READ MORE »

EDUCATION

Visit Graduate Schools from Your Living Room

AAUW's first-ever Virtual Graduate School Fair is February 9. It's free for students, and there's still space for exhibitors. Sign up today!

READ MORE »

ANNOUNCEMENTS

Hear from Executive Director Linda Hallman about why we need campaign finance reform, and sign the petition for the Democracy for All Amendment.

Put a name with that lovely face! Personalized AAUW name badges are available now on ShopAAUW.

The Global Summit of Women is May 14–16. AAUW members get a discount on registration (code AAUWXY15).

Equal Pay Day is April 14, 2015. Save the date, and start planning your events now.

The final deadlines for AAUW fellowships and grants are rapidly approaching. Applications are due January 10 for Selected Professions Fellowships and January 15 for Community Action Grants. Members are eligible to apply.

Give to AAUW

1111 Sixteenth St. NW • Washington, DC 20036

in *Mission & Action*. To make members care about the mission, it has to be made exciting to them and shown how it is playing out in the work we do every day. New criteria were developed—to be included, a piece has to show a concrete result of mission-based work *or* be something that members could take action on immediately. A revamped masthead was created, fabulous pictures for the now fewer items included, and it was made mobile-friendly. The result? It has steadily maintained an open rate of at least 40 percent, while click-throughs consistently number in the double digits. (See Exhibit 15.2.)

So what is the most important message in this section? Do not abuse a captive audience. Find out what their areas of interest are, speak to their needs, and don't forget to include the ways and means of engagement. What works for your member audience? Can't say it enough—ask them.

Online Communication—Member Opportunities and Challenges

The online communications landscape for nonprofit, membership-based associations is filled with rapidly evolving opportunities and challenges. The changing technologies and technological infrastructure (high speed and broadband Internet, Wi-Fi, smartphones, etc.) offers never-before-possible means to reaching and engaging current and prospective members and building online member-based communities covering the issues and topics they care about. Along with these rapidly evolving changes in this sector, there is a corresponding rise in media noise and competing chatter—a virtual clutter of available information. Simultaneous to these channel challenges, changing programmatic priorities and purposes also occur and the demographics of both membership and constituencies morph.

New technologies have dramatically improved an association's ability to listen to and speak with an exponentially larger number of people and segment messaging to better targeted audiences delivering the most relevant content on demand in real time and at a fraction of the cost. The proliferation of channels has also dramatically improved an organization's ability to be more timely in their responsiveness and transparent in their operations. Building online communities around membership, allies, supporters, peers, and fellow-travelers is a key online communications objective (see Chapter 14, Digital Engagement).

Building Communities

We must know who and where our members, prospective members, and supporters are and "be" right there with them. If they are online, we must be online. If they're on Facebook, then we should be, too. If they use Twitter or Instagram, Snapchat, Google+, or LinkedIn, you need to be there, too. But "being there" isn't all it takes. You have to participate in the conversations that they care about on these channels and share both their content and your own on these channels.

Exhibit 15.2. Mission and Action Newsletter After

This year's National Conference for College Women Student Leaders drew nearly 1,000 attendees.

AAUW NEWS

NCCWSL Attendees Ready to Redefine Leadership

With nearly 1,000 attendees and speakers like Chelsea Clinton and Judy Smith, the National Conference for College Women Student Leaders, held June 5–7, was a huge success. A special thank-you goes to all the generous donors, the AAUW college/university partner members who sent their students, and the legion of volunteers. Together, we empowered these women leaders. Did you send a student to NCCWSL? Let us know if we can help you start making plans for next year.

Sorry, Not Sorry: Tackling Stereotypes and Biases on Campus

This fall, AAUW's Campus Action Project grants, sponsored by Pantene, will empower college women across the country to take action on their campuses against the harmful stereotypes and biases that stand in their way. Learn more about the program, and sign up to take action on your campus.

Want to Go to AAUW's Convention for Free? Pledge to Register!

What's better than attending AAUW's 2015 National Convention in San Diego? Not paying a dime for your registration! If you "pledge to reg" now and then complete your registration before January 1, you could win a free registration. So pledge to reg today, and tell your friends to join the wave too.

Why Don't You Run for the AAUW Board of Directors?

Research shows that women don't run for office because they aren't asked — so we're asking. Will you run for AAUW national office? It's your chance to get involved in AAUW issues at the highest level as president, vice president, or one of 10 elected directors. Applications will be available July 1, and the deadline is November 1.

Favorable Decision Upheld in Discrimination Case

The Massachusetts Commission against Discrimination recently upheld a 2011 decision in favor of Legal Advocacy Fund-supported plaintiff Associate Professor Lulu Sun, concluding that the University of Massachusetts, Dartmouth, engaged in unlawful discrimination in denying Sun, an English professor, a promotion. AAUW is thrilled by the decision and proud to play a part in supporting her case.

White House Takes Action on Student Loan Debt

AAUW was at the White House when the president signed new executive actions to help lift the burden of student loan debt, which disproportionately affects women due to the pay gap. One new law will allow an additional 5 million borrowers with federal student loans to cap their monthly payments at 10 percent of their income. Learn more.

AAUW Testifies at Senate Round Table on Sexual Assault

AAUW took part in a Senate round-table discussion on campus sexual assault prevention. The discussion was hosted by Sens. Claire McCaskill (D-MO) and Richard Blumenthal (D-CT). Sen. Jon Tester (D-MT) also participated. Watch AAUW Government Relations Manager Anne Hedgepeth's presentation and learn more.

AAUW Honors Title IX Champions on Capitol Hill

On June 17, AAUW celebrated the 42nd anniversary of Title IX by recognizing Sen. Tom Harkin (D-IA) and Rep. George Miller (D-CA) as Title IX champions for their legislative legacy of improving gender equity for students across the country. Continue their fight and go to bat for women and girls in sports. Do you have any Title IX champions in your area?

Human Trafficking Bills Pass House

Five bills offering measures to stop human trafficking passed the U.S. House of Representatives easily with bipartisan support in May. One of the bills, the Stop Exploitation through Trafficking Act, would encourage states to treat children involved in sex trafficking as victims, not as criminals, and would allow victims of trafficking to be eligible for Job Corps. Learn more about the scope of trafficking and how it affects all of us.

TAKE ACTION

Title IX Know the Score Program in a Box Now Updated

Taking action to help schools in your community reach Title IX compliance has never been easier. More than 40 years after Title IX became law, the majority of federally funded schools still don't comply. Use Know the Score to check out your local schools today. Remember, grassroots advocacy is one of the best ways to address noncompliance.

November Midterm Elections Right around the Corner

How will you get out the vote in your community this fall? Learn more about what you can do, and tell us about your upcoming events. Contact VoterEd@aauw.org if you have questions.

Have a WNBA Team in Your Area?

AAUW joined forces with the Washington Mystics this month to sponsor a workshop for girls highlighting Title IX and access to higher education. Student athletes from AAUW college/university partner member schools gave tips on overcoming obstacles, and AAUW's "You Throw Like a Girl" video was featured. AAUW of California also recently hosted an event with the Los Angeles Sparks. Contact your local team today and find out how you can work together.

The Motherhood Penalty for Working Women

June 12 was moms' Equal Pay Day, the symbolic day when moms' earnings catch up to dads' from the previous year. It takes so long because working mothers typically are paid 69 cents for every dollar working dads are paid. June 16 is African American women's Equal Pay Day, and November 12 is Latinas' Equal Pay Day. Mark these days with activities in your community, and tell Congress to pass the Paycheck Fairness Act.

AAUW ON CAMPUS

Know a Recent College Grad? Give the Gift of AAUW
Empower graduates with the ability to expand their networking opportunities and future careers. The Give a Grad a Gift program enables members to give free, one-year national AAUW memberships to recent college graduates — at no cost to you or them. Give your grad the perfect gift today.

Student Candidate Makes History at Rutgers
After getting trained to run for office at Elect Her–Campus Women Win, Kristine Baffo was elected this spring to be the first woman president and the first African American president of the Rutgers University Student Assembly. Share your congratulations on Facebook, and help AAUW spread Elect Her to more campuses.

MEMBER NEWS AND RESOURCES

Are You a STEM Leader? Make It Official
Many branch and state organizations have made science, technology, engineering, and math (STEM) education a priority, and now you can designate an official STEM chair for your branch or state by visiting the Member Services Database. Your STEM chair will be added to an e-mail list to facilitate communication with other STEM chairs and the national STEM Task Force.

July 15 Call: What You Need to Know about Supreme Court Decisions
Sign up today for a call wrapping up the U.S. Supreme Court's latest term. Federal courts are sometimes the last, best hope for women who have experienced discrimination. On this call, Legal Advocacy Fund staff will highlight decisions from the past year that will affect the rights of women and girls. LAF had a terrific call last fall laying out the issues before the court — don't miss this chance to hear what the justices actually decided. Registration closes July 8.

FELLOWSHIPS, GRANTS, AND AWARDS

Tell Students to Apply for Grad School Funding
Expand your outreach to graduate students, researchers, and those working to improve their communities by spreading the word about AAUW fellowship and grant opportunities. You can order our new brochures (coming soon!) and bookmarks online. Applications for 2015–16 funding will be available August 1.

Ever Wonder How Fellows Are Selected?
AAUW's selection panelists are seasoned academics and professionals who analyze the thousands of applications AAUW receives for our competitive fellowships and grants. We are always seeking new talent and expertise. Learn more, and pass the information on to your local colleges and your networks.

AAUW Fellows Change the World

Find out what amazing things AAUW alumnae are up to by reading about them on the AAUW blog. From increasing widows' access to legal rights in Cameroon to redefining feminism's role in civil rights, AAUW fellows do truly amazing work.

AAUW MEMBER BENEFITS

Raise Your Hand If You Read Magazines

Now, raise your hand if you order yours through MagazineLine. MagazineLine has thousands of titles and the guaranteed lowest pricing. When it's time to renew, do it through MagazineLine and support AAUW with every subscription. (Right now, *Smithsonian* magazine is only $12!)

Travel with AAUW Leaders and Members to Poland

You'll never have the opportunity to walk in the footsteps of Marie Curie with better travel partners than fellow AAUW members. This delegation, November 1–9, was designed specifically for AAUW and includes highlights from Curie's childhood, meetings with women in science and academia, and cultural events such as a private concert featuring the music of Frédéric Chopin. Call Professionals Abroad today at 877.298.9677 for more information.

AAUW
1111 Sixteenth St. NW
Washington, DC 20036

Unsubscribe

Fundamental Concepts

Do the member and the affiliate feel like they are a part of the wider community that is your organization? Branding, multi-channel approaches, understanding how today's demographics want to belong—all of these and other factors contribute to a sense of belonging if the communication strategy is tied in:

- Solid, consistent, high-quality branding across all channels (online and offline) matters. Name, logo, color, and editorial-style consistency help members feel a part of the whole, the larger organization. It also helps elevate smaller entities (state and chapter organizations) to the national and even international level.

- Multi-channel output requires that robust standards and values be identified and rigorously enforced.

- The pace of change and demand for business unit visibility require a nimble production mechanism and logistical flexibility.

- Maintaining institutional integrity and message cohesion require oversight and coordination across all channels.

- Flat or declining resources (staff, dollars, infrastructure) require creativity and innovation to meet the new demands of the changing communications landscape.

Challenges

- When we must serve dozens of distinct interests, and each requires ever-increasing visibility and premium, while we often have limited "space" on new online platforms and each unit has content-sharing needs each day (sound familiar?!), we must innovate in the planning, pacing, production, and scheduling of this content.

- On any given day, any interest may desire content, ranging from a single tweet, a mere "like us" or "follow us," to a much more complex, cross-platform online campaign.

- The core challenge is "How do we do it all, and do it all well?"

Components of Success

What does success look like? How do you know you're headed in the right direction with the mechanisms you've put in place to build a strong internal communications infrastructure that meets the often very broad and diverse needs of our members and supporters?

- A plan forward begins with broad buy-in for our approach from institutional leadership, colleagues, and volunteer leaders.

- Maintaining that initial buy-in requires transparency in the logistical operations and being open to feedback and willing to adjust the approach if necessary so that it meets expectations and aspirations.

- When production operations are structured and executed in an organized and open manner, the organization delivers higher quality communications on a greater number of channels in a more consistent, cohesive, and coordinated manner and simultaneously serves broader organizational messaging goals.

- The organization also becomes *more* nimble, not less, because the inevitable and unexpected, but necessary, exceptions to the process can be more quickly and fairly addressed (breaking news, rapidly changing circumstances, etc.) while inflicting fewer negative and counter-productive effects on overall messaging plans and needs organization-wide.

The Use of Video

Video is becoming more and more of a membership communication tool, whether for prospects or current members. The more an individual (or company) understands your mission, learns that your activities are there to be engaged in, or sees like-minded individuals in a given video—that builds community across interests, distances, and demographics. Video is one of the most powerful tools a communicator can use. Rather, good video is! Whether you have an in-house team or contract this important work out, video simply has to answer the same questions asked earlier regarding audience and messaging. Many associations now produce short, one-minute videos and 15-minute videos for different audience segments. The best videos speak very clearly, with ONE intended result, to ONE audience only.

Once you have created wonderful videos, use them every time it's appropriate. AAUW repurposed many videos by linking to them in blogs, embedding them on web pages, and listing them under the member resources tab on our website. Each video has drop-down menus explaining how they can be used for different audiences in different scenarios. Again, this is a case of the national organization offering engagement tools to its chapters while communicating how we prefer they be used.

Engaging Member Volunteers in Communication

Your volunteers are key partners in any communication effort you plan and implement for your association. They can (and many do) run online communities, lead your Facebook or other social media efforts, staff a table at events for non-member outreach, use an "elevator speech" wherever they can to share the mission and activities of your organization, and, most importantly, they are crucial for member engagement and retention. A good general resource to review is *How to Engage Member Leaders in Member Retention*.[18]

Training Members in Communication and Marketing

Investing in training your volunteer leaders in communication and marketing techniques is well worth the energy. Whether through workshops at your conferences, resources available online, face-to-face training, having your leaders understand the importance of knowing how to reach their audience (whether current or potential) is crucial to membership recruitment, engagement, and retention. Don't assume they know! Even PR professionals may know how to showcase a specific product, but have no clue how to do the same for intangible benefits often found in associations. Teach them.

An insight learned from experience—don't just hand over written or visual resource tools to your volunteer leaders and expect them to read them and then implement your suggestions or examples. Won't happen! Training them how and when to use any resource is integral for success.

AAUW created a presentation entitled *How to Market Your Branch*, which was an instantaneous success. Volunteer leaders were trained using this as a tool, and actually were thrilled they would be part of a much broader outreach than using staff alone. Additional communication vehicles were also created to both inform and train volunteers to help with recruitment and retention. This communication occurs from the national membership staff to volunteer leadership via monthly e-newsletters; webinars, a special section of the website (8 Leader Essentials for Membership Vice Presidents[19]), an online resource tool kit, as well as through peer-to-peer communications (member leaders regular contact among the branches, Google hangouts between branches, share and learn calls).

Webinars are great training tools for volunteer leaders. AAUW holds a specific series of three that focuses on recruitment, engagement, and retention. Gone are the days when a webinar was simply a voice-over-PowerPoint presentation. Engaging your leaders is just as important as sharing tools with them. Of the hour presentation, the last half is an "open mic (aka phone)" session for asking questions and sharing problems or successes. Volunteer-to-volunteer with staff participation works well in "phone-and-share" sessions that are easy to use and generally are more inexpensive. What would work for your volunteers?

Demographics are changing, communications technologies are changing, and members' perceptions of value and community are changing. Do your volunteer leaders recognize this? Association volunteers as well as membership professionals must consider all these issues and develop plans to reach current and prospective members with communications tailored to different needs in the marketplace. The best association communications are based on a clear vision of the association's mission and value proposition and are supported by research and member feedback. This is a critical point your volunteer leaders, as well as staff, must understand.

Notes

1. James Dalton; Alan Balkema. *Environmental Scanning for Associations: The Everyday Guide to Capturing, Analyzing, and Interpreting Strategic Information.* (ASAE Association Management Press, 2012).

2. *7 Measures of Success: What Remarkable Associations Do That Others Don't* (revised and updated edition). (ASAE Association Management Press, 2012).

3. Sheri Jacobs. *The Art of Membership: How to Attract, Retain, and Cement Member Loyalty.* (ASAE Association Management Press, 2014).

4. John Barnes, Jenny Nelson, Dean West, Sheri Jacobs, Susanne Connors Bowman, and Lisa Dicke. *Exploring the Future of Membership.* (ASAE Association Management Press, 2014).

5. *The Future of Association Engagement.* (Association Laboratory, 2014).

6. Paul Taylor; Pew Research Center. The Next America: Boomers, Millennials, and the Looming Generational Showdown. (*PublicAffairs,* March 4, 2014).

7. Sheri Jacobs. *The Art of Membership: How to Attract, Retain, and Cement Member Loyalty.* (ASAE Association Management Press, 2014).

8. Going International. www.goinginternational.com

9. Anna Caraveli. Member Engagement: From Participation to Relationships. *Associations Now,* March/April 2015.

10. Carrie Kolar. Successful Communication Strategies for Associations. (The Association Blog: News and Resources for Association Executives. April 14, 2015).

11. Carrie Kolar. Most Common Methods to Communicate with Association Members. (The Association Blog: News and Resources for Association Executives. May 12, 2015).

12. Allyson Kapin. Top 5 Tips for Standing Out from the Crowd: Are your non-profit communications emotional, empowering, authentic, challenging, or newsworthy? (Wild Apricot Blog. March 13, 2015).

13. Leo Widrich. The Science of Storytelling: Why Telling a Story Is the Most Powerful Way to Activate Our Brains. (Lifehacker, December 5, 2015).

14. *Making an Impact with Your Membership Materials: What Works, What Doesn't, Part 1.* (ASAE, June 1, 2015).

15. Making Membership Relevant. (*Association Impact,* April/May 2015).

16. Bryan C. Harrison. *A Guide to Recruiting and Retaining Next-Gen Association Professionals.* (ASAE, April 6, 2015).

17. *Mission & Action.* AAUW. Bimonthly e-bulletin. www.aauw.org/resource/aauw-mission-action/

18. Michele F. Liston. *How to Engage Volunteer Leaders in Member Retention* (ASAE, April 20, 2015).

19. 8 Leader Essentials for Membership Vice Presidents. *Leader Essentials: A Collection of Resources for AAUW Officers.* AAUW. www.aauw.org/resource/leader-essentials/

About the Author

Christy Jones, CAE, is the vice president for membership and direct response marketing for the American Association of University Women (AAUW), Washington, D.C. She has worked in trade, professional, and now philanthropic associations, focusing on membership and communications. Active in ASAE, she is a past chair of the International Section Council and was a member of the Membership Section Council. Email: jonesc@aauw.org.

Acknowledgements

Special thanks to Peggy Woods Clark, website manager, AAUW, and to Elizabeth Bolton, associate director of arts, editorials, and media, AAUW. I would also like to recognize Cordy Galligan, Alan Callander, Claudia Richards, LaToya Millet, and Rachel Berryman from AAUW for their help and support with various sections.

APPENDIX I

AAUW Web Survey

Goals and Mission

1. What are the basic goals of the AAUW website? Does the website currently serve that purpose?

2. What are the basic goals of the redesign project?

3. What is the revenue or cost savings goal or objective, if any?

4. What outcomes will make the redesign project successful?

Audience

1. Who is the primary target audience, and how would you describe them? Include demographics, technical skill, and knowledge base details, and other adjectives to develop an audience "persona."

2. Who is the secondary target audience? Other audiences? How would you describe them?

3. What types of visitors are we trying to attract? What are the site goals for each type of visitor?

4. Why would a first-time visitor come to the site? What would make him or her a loyal return visitor?

5. From the homepage, name the five most important tasks visitors should be able to complete (e.g., join AAUW, login to the member area, etc.)?

Form and Function/Look and Feel

1. What currently works well on the site? What currently isn't working well on the site? Please provide specific technical, structural, content, or design examples.

2. What new technologies should be implemented on the site and why? How will these technologies enhance the user experience?

3. If the world were your oyster and you could have anything you wanted, what would the site look like and what would you want it to do? Describe the site experience you want to create.

4. Use three adjectives to describe how the website should be perceived by the user (i.e., progressive, professional, informative, etc.). Is this different from the current perception of the website?

5. Who are our biggest "competitors" or others in the same industry? What do you like/dislike about their websites?

6. Find three high-quality sites on the web that relate to our redesign project in terms of mission, audience, design quality, and functionality that you feel we should emulate. List the URLs, explain why the sites are appealing, and explain how they relate to our redesign project.

Additional Comments

APPENDIX II

AAUW's Quad Process

Liz Bolton, Associate Director, AAUW's Art, Editorial, and Media Department

We came up with the Quad, which is basically just the four foundational marketing questions in a user-friendly form: Who are you targeting? What are you trying to tell them? Why should they care? and How are you going to get the info to them? We ask anyone who wants to put content up online to answer the first three questions and offer any suggestions they have for the fourth question. They pitch the content at a standing weekly meeting, and afterward the "communications staff" meets to discuss channels further, if necessary, and scheduling. The process allows us to accommodate a huge amount of content (about three daily posts on top of about 300 print projects a year) with the resources we have. It allows us to prioritize and to keep a deliberate eye on the results of each piece.

AAUW Staff Resources

INFORMATION TECHNOLOGY   **COMMUNICATIONS**   HUMAN RESOURCES   MARKETING MATERIALS

Online Content Quad

Item Name *

Where should time on this project be billed? *

Administrative Services (1100)

Your Name *

E-mail *

Purpose/Outcomes/Goals *

If your content is wildly successful, what happens? How will you measure success?

Audience *

Who is most likely to be moved by your content?

Message *

What story are you telling?
What kind of values, problems, solutions, and actions are involved?

Channels/Strategy Suggestions

Financial Metrics, Management, and Budgeting for Membership

16

By Susanne Connors Bowman, CAE

Understanding membership metrics and how to use them is a critical skill for today's membership professional. Metrics will help you tell the story of the current health of your organization, forecast future needs, judge return on investment of programs/services, and identify challenges.

This chapter covers:

- Key membership metrics;

- Examples of how metrics are calculated;

- How metrics might be best used to measure health and forecast future growth;

- Cautions on how best to interpret metrics; and

- Trends in metrics.

Regardless of role within the organization, it is essential for association executives to have a solid understanding of finance as it relates to the membership function. While some departments may have oversight or responsibility for adhering to the budget, there is clear synergy between the membership and finance functions. This chapter will also address billing cycle differences and revenue projections.

Performance Metrics in General

The intent of performance metrics is to monitor progress toward goals. Metrics tell the story of what was expected to happen versus what actually happened. Good performance measures go beyond "a numbers game." They should be put in context so that others within the organization, including volunteer leaders, can understand the reasons behind the results, whether positive or negative. Good performance measurements must be:

- Credible and backed by data.

- Useful to the membership department and senior management.

- Easily understandable by volunteers and other staff.

- Attributable—where did the information come from?

- Accurate—your data sources should be audited periodically.

- Balanced—look at data in several different ways. As an example, look at average renewal rate across all members, but look at renewal rates by member segment.

Financial Metrics

Performance measurement consists of two classes of metrics: operational effectiveness/efficiency and measuring mission attainment. This chapter concentrates on metrics relating to inputs, activities, processes, and outputs, that is, operational measurements. But we have a few words to say on trends for the future later in the chapter.

Historical (and Still Useful!) Metrics

Acquisition Metrics—How Much Does It Cost to Acquire a New Member?

New members contribute to the financial health of any membership organization. But it's important to understand how much acquiring new members is costing the organization. Many membership departments adhere to the belief that it is cheaper to keep members than to acquire them. While digital and social marketing tactics may appear to require fewer resources and cost less than direct mail or print advertising,

Table 16.1. Calculating Gross Acquisition Costs from a Direct Mail Campaign

Key Information	Costs
Total costs of direct mail campaign	$4,825.92
Number of new members	120
Campaign cost	$40.21 per member
Fulfillment cost	$3.50 per member
Average Acquisition Cost	**$43.71**

there are still costs associated with digital and social marketing, such as staff time to develop messaging and costs associated with the software. See Table 16.1 for how to calculate these costs.

Terms to Know and Understand

- Acquisition costs are considered on a per member basis.
- Fixed costs do not change based on volume. As an example, the creative fees associated with developing the artwork or messages will not change based on volume.
- Variable costs will change by type of campaign. Examples of variable costs are list acquisition, postage, printing and mailing services. and paper.
- Average acquisition costs are total acquisition costs divided by the number of members who respond to your campaign.
- Net acquisition costs factor in members who request a refund, or do not ultimately pay their full dues amount.
- Fulfillment costs are costs associated with welcoming the new member. Examples of fulfillment costs include membership cards, welcome letters (paper/printing), and postage.

Cost to Serve a Member

The cost to serve a member is an important calculation when considering the setting and maintaining or raising of membership dues. At a minimum, the following expenses must be included in the calculation (see the examples in Tables 16.2 and 16.3):

- List acquisition
- Expenses related to member publications and communications
- Membership staff (and member service) salaries, benefits, and training
- Call center support if outsourced
- Communication expenses (web and email marketing automation, including email and website landing pages)
- Research relating directly to membership, such as member satisfaction or needs surveys

Table 16.2. Example 1: Costs to Serve Members

Direct Membership Costs	$250,000
Number of Members	1,500
Basic Cost to Serve Members (Direct costs/# of members)	$167
Dues	$180
Relationship Between Dues and Cost to Serve	$13

Table 16.3. Example 2: Cost to Serve Members

Direct and Indirect Membership Costs	$500,000
Number of Members	1,500
Broader Cost to Serve Members	$333
Dues	$180
Relationship Between Dues and Cost to Serve	($153)

Organizations can adjust the cost to serve a member by allocating a portion of rent, general/administrative, executive salaries, and governance expense.

Caution: Have a Clear Understanding of What Is Truly Related to Serving Members vs. Overhead

Whether or not to have dues level cover the full cost to serve members is a strategic decision to be made by the organization's leaders. When dues do not cover the costs to serve members, then non-dues revenue will be needed to ensure the organization's continued financial viability. This metric will vary widely by organization type (professional, trade, or philanthropic). In a typical professional organization, a commonly accepted cost-to-serve ratio should be no more than 50 percent of your dues.

Cost to Renew a Member

The cost to renew a member is significantly less than the cost to acquire a member. Why? In acquisition, you spend resources to identify prospects and create content. But the biggest variable is the response rate. Current, especially engaged, members have a much higher propensity to respond. Current members are also much more responsive to email-centric strategies. But you do have to apply the same methodology to determine your cost to renew as you do to your cost to acquire. Factors to be considered are:

- Graphic design
- Incentives
- Print costs
- Postage

- Mail services
- Email software/services
- Database management
- Call center
- Staff time

Tip: If resources are limited, focus on your renewal strategies, FIRST!

Return on Investment (ROI)

For membership professionals, return on investment (ROI) is most commonly applied when looking at acquisition metrics. ROI formulas can and should be applied to renewals and to programs and services such as conferences and publications. ROI is the ratio between expense and revenue. Examining ROI is the first step in the determination of whether a program/service should be continued or not.

Lifetime Value of a Member

Lifetime value of a member (LTV) is a critical metric. LTV estimates a member's *financial* contribution to the organization over the life of his or her membership. It is a fair measure of the member's financial contribution because it takes into consideration dues and non-dues income. The data points you need to calculate LTV are:

- *Dues level.* If you have multi-level dues and member categories, you can do separate LTV calculations for each member type. Or you can average the dues level by multiplying the number of members (at each level) by their dues, totaling those numbers, and dividing by the total number of members.

- *Average member tenure.* This is the average number of years a member stays with the organization, by dues category or audience segment.

- *Total non-dues revenue.* This may include conference registrations, publication sales, advertising, sponsorship revenue, and any fees from affinity relationships.

- *Cost to serve a member.* See the earlier section in this chapter.

One of the barriers frequently heard is that the association management system (AMS) will not provide these data points. This is an important consideration in the selection of a new AMS or an upgrade to an existing AMS. Related terminology is spelled out in Table 16.4. A sample calculation is provided in Table 16.5.

What Does the LTV Calculation Tell You?

LTV helps you determine how much you can spend to acquire new members because it allows you to view your break-even point. What should your LTV look like? LTV is dependent on the relationship between the dues amount and the amount members contribute as a result of participation in the associations' programs and services. For a professional organization, it should be 7 to 10 times your annual dues amount.

Table 16.4. Terminology Relating to Lifetime Value of a Member

Measurement	How to Calculate
Lifetime Dues Value of a Member	Annual dues per member times average member tenure
Annual Non-Dues Revenue/ Member	Total non-dues revenue divided by the number of members
Lifetime Non-Dues Value of a Member	Annual non-dues revenue divided by number of members times average member tenure
Gross Lifetime Value of a Member	Lifetime dues value plus lifetime non-dues value
Lifetime Cost to Serve a Member	Annual cost of serving members times average member tenure
Net Lifetime Value of a Member	Gross lifetime value of a member minus lifetime cost to serve member

So what does this tell you? You have a positive relationship between dues charged, non-dues income, and the value of a member during his or her tenure. Get that message out in terms of budgeting for acquisition expense!

Membership Renewal Calculations

Key metrics concerning membership renewals are the "renewal rate" and the "lapse rate." They are the inverse of each other. Renewal rates reflect those who remain with the organization; lapse rates reflect those who do not continue. Retention and

Table 16.5. Example of Lifetime Value Calculation

Number of Members	12,000
Annual Expenses	$4,000,000
Direct Membership Costs	$1,800,000
Average Dues Level	$250
Annual Dues Revenue	$3,000,000
Annual Non-Dues Revenue	$2,000,000
Average Member Tenure	9.5 years
Lifetime Dues Value of a Member	$2,375
Annual Non-Dues Value of a Member	$167
Lifetime Non-Dues Value of a Member	$1,586
Gross Lifetime Value of a Member	$3,961
Annual Cost to Serve Member	$150
Lifetime Cost to Serve Member	$1,425
Net Lifetime Value of a Member	$2,536

renewal often are used interchangeably. Actually, renewal is the process of retaining the member. Along the same lines, invoice and renewal notice are also used interchangeably and incorrectly. Invoices establish an obligation on the part of a purchaser to pay, creating an account receivable. When membership is up for renewal, there is no obligation to pay and therefore no account receivable. A personal bias is that the term invoice really equals a "bill to be paid." Is that really the type of relationship you want to convey to your members—we are bills to be paid?

When Should You Measure Renewal Rates?

At least annually at the beginning of two consecutive periods. Other common measurement times are:

- For anniversary billing cycles, compare this month to the same month last year. Compare this year-to-date to last year-to-date.

- For calendar year billing, examine yearly payers. Who is renewing from which notice?

Other considerations include eliminating members who do not renew because of reasons such as retirement, leaving the profession, death, or because they no longer meet the organization's membership criteria.

Renewal Calculation Example

Assumptions for the example in Table 16.6 are that memberships are billed on a calendar year basis and that membership eligibility is based on full dues payment. New members are prorated and are not paying the full year's dues. On January 1 there were 425,000 members who were paid in full. On December 31 of the same year, there were 405,000 members paid in full. Renewal rate plus lapse rate always equals 100 percent.

Using an "average" renewal rate can mask some serious problems. Table 16.7 outlines an example of the intelligence a segmented renewal can provide. An association has an average renewal rate of 81.64 percent, a number of which their board is very proud. When new members were pulled out of the average rate, the numbers told a much different story. New members were defined as being in the first two years of membership.

Table 16.6. Calculating Renewal Rates

Measurement	How to Calculate
Renewal Rate: 95.29%	Divide current number of paid members at the beginning of the period (BOP) by the number of paid members at the end of the period (EOP).
Lapse Rate: 4.71 %	Subtract members at EOP from members at BOP; then divide by number of members at BOP.

Table 16.7. Segmented Renewal Rate: Examining by Tenure

Total Number of Members	25,000
Number of New Members	3,000
Tenured Members	22,000
Total Number Renewing Members	20,410
Average Renewal Rate	81.64%
New Members Renewing	1,050
Tenured Members Renewing	19,360
New Member Renewal Rate	35%
Tenured Member Renewal Rate	88%

This data illustrates new members are not renewing at anywhere near the level of tenured members. Membership professionals can use this information to examine the flow of communications to new members, as well as the content of those communications. Perhaps a different engagement strategy is warranted.

Other elements on which to examine a segmented renewal rate are:

- Category of member (using ASAE as an example, CEO members, association staff professionals, industry partners, and consultants)

- Geography (Texas Society of Association Executives segments renewal rates by those members living in Austin, versus those living outside of Austin)

- For trade organizations, type/size/budget of member organizations

---

What Should Your Renewal Rate Look Like?

The answer is—it depends. Renewal rates can be impacted by:
- The economy
- Dues increases
- World events such as natural disaster and terrorist attacks
- (For trade organizations) mergers/acquisitions in your industry
- (For trade organizations) regulatory change
- (For professional organizations) aging of your members
- (For professional organizations) changes in your profession

Bottom line, developing renewal trend data will help you quickly identify problems and negative trends and take actions to remedy them.

Tracking and Presenting Metrics

Dashboards are a commonly used tool helping staff and boards organize and understand data regarding associations' performance. Dashboards can track metrics over time (such as new and renewing members) or they can provide a broader picture of a snapshot in time. Dashboards tell a story to the readers, offering them the data in a visual presentation that is easy to understand.

American Academy of Pediatrics: Rebuilding Our Membership Dashboard

By Melissa Walling, IOM, CAE

The American Academy of Pediatrics is a 64,000 member professional association with a charitable mission to advance children's health. With an increasing number of members working in larger healthcare institutions and specializing to increase their knowledge and earning power, it was imperative that we take a fresh look at the definition of membership growth. Also, with increasingly busy volunteers, we needed to build an easy-to-interpret membership dashboard that clearly and succinctly articulated our membership story. Decision-makers need to be able to quickly digest membership metrics to make informed business decisions in this dynamic environment.

Our first step in building a dashboard was to ask staff, the board, and other volunteers the following:

- What influences membership growth (e.g., retention and recruitment)?
- Are there other vital signs of membership health (e.g., diversity or demographics)?

While these questions seemed simple, they generated diverse opinions on the membership environment of our organization. We next identified which of these metrics we could accurately define and track and then got to the fun part—building the dashboards.

While some associations have one membership dashboard, we realized that our member groups need different information, so we created two primary dashboards. Since some metrics held value for staff, others for volunteers, and some for both, having multiple dashboards provided us the flexibility we needed. For example, the board of directors has a fiduciary responsibility and should review dues trends and needs to be able to closely track membership data, whereas a national committee may only need to understand the composition and diversity of membership at a certain point and doesn't need to track or monitor this information. We therefore developed two primary dashboards to meet these needs:

- A membership infographic (Figure 16.1) that visually shows the diversity of our members by membership categories and demographics at a certain period in time.
- A membership dashboard for our board of directors (Figure 16.2) that aligns with strategic priorities and is better used as a tracking tool to monitor trends. Including visual images like graphs and arrows helps volunteers understand trends.

We used a variety of tools such as spreadsheets, charts, images, and data visualization software to build our dashboards. The goal was to highlight only the critical metrics for each group to tell our membership story quickly, efficiently, and visually. We didn't want to burden our volunteers with sorting through unnecessary information to find the highlights and trends but instead clearly outline key information. And we want the dashboards to evolve over time so we have empowered our volunteers and staff to give us regular feedback on what they need to do their jobs better. Ultimately, the membership dashboard should be a key tool in helping volunteers and staff support the membership goals of the association and make knowledge-based decisions.

Figure 16.1. Sample Membership Infographic

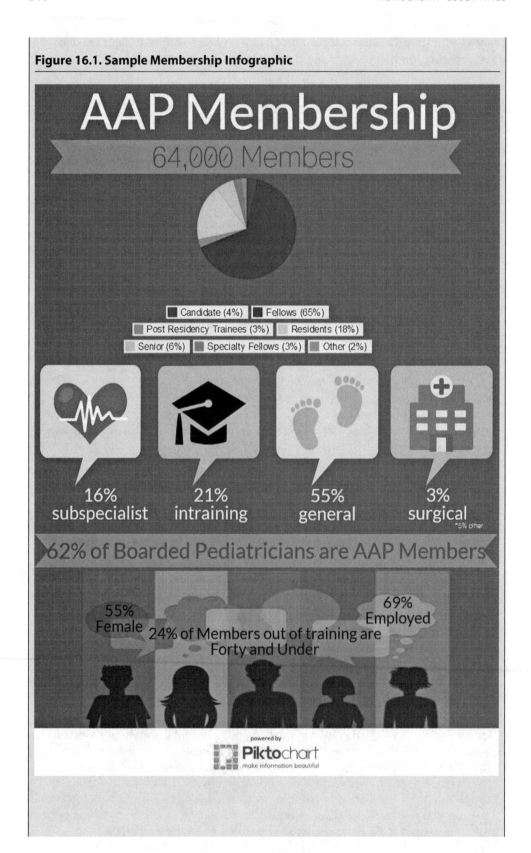

See Figures 16.2, 16.3, 16.4, and 16.5 for different ways to look at your data and remember to include targets

Figure 16.2. AAP Membership Counts January 1, 20xx

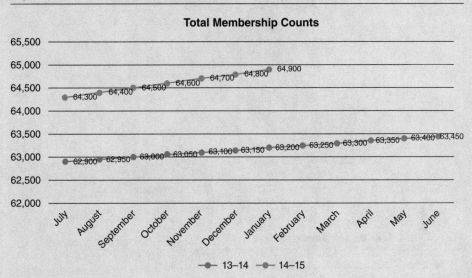

Membership Count	64,000
Voting Members	48,000
YTD Renewal Rate for Voting Fellows: 85.4%	*85.4% (on track with previous year)*

*Membership metrics have been modified for the purposes of publication.

Membership Count Dashboard					
	1/1/2013	1/1/2014	1/1/2015	3 year Average	% Variance from Average
Fellows	40,000	41,000	42,000	41,000 ⬆	2.44%
Specialty Fellows	3,000	3,500	4,000	3,500 ⬆	14.29%
Seniors	4,000	5,000	6,000	5,000 ⬆	20.00%
Associates	100	100	100	100 ⬆	0.00%
Candidates	4,000	5,500	5,000	4,833 ⬆	3.45%
International	500	600	700	600 ⬆	16.67%
National Affiliate	100	150	200	150 ⬆	33.33%
Post Residency Trainees	2,000	1,000	1,500	1,500 ⬆	0.00%
Residents	8,000	6,000	5,000	6,333 ⬇	-21.05%
Other*	300	350	400	350 ⬆	14.29%
Total:	62,000	63,200	64,900	63,367 ⬆	2.42%

*this includes honorary and corresponding fellows

Figure 16.3. Total Market Share

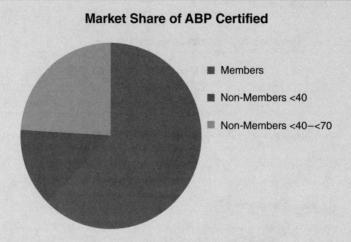

2015 ABP Market Share: 65 percent (*same as previous year*)

Figure 16.4. Sub-Board Market Share

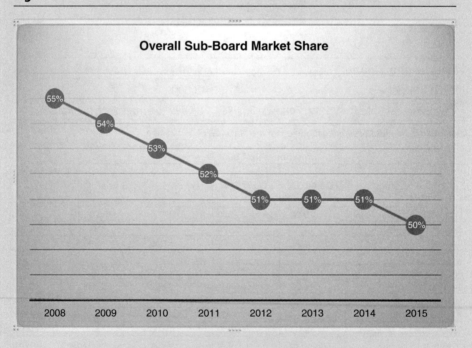

2015 ABP Sub-Board Market Share: 50 percent (*decline from previous year*)

Figure 16.5. Early Career Retention Conversion Rate for 2014 Graduating Residents

June 30, 2015 Goal: 53.00 percent

January 1, 2015: 48.12 percent

January 1, 2014: 47.05 percent

Trending Metrics: Things to Think About

Historically, metrics most commonly track financial performance, but they are being expanded to non-financial performance.

Member Engagement

Increasingly, organizations are seeing the value of tracking member engagement. We know that a more engaged member is most likely to renew, to volunteer, and to become a promoter of the organization. The basic tracking of engagement begins with transactional tracking such as:

- E-newsletter open rates
- Purchases (frequency, type, amount)
- Program attendance
- Credential/certification acquisition
- Unique web page hits
- Participation in list serves or online communities
- Length of membership
- Volunteer activity

Organizations commonly assign values to elements and create indices. A more cutting-edge process looks at engagement through the lens of value provided to members (as defined by members). Bill Lee writes in his book, *The Hidden Wealth of Customers*, engagement programs often fail because the organization has a limited goal "to induce customers to buy more stuff." We also see the opposite . . . that membership organizations are content to have large numbers of what we term "checkbook" members.

Social Return on Investment

Social return on investment (SROI) is used to measure performance against the social or member focused mission of the organization. SROI is outcome focused. Outcomes can be related to social structures, the economy, and the environment. There are two types of SROI: evaluative and forecast. *Evaluative* SROI is retrospective, based on activities that have already taken place. *Forecast* SROI predicts how much social value will be created if activities meet their intended outcomes. There are four main elements to include in measuring SROI:

- *Inputs*—resources invested in your activity (such as the costs of running a program)
- *Outputs*—the direct and tangible products from the activity (such as the number of people receiving a certification)
- *Outcomes*—the changes people are reporting from the activity (such as better/new jobs, better income, improved quality of life)
- *Impact*—the outcome less an estimate of what would have happened anyway (for example, if 10 people were to find new jobs, but 3 would have anyway, the impact is based on the 7 people who found jobs as a result of a job readiness program)

> ## Exhibit 16.1. Social Return on Investment Case Study
>
> KaBOOM! is a national nonprofit dedicated to giving all kids the childhood they deserve, filled with balanced and active play, so they can thrive. For almost two decades, their mission has been to create play spaces with Community Partners. In 2013, KaBOOM! expanded their mission and adopted a new strategy: to catalyze and create great places to play, empower advocates to promote and protect play, and elevate public discourse around the importance of play. They set out to prove that play can help tackle a number of urgent issues plaguing our society—especially those endemic among low income communities. Only one in four children gets 60 minutes of physical activity or play daily. As play has decreased, obesity rates and behavioral/cognitive disorders have increased. In their annual report, KaBOOM! noted:
>
> > We created and catalyzed others' work to create great places to play. KaBOOM! led 165 playground builds, engaging 36,316 volunteers who contributed 218,000 hours of service to communities in 37 states, D.C., Puerto Rico, Canada, and Mexico. All to serve more than 303,000 children. We provided 631 local, community organizations with a total of $3,972,500 to assist with the construction of 125 new play spaces, to maintain and improve 520 existing play spaces, and to help open 131 otherwise locked playgrounds for broader community use. These projects served an estimated 558,100 children and engaged 14,703 volunteers.

Budgeting as It Relates to the Membership Function

Membership professionals play a key role in the development of the organization's budget.

Accounting Methods

One of the first things with which to acquaint yourself is the type of accounting method your organization uses: cash basis or accrual. The difference is the timing when the revenue or expense is recognized.

Cash Basis

Cash accounting is based on real time cash flow. Income is recorded when it is received and expenses when they are paid.

Accrual Basis

Accrual accounting records income when it is earned. Likewise, expenses are recorded when the obligation is made, not when you pay the bill.

Hybrid

Less frequently, associations take a hybrid approach to accounting, using the accrual basis of accounting but recoding membership revenue on a cash basis and deferring the income throughout the year. Or your organization might accept partial dues payments. The balance due is recorded as accounts receivable. Accrual basis is considered to be a best practice for membership organizations.

Terminology and Practice

Deferred Income

Using a dues payment as an example, some organizations recognize the total dues payment in the month in which it is received. Others use a deferral system where one-twelfth of the income is recorded each month. This is important when working with multiple-year memberships or life memberships.

Audit

While Sarbanes-Oxley does not directly apply to nonprofit organizations, many associations have voluntarily complied with some of its requirements. An external audit provides your board and members confidence that the assets of the association are being properly handled. During an audit, usually a random selection of membership payments are chosen and tracked back through the dues payment processing.

Internal Controls

Segregation of duties or accounting controls is necessary to avoid any appearance of mismanagement or the possibility of theft. For example, payments are received in the accounting department and a batching process records the receipts. The same person does not create invoices, enter payments, and post payments to the general ledger. A person from membership performs data entry of payments, while another records the batch as being complete.

Calendar Year vs. Anniversary Year Billing Cycle Differences

If your association operates on a calendar year, budgeting and invoicing are tied to the beginning of the year, and all members are on the same annual cycle. Anniversary year is tied to when the member joined the organization. Things to consider are noted in Table 16.8.

Table 16.8. Considerations for Billing Cycle

Calendar Year	Administrative process is compact.
	Need to manage a large influx of cash at one point in the year.
	Payment processing delays may occur, with adverse member reaction.
Anniversary Year	Invoicing is spread throughout the year.
	Less complicated to staff because it is a function throughout the year.

Changing from one process to the other requires extensive analysis and adherence to process. It's not a decision to be taken lightly!

Projecting Revenue

Your projections regarding revenue will be the foundation for the association's overall budget. Working with anniversary billing is more complex, because renewal/lapse decisions occur monthly. If your organization has multiple dues levels, that too increases your projection's complexity!

Our sample association in Table 16.9 has an anniversary billing cycle. There are three types of members: professional members, student members, and supplier members, all with differing dues levels and retention rates.

Using this data and Excel, you can project revenue as follows in Table 16.10.

Table 16.9. Example Data

Member Type	Total Members	Retention Rate	Dues Amount
Professional Members	10,000	75%	$250
Student Members	4,000	90%	$10
Supplier Members	2,500	60%	$300

Table 16.10. Sample Quarterly Budget Projection

Month	Category	# Members	Retention	Dues Level	Total Dues	Projection	Budget Recognition
Jan	Professional	600	75%	$250	$112,500	$ 9,338	December
	Student	100	90%	$10	$900	$75	December
	Supplier	45	60%	$300	$8,100	$672	December
Feb	Professional	300	75%	$250	$56,250	$4,669	January
	Student	0	90%	$10	$ —	$ —	January
	Supplier	150	60%	$300	$27,000	$2,241	January
Mar	Professional	75	75%	$250	$14,063	$1,167	February
	Student	0	90%	$10	$ —	$ —	February
	Supplier	300	60%	$300	$54,000	$4,482	February
First Quarter	All	1,570		$1,680	$272,813	$22,643	

Note: The projections in this table are total dues times the decimal equivalent of 1/12 or .083. Depending on how far you extend .0833333333 or how you round up/down dollars, your projections may differ slightly.

Revenue Mix

Revenue mix is the balance between the level of dues revenue and revenues coming from various programs and services. Membership professionals should understand the concept, because it can alert them to potential problems. Reviewing revenue mix is an important part of budgeting and should be examined at least annually. The percentage of dues to total revenue mix will vary widely between professional and trade organizations.

Terminology

Non-Dues Revenue

Any activity generating revenue for the association (other than dues). Examples of non-dues revenue are:

- Sponsorships
- Exhibit booth fees
- Conference registrations
- Publication sales
- Advertising
- Affinity program royalties
- In-kind donations

In larger associations, management of non-dues revenue may fall outside the membership department. It is important for membership professionals to understand how membership dues fit into the larger financial picture.

Unrelated Business Income Tax (UBIT)

The Internal Revenue Service (IRS) has created a complex set of rules surrounding UBIT. If the association does not comply with UBIT reporting, its tax-exempt status can be at risk. Income from affinity programs and portions of advertising revenue are generally considered UBIT. ASAE's *Association Law Book* (5th ed.) and the *ASAE Handbook of Professional Practices in Association Management* are excellent resources for more detailed information.

Communicating How Membership Dollars Are Spent

It is increasingly more common for members to question how their organization manages its resources. Below is a sample graph.

Figure 16.6. How Membership Dues Are Spent

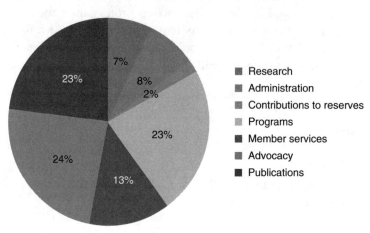

How Membership Dues Are Spent

■ Research
■ Administration
■ Contributions to reserves
▨ Programs
■ Member services
■ Advocacy
■ Publications

The membership function is both an art and a science. People entering our profession can be quite excited about the "creative" part of the job but neglect the quantifiable element. Becoming a membership expert is a process involving trial and error and evaluation. By having a clear understanding of how these metrics are calculated and what they tell you, you will be in a much better position to be proactive in developing strategies as they relate to membership acquisition and retention. Tools such as dashboards can help you establish consensus among your leadership as to how strategies will be evaluated.

Additional Resources and Suggested Reading

Bowman, Susanne Connors, Haefer, Wayne F., & Blanken, Rhea. *New Realities Existing Within Converging Trends: The Future Is Now*. Washington, DC: ASAE Foundation, January 2014. http:///www.asaecenter.org/foundation2/downloads/haeferBlankenreport.pdf

Caraveli, Anna, & Engel, Elizabeth Weaver. *Leading Engagement from the Outside In: Become an Indispensable Partner in Your Members' Success*. Monmouth Junction, NJ: Spark Consulting, May 2015. http://www.getmespark.com.

Epstein, Marc J., & Buhovac, Adriana Rejc. *Performance Measurement of Not-for-Profit Organizations*. Mississauga, ONT, and Washington, DC: The Society of Management Accountants of Canada and the American Institute of Certified Public Accountants, 2009.

Lee, Bill. *The Hidden Wealth of Customers: Realizing the Untapped Value of Your Most Important Asset*. Boston: Harvard Business Review Press, 2012.

Seibert, Larry J. *Measuring Member Engagement*. Anderson, IN: Association Metrics, n.d.

About the Authors

Susanne Connors Bowman, CAE, is co-owner of The Haefer Group, Ltd. Her consulting practice focuses on helping membership organizations evaluate and articulate their value propositions. She has served as the chair of ASAE's Membership and Consultant Section Councils and as the immediate chair of ASAE's Membership Development Committee. She is a current faculty member of ASAE's Center U, teaching membership-related courses.

Sidebar author **Melissa Walling,** IOM, CAE is the director, Division of Membership Services, Data & Analytics, at the American Academy of Pediatrics. She has been working as an association professional since 2005. Her career has been focused on membership, analytics, chapters, and customer service.

Legal Considerations

17

By Jefferson C. Glassie, Esq., FASAE

Membership associations are generally not high-risk organizations. Trade and professional associations and, of course, charitable organizations, are extremely valuable for society and for the industries, professions, and causes they represent. They benefit their stakeholders, the public, and even the economy more than is probably understood. They are not subject to significant liability risks, because they are primarily doing good things and not usually causing damage.

Of utmost importance is their integrity. They must have the trust and confidence of their members, constituencies, and the public to operate successfully. In other words, they must have a respected brand. There are many aspects to this, but one key factor is to act consistently with applicable laws and best practices. An organization that reneges on contracts, fails to make corporate and tax filings, and skirts the law won't be viable for long.

So when considering some of the essential membership considerations for associations, legal issues are important. Association executives, especially those who hold or aspire to the Certified Association Executive (CAE) credential, must be aware of the gamut of concerns from a legal perspective when managing their organizations.

We're going to cover some important legal issues related to membership in this chapter, including corporate, tax exemption, antitrust, due process, and intellectual property, although some other chapters may also touch on these legal points.

Corporate

Most associations are nonstock corporations, meaning they have no stock or equity shares. Thus, there really are no owners of an association. Many have said that the members are the owners of an association, and that may be true from the practical perspective that members usually elect the board of directors and have the ultimate say-so about the purpose of the association and how it is operated. Members have no rights to the assets of a nonstock association, however, so they are not legal owners. If tax exempt, the Internal Revenue Code (Code), regulations, and rulings by the Internal Revenue Service (IRS) clearly hold that members can't simply divvy up all the assets of the corporation if dissolved, but remaining assets must be distributed to another tax-exempt organization.

Most associations are also nonprofit (or not-for-profit, which terms are basically interchangeable) corporations, which means they must have a nonprofit, rather than a commercial profit-making, purpose. Traditionally, members of an association view this as important, because they want to contribute their resources to an organization dedicated to the good of the industry, profession, or public, rather than for private gain. However, the Internet age has brought a new mindset to many about what they want to receive from an association. Many now don't seem to care about the nonprofit (or even tax-exempt) status of an association, as opposed to the benefits they can receive, many of which may be readily available online from other sources. These issues obviously pose challenges to associations because potential members may be able to obtain similar benefits elsewhere.

The typical governing documents for an incorporated association are articles of incorporation, which are filed with state authorities to set up the corporation, and bylaws, which are the internal governing rules of the organization. The articles are like a contract with the state, under which the state confers limited liability protection in return for following the corporate law, and bylaws are like a contract with the members. The articles often state whether the corporation will have voting members or not, but it is advisable to have most details about membership in the bylaws. Generally, basic membership classifications, eligibility, voting rights, and other privileges will be set forth in the bylaws. It is not unusual to have certain classes of members with the right to vote, typically the active or main members, and other classes without the right to vote, such as suppliers or students, for example.

In the traditional model, members with voting rights elect the board of directors and officers. There are variations on this and, nowadays, it's common to see nominating committees propose a single slate of candidates for approval by the members to identify the best candidates and avoid electioneering that can cause division and dissension among the membership. In addition to voting, members also have the power under state laws to approve amendments to articles of incorporation, mergers, transfers of all or substantially all the assets of the association, and dissolution.

Typically, members also have the right to amend bylaws, although this is generally not mandated by state law. Many associations allow the board of directors to amend the bylaws, which can be more efficient as a practical matter. It is sometimes difficult for associations to achieve the requisite number of members voting, particularly if the quorum stated in the bylaws is relatively high. This is the reason a low quorum for membership votes is often advisable (as low as the corporate statute allows, which could be 2 percent or 5 percent, or in some cases, however many members show up).

Under most state laws, members are able to vote in person at a meeting or by proxy (which generally can be electronic). Members are also typically permitted to participate in a meeting and vote by conference call, where all can simultaneously hear one another. Some state laws allow members to vote by ballot without a meeting, including electronically. And a number of states otherwise permit votes by members without a meeting, but may require unanimity or perhaps over 50 percent of the members voting. (Unanimous written consent is typically permitted for voting by boards of directors, although it can be difficult to obtain votes all in favor from all directors. Note that member voting is generally more flexible than board voting, because directors have fiduciary duties to deliberate, and the law frowns on directors managing organizations or companies without such deliberation, either in person or telephone/video conferences. This is also why proxy voting by directors is generally not permitted.)

Associations often are structured on a regional basis, with components (chapters or affiliates) at the local, state, or regional level. Seats in a house of delegates or on the board may be allocated to components for selection. Generally, the membership requirements and classes of components will be similar to the national association, although not always. Membership in a component is sometimes required for national membership (note, this should not be an antitrust problem, as discussed below). Dues may be payable to the national association or to the component, or separately payable to each. Components are generally separately incorporated and will either have their own tax status or be part of a group exemption under the national association. Sometimes, tax status will be different depending on the situation, but components usually have the same tax exemption status as the national association. Components can be valuable for membership engagement and to help further the national association's mission.

The board of directors of an association has the ultimate authority to manage the association, including usually setting dues for members and approving the budget. The board also usually has the right to discipline members, including terminate members for bad conduct or violation of law or a code of ethics. Such actions are subject to due process principles and potentially antitrust law, as discussed below.

Tax Exemption

Most nonprofit membership associations are also exempt from federal income taxation. They must be organized and operated for stated public purposes to achieve tax exemption. The two main Code sections under which associations gain exemption typically are 501(c)(6) and 501(c)(3). The former are described as business leagues, chambers of commerce, and similar organizations, and most trade and professional associations will be eligible for exemption under section 501(c)(6). Charitable organizations are described under section 501(c)(3). Usually, 501(c)(6) associations will have members, but it is not required. Section 501(c)(3) organizations often don't have members, but certainly they can, and there are many 501(c)(3) membership associations.

Dues paid to 501(c)(6) associations will generally be tax deductible to members as ordinary and necessary business expenses under Section 162 of the Code, as are other expenses of a member in attending association conferences and meetings, purchasing publications, and so forth. However, amounts paid to a 501(c)(6) organization are not deductible as charitable contributions; only amounts contributed as donations to 501(c)(3) charitable organizations are so deductible. But payments for meetings, educational publications, and such to charities also may be deductible as ordinary and necessary business expenses, as applicable.

Dues paid by members to 501(c)(6) associations that lobby or engage in political activities are non-deductible to the extent of the proportional lobbying and political expenditures by the association. Such associations must provide notice to members of the percentage of lobbying expenses and advise that such percentage of dues is not deductible. As an alternative to giving members this notice of non-deductibility, such associations may elect to pay a "proxy" tax at the highest corporate rate on the amount of lobbying and political expenses.

501(c)(6) associations may conduct unlimited lobbying, operate political action committees, and engage in political campaign activities. Section 501(c)(3) organizations may only conduct minimal lobbying, although they may make the 501(h) election to permit more government relations activity under specific expenditure amounts. Note that 501(c)(3) organizations may not conduct any political campaign activity; the IRS has a zero tolerance policy on political activity by charities.

Neither type of organization is permitted to allow "private inurement" (gain) to those in positions of influence with the organization. Of course, however, such exempt organizations may pay reasonable value for products or services rendered, including to members or even officers or directors (although most volunteers are not paid compensation for their services to the association). If payments are made to such "insiders" of 501(c)(3) organizations, there are specific safe harbor rules promulgated by the IRS to ensure any payments are reasonable and consistent with market value. So payments to officers, directors, and staff in certain executive positions (CEOs, CFOs, etc.) may have to be approved by members of the board or executive committee without conflicts of interest upon review of comparability data ensuring market payments and memorialization of the vote in meeting minutes.

Further, tax-exempt organizations do have to pay tax on net revenue received from unrelated business activities. This tax, referred to as the unrelated business income tax (UBIT), is applicable to activities generating revenues, such as advertising or individual/consulting services, where the underlying activity is regularly carried on, unrelated to the exempt purpose, and constitutes a trade or business. An excessive amount of UBIT, perhaps 40 percent or more of an organization's revenue, could threaten tax-exempt status. Some associations with significant non-exempt activities, such as marketing and affinity programs, set up a separate corporate subsidiary to conduct such activities.

Tax-exempt organizations are required to submit annual reports on Form 990 to the IRS (either the full form or a short form 990-EZ or postcard, depending on the financial size of the organization). UBIT is reported on the Form 990-T. A discussion about the Form 990 is beyond the scope of this chapter, but it is important to know that the Form 990 for the prior three years, as well as the organization's tax exemption application and IRS determination letter, must be made available to anyone in the public (not just members) upon request. This is distinct from state corporate laws that typically require that certain books and records, including minutes, membership lists, and financial information, be provided to members (not the general public) who may request such information.

Associations that have tax-exempt status are advised to be knowledgeable about the Code and IRS rules to preserve and protect this beneficial status.

Antitrust

The antitrust laws apply to associations in several significant ways. The U.S. government, represented by either the Department of Justice (DOJ) or the Federal Trade Commission (FTC), can enforce the antitrust laws, and there are also private rights of action, so that individuals or organizations can bring suit also and collect damages (often tripled in antitrust cases). Most executives are aware of the prohibitions on price fixing, which are per se illegal under the antitrust laws. While only actual agreements to set, raise, or lower prices are technical violations, even implied agreements or evidence of parallel action can constitute violations, too. For this reason, most associations have antitrust policies that prohibit members from even discussing prices, fees, salaries, and so forth at association meetings or social media.

In addition, the antitrust laws prohibit "boycotts," referred to as concerted refusals to deal with another or only on certain terms. If association members agree not to do business with certain companies, such as suppliers or retailers, that could be considered a boycott, which also can be per se illegal. Even if the association was not part of the agreement, if the members made their agreements at an association meeting or using association media or resources, the association itself could be implicated. As a result, most associations also include prohibitions on discussions about specific competitors, suppliers, retailers, and others in their antitrust policies.

Rejecting a person, company, or firm for membership, or revoking membership also can be alleged to be a violation of the antitrust law on the basis of a boycott. Discipline of a member, or a certificate of a certification program or an accredited entity, also could bring antitrust boycott claims. Providing adequate due process, as discussed below, can help ameliorate the likelihood of such claims. Note that agreements to divide or allocate markets among members also can give rise to antitrust concerns.

Sometimes associations also require membership in order to obtain a product or service, such as certification or a valuable report. These restrictive policies can also be challenged as boycotts, or as tying arrangements (requiring product/service A to get product/service B). It's fine to have certain "members only" sites or benefits, but the general rule of thumb under the antitrust laws is that non-members should have access to association products and services (especially those that are valuable), but may be charged a higher fee, as long as it is not so high as to compel membership. It is important for associations to be cautious when excluding a person, company, or firm from membership, revoking membership, or requiring membership to obtain certain products or services. Note that integrated associations that require membership also in a component, as discussed above, generally are not viewed as problems under the antitrust laws, because of the procompetitive effects of such tiered memberships.

Finally, dissemination of data about members and prices, salaries, costs, expenses, or fees must be carefully controlled for antitrust purposes. Survey reports on such information can be disseminated, but the FTC and DOJ have promulgated "safety zones" to avoid distribution of data that might be used to inappropriately lead to price fixing. The safety zones require that such price and fee related data be compiled by a third party (which can include an association), be at least three months old, and that there be at least five providers reporting data, with no individual provider's data representing more than 25 percent of that statistic, and any information sufficiently aggregated so that it would not allow recipients to identify the prices charged by any individual provider. Following the safe harbor provisions for price, salary, or fee-related surveys is a best practice for associations.

Due Process

Association membership is a privilege, not a right. There can be situations in which membership is extremely important, which can exacerbate antitrust problems. In addition to antitrust claims by individuals who may be denied membership or those whose membership is revoked, legal challenges can also be brought by such persons or entities on the basis of common law fairness principles, generally referred to as "due process." These claims can allege substantive due process violations, meaning the membership requirement or criteria are not fair or are too restrictive. Such claims would generally be difficult to bring, as membership criteria are usually reasonable and tailored so that members will be aligned with the association's mission.

More important, however, is procedural due process. The key elements of due process are notice of the reasons for the action or the charge, an opportunity to respond, a fair and impartial decision-maker, and usually the opportunity to appeal the action to a separate body within the association. Denials of membership don't require extensive due process, because the applicant has not obtained membership yet. Once a member, however, there may be a more legitimate claim that a right is being taken away, which requires more thorough due process procedures. Discipline of a member for violation of a code of ethics or conduct also should be conducted consistent with due process principles. For a certification or accreditation program, where the designation granted is considered to be a right, revoking the designation mandates substantial due process. The nuances of due process requirements are complex and beyond the scope of this chapter.

Membership Information

In the Internet age, information is plentiful and easy to access. Private companies accumulate myriad data for marketing purposes, but associations also are in the data business. More and more, data drives association strategic decisions, and all this data becomes valuable. There are risks with acquiring, using, and holding data, however, and here are some things for executives to think about.

A lot of the information that associations compile does not generally give rise to legal issues. Data on business, sales, products, and services in the profession or industry is not likely to evoke legal privacy concerns. Data obtained from members for statistical and research purposes usually is disseminated only in aggregate form. There are a few reasons for this. Of course, such data is confidential to the companies, who do not want their private information revealed to competitors and others. As mentioned above, dissemination of price- and fee-related data gives rise to antitrust issues.

Specific types of information may fall within the protections of certain federal laws. For example, information about patients is covered by the Health Insurance Portability and Accountability Act (HIPAA) and restricted for unauthorized disclosure. Information about financial transactions is protected by the Gramm-Leach-Bliley Act. And there are federal statutes that protect information about children. These laws affect personal information on a vertical basis and, unless an association has such information, these laws likely will not be applicable.

There is concern, however, about personal information that can be used for nefarious purposes if disclosed without authorization, such as identify theft, cyber crime, or other illegal goals. Many states have laws that restrict use, access, and dissemination of "personally identifiable information" (PII). PII is information that can be used to identify, contact, or locate a person. This may include a person's name in combination with his or her Social Security number, driver's license number, bank account information, credit or debit card number, or taxpayer identification number. In some states, such as California and Florida, the definition of PII is even broader.

If an association only holds basic publicly available information like name, company, title, office address, phone number, or email, that information is generally not considered sensitive PII. This information may be available publicly in association directories or websites, or used or even rented in the form of mail or email lists (for example, for use in affinity programs). While it is advisable that an association have permission to use or rent member or other lists from the individual (which permission might be included in membership applications, renewals, or invoices), the use of such data does not raise significant legal issues. There should be an agreement in place to state the accepted uses of any lists or similar information. It is not the case that an association legally owns such data, because it is typically not subject to copyright protection, being just facts, but if an association has the data, it should control access to it. If the association has PII, however, it must take diligent steps to protect such information to avoid not only problems for the individuals whose data might be released or accessed, but also to minimize legal liability to the association.

There is no law requiring that associations have published privacy policies for their websites, but certainly having such policies in place is a best practice. The FTC has investigated privacy policies and essentially wants those promulgating such policies to ensure they are accurate. The policies should describe what types of information the association collects and how it treats and uses the information.

Associations must be particularly vigilant about PII, because there are many ways in which such information can be hacked, attacked, or even inadvertently disclosed. It is a mistake for association executives to think that only large companies are targeted. Hackers are going after any data they can get their electronic hands on to steal for criminal purposes or so they can install malware on users' computers and take them over. Associations are not immune, and many have been targeted and suffered breaches through malicious hacking, phishing schemes, and other plots. Breaches can also occur when staff members leave computers or personal devices unattended. Some associations have basically given away member lists when simply asked by a spoofer. A word to the wise here: "Plan to fail well." In other words, all organizations should expect to suffer a computer system breach at some point, sooner than later, and must be prepared.

There is no broad federal law covering PII, but many states now have adopted laws regarding security breaches. Since most associations (or certification bodies, which typically accumulate sensitive personal information on certificants) have members from multiple states, they will have to comply with the data breach notification laws for each state in which they have a member. These laws may impose different requirements on when and under what circumstances notification is required, and on the method and the content of the notification. Certain state laws (such as those in Massachusetts and Maryland) now require business organizations, including associations, to design and implement a written information security plan (WISP) in advance for safeguarding PII and certain other data. For this reason, it is imperative that associations proactively take all necessary steps, including developing a WISP, to protect their organizational data and PII before a breach occurs.

Associations should also ensure that they have systems and controls in place to screen suspicious URLs and IP addresses and to block malicious materials. It is important for associations to make sure policies and procedures are also adopted for staff to avoid inadvertent breaches. Training programs to educate staff members about cybersecurity issues and how to protect against lapses (such as clicking on unknown or suspicious links) should be implemented. Staff should also be instructed not to transmit important data without first verifying the identity of the recipient.

Association executives should also make sure the association's insurance policies protect against losses that may arise from cyber-breaches. Policies are available that will cover losses (including attorneys' fees) for responding to third-party claims brought by those whose information may be stolen and also to reimburse for the so-called "first party" costs incurred by the association in providing notification and remedies to those who've been hacked.

There are international implications from use of PII, as well. Any use of a broad category of PII about European residents requires their affirmative consent, or "opt-in," under the European Union policy directive. Such information cannot even be transmitted out of Europe and brought to the United States and held in servers here without consent. Other countries also have cyber-breach laws that would apply in the event of an inadvertent disclosure.

Associations also have to be vigilant about compliance with laws in the United States and elsewhere that attempt to limit unwanted, or spam, emails as well as telephone calls, texts, and faxes. The United States has adopted the CAN SPAM law, which applies to commercial emails and prohibits false or misleading emails (header or subject line information), requires identification of ads, requires disclosure of a physical address, and also requires providing an opt-out from receiving further emails. Relevant to associations, there is an exemption for "transactional" or "relationship" messages that applies to prior transactions or relationships, which should generally include association membership. The FTC is tasked with enforcement of the law, although there is no private right of action. The FTC also enforces the U.S. do-not-call, text, or fax laws, although there are exceptions for certain charities.

Note that other countries often have more strict laws, such as Canada, which requires an affirmative opt-in to send emails to individuals. Also note that there are standards applicable to the secure use of credit card information, known as the Payment Card Industry (PCI) Data Security Standards, and associations should be in compliance if they accept credit card numbers for payment for association products and services.

Intellectual Property

Certain laws and legal principles related to intellectual property relate to association membership. Intellectual property is also referred to as "intangible property." It is not real property (like land) or personal property (like computers, desks, and equipment), but property based on legally created rights and obligations. Associations typically have valuable intellectual property in the form of copyrights (books, journals, newsletters, magazines, white papers, and educational content) and trademarks (the association's name, acronym, logo, and slogans). A patent is another form of intellectual property that grants exclusive rights to the inventor of a product or process, although not many associations have patents. But let's begin the discussion of intellectual property by talking about lists.

Associations typically have lots of lists, such as membership lists, attendee lists, non-member lists, exhibitor lists, potential exhibitor lists, mailing lists, and email lists. These lists are critical for association operations, because they allow associations to communicate broadly to members and others about programs, conferences, products, and services. Proper accumulation, maintenance, and use of lists are important for successful associations.

An interesting fact, however, is that such lists are not considered to be any particular form of intellectual property. In actuality, there is no real ownership of such lists, because—unless comprising PII—most lists are comprised of public information that cannot be legally owned, such as a person's name, company name, address, phone number, or email address. Rather, the information in such lists is controlled, and therein lies the practical right to use the information. An association may compile various types of lists and use them for its own communications purposes or potentially "rent," or license, use of the lists to others on certain terms as a contractual matter.

Some may think lists are subject to copyright protection, but that is generally not the case. Copyright law does not protect ideas or facts, and most lists are simply a compilation of facts. So a member directory, similar to a phone book (remember those?), are not protected by copyright law, and this has been made clear by the courts. One case held that copying and use of the contact information in an association's membership directory without authorization did not constitute a copyright violation. Only if the directory is extremely creative in its design might there be some limited copyright protection. An automated database, where software manipulates the data, may have copyright protection, depending on the facts. Mentioned above was the idea that renting of lists is a contractual matter, so associations can achieve some ability to control use of their lists by entering into contracts with users subject to certain terms and limitations.

In many cases, trademarks will be an association's most valuable property. The name, acronym, and logo of the association represent the brand and integrity of the organization. Members recognize the association's programs, conferences, products, and services through use of the marks. Members may also be permitted to use certain versions of the association's marks to identify themselves as members. In that respect, it may be legally considered a "collective membership mark," which is one of several types of trademarks. Associations must always impose terms and conditions for any use of its marks to preserve the style and quality of the mark, or risk diminished value or losing rights in the marks. Terms and conditions of use can be included on the association's website and contractual enforceability ensured through reference to compliance with association policies on membership applications and dues invoices. While rights to trademarks arise from use in commerce of the marks, enhancing protection through registration through the U.S. Patent and Trademark Office is usually recommended.

As to copyrights generally, the author, artist, photographer, or other creator of the work is the owner of that work. It's just that simple, except that employees automatically transfer rights to any copyrights created within the scope of their employment to their employer (including association employers). So if any members, volunteers, or contractors create copyrighted materials or content to an association, they own the copyright to that content. This means that associations should either obtain a license or assignment of the work from the member, volunteer, or contractor. A license, meaning legal permission, to use a copyrighted work can be oral or implied, but it is always advisable to obtain such a license in writing. Many associations obtain signed license and release forms from member or volunteer authors and contributors. A license is limited, however, so many associations prefer to own the works and therefore would need to obtain a signed written assignment, that is, a transfer, of the copyrighted work to the association. This is generally advisable. The same holds true for contractors and consultants. They own the right to any work they created unless assigned to the association. Registration with the U.S. Copyright Office to enhance legal protections is also advisable, particularly for important works and publications.

Social Media

Finally, one might say that the defining transformation in society has been the Internet and its business, personal, and social aspects. Associations have always been about community. In the past, conversations and communications among members and other constituencies took place in person, by telephone, in print, or by mail. The Internet has transformed the communications among association members and stakeholders. There are legal risks associated with electronic communications and social media. Here are a few key concerns. As discussed above, associations are susceptible to antitrust risks. Emails or social media posts discussing prices, fees, or particular companies or competitors can lead to problems and should be avoided. Also, members and others seem more likely to make critical, disparaging, or impolitic comments online, which give rise to the risk of defamation claims. Some posts also could be considered discriminating, harassing, or otherwise injurious. While these comments are more problematic in the employment context, volunteer leaders can also be subject to employment claims of these types. For all these reasons, associations should have social media policies in place and enforce them. Members or others should not be permitted to make anticompetitive, defamatory, or other offensive comments online on association social media platforms. If they do, their use privileges should be constrained or removed.

About the Author

Jefferson C. Glassie, J.D., is a partner and co-chair of the nonprofit organizations and associations group at Whiteford, Taylor & Preston. He represents associations and nonprofit organizations on a wide range of legal matters, including antitrust, tax, certification, accreditation, contracts, employment, mergers, intellectual property, and corporate issues. He has significant experience in international legal issues and is the author of *International Legal Issues for Nonprofit Organizations*, published by ASAE. He is also co-author with Jerry Jacobs of *Certification and Accreditation Law Handbook* (2nd ed.), and with his partners Eileen Johnson and Dana Lynch of *Intellectual Property for Nonprofit Organizations and Associations*. He has served on several ASAE section councils and committees and is an ASAE Fellow. Email: jglassie@wtplaw.com.

Innovations and Potential Directions for Membership-Based Organizations

18

By Lowell M. Aplebaum, CAE,

Greg Melia, CAE, and

Melody A. Jordan-Carr, MS

Introduction

As previous chapters have detailed, "membership" is an essential component of professional societies, business leagues, and trade associations. Membership typically defines who has a voice in the positions adopted by the organization, the goals it pursues, and who has rights of access and participation. But as we have seen across the globe—in the political revolution of Arab Spring, crowd-funding initiatives like

Kickstarter, engagement platforms like change.org, and fan-selected "all-star" rosters—technology and evolving notions of alternative structures are disrupting traditions and introducing new models for affiliation, participation, and relationships. This chapter looks at a few of the factors driving associations to change and highlights a few examples of associations that are adopting approaches that challenge or reinvent the status quo. Time will tell whether these adaptations survive, but each provides an insight into how an organization can adjust its membership model to survive in a new, more competitive world.

> "It's important to learn the sheet music and the harmonies, but after you've learned them, it's equally important to throw them away."
>
> *John Kao, former Harvard Business School professor, accomplished jazz pianist,*
> *and innovation activist*

ASAE's 2012 Great Ideas Conference

At this point, you've probably invested a good deal of time reading the insights and instruction from the preceding chapters of this book, much of which reflects current approaches to the discipline of membership. As John Kao outlines for jazz musicians, it is equally true that innovation in membership association models can only come when we have learned these approaches in such a way that we can identify viable opportunities to riff on traditional precepts. So what are the elements of the traditional association membership model?

- Membership for either individuals (professional societies) or companies (trade associations).

- Serving a professional or industry niche, typically defined by an individual's predominant role or an organization's primary function.

- Dues paid on an annual basis (whether calendar or anniversary).

- Dues schedules, in which members pay dues based on an established matrix defined by characteristics such as position level or salary for professional societies, or revenue, production levels, or FTEs for trade associations.

- Relatively uniform rights and benefits for all members, including discount levels, committee service, website access, mailed materials, etc.

- A tendency to include as "free" member benefits activities or services that are used by only a portion of members.

- Frequent marketing outreach to members selling additional activities and services throughout the year to increase both engagement of the individual and revenue to the association.

- A focus on members, with limited outreach, engagement, and/or service to those who are not members.

In short, many associations have used the "one size fits all" approach, offering a membership relationship on the terms that work best for it as an organization. This model worked well for a very long time, as the alternatives to associations were often difficult to find, limited in scope, more expensive, and/or lacked the reputational benefit afforded by being identified as an association member.

However, the world in which associations operate has changed. The Internet has made it simpler to find alternatives, which can often be delivered in customized, cost-effective ways, allowing buyers to purchase exactly what they need and not pay for "benefits" that are never used. Yelp, Angie's List, Glassdoor, LinkedIn, and numerous other sites are often the source of reputational first impressions—the "zero moment of truth" that occurs when a potential client or employee searches for information on the Internet. These elements have irreversibly changed consumer expectations, increasing the assumption that a better solution is out there to be found, determined by the buyer's perception of "the right fit" and suitable return on investment—exactly opposite to the notion that one size fits all.

As the operating environment and consumer expectations have shifted, the discipline of association membership has evolved as well. Sheri Jacobs' *The Art of Membership,* available from ASAE, accurately reflects that it has become an art form, in which the membership director considers the design of a membership strategy in much the same way that an artist considers the design of a piece. This includes considering the perspective of the potential member's viewpoint; the feelings evoked by the offer; the details and flourishes to which members and perspective members relate; and, above all, an intentionality of the artist—that is, what is the membership strategy designed to represent or do? Is the strategy designed for stability, growth, deepening relationships, political clout, or another goal? How can the model be more relevant to specialized niches and needs?

The following examples highlight questions like these to go beyond "business as normal" to create variations from traditional association membership model assumptions.

Associations Looking at the Book Ends

As more associations explore the segments that compose the population of their industry, there is increased focus on two particular segments that, interestingly enough, are the least likely to pay "full" membership dues—students and retired members.

Students

Those still in school may have the least resources and are not focused on their future profession in a full-time capacity. Yet, as associations experience a shift in their membership base as long-time members begin to retire, students start to fill their pipeline of future leaders and community participants. Although many associations offer lower student dues, a number of associations have tried to eliminate those dues, often to the result of increased student membership numbers. (Who doesn't like free?) Three issues arise at this point:

1. There is no revenue offset from whatever the minimal amount of student dues once was. They are not going to be consumers of non-dues revenue sources unless required by a class/professor.

2. There are minimal levels of increased engagement, despite higher numbers of members.

3. The association reflects a steep drop-off upon graduation and may conclude that the effort to recruit young was a failure.

Associations looking to invest in the future by creating a robust student program today are meeting these challenges through a number of alternative approaches.

Revenue Offset

Instead of simply eliminating student dues, some associations, or their respective foundations, are creating programs of corporate sponsorship of association dues. Companies, who often also minimally have an interest in the rising generation as their next influx of employees, can find value in such a program through a simple approach of assessing their need for access and recognition. If they have internship programs, associations can promote those internships to their student members, which is also a value to the students. If the companies have specific areas of expertise, they can create virtual learning sessions that can give insight into their area of focus.

In turn, the association can acknowledge their commitment through various media, such as including their logo on marketing materials, and web presence. Arrangements can also be made to give the company priority in a virtual career fair or to directly connect with rising student leaders for introductions. Tiered sponsorship can increase the investment further—and an investment is truly what it is. The shift from "free student membership" to "sponsored student membership" is a significant one. Students are not just getting another freebie. Instead, companies, through their commitment to the association, are investing in the students—in their careers and their futures. That alternate approach can change the whole premise of joining the association without paying dues.

Engagement

The idea that the value an association delivers has to be targeted to its respective member segments is not a novel one. Yet, for some reason, there is all too often a disconnect when associations create their packages for students. Those programs, products, and services geared toward those already working could serve to provide insight for students into the profession they are going to enter, but do not necessarily provide them with solutions of stepped-up improvements from where they currently are in their lives.

If the association is serious about creating a robust student program, then they make a commitment to create value specifically for the student population. This may be through training at the introductory level, through creating connections to mentors and/or future colleagues, or probably the most impactful—through helping them find their first jobs. Whatever the components of the student package may be, they should be the next step of creating a feeling of investment on the part of the students—a feeling that the association is focusing on them for who they are and not as a secondary market because they don't (yet) have the same buying power.

Drop-Off

There are some natural causes for a gap/drop-off in belonging once a student graduates. Some will take some time off before joining the workforce; others may not actually enter the industry that they pursued in school. Some will not want to pay for what was previously free, and others will think of the association as part of their "student" lives," rather than life post-graduation.

Associations that succeed in creating a transition are those that don't focus on the reasons why it doesn't happen and instead embrace the need to create a community and "home" for those graduating that is distinct from the student experience, but builds on the support that existed while the new professional was in school. A dual focus on creating a distinct virtual community for those early in the profession where there can be a more informal approach—recognizing needed learning, peer achievements, connecting social media outlets—with targeted local connections and programming. Most associations can target where there are larger pockets of professionals. If the association can help create a smooth transition into these new communities for those who just graduated, then there is a transition of "belonging."

Case Study: The American Institute of Chemical Engineers (AIChE)

AIChE has created a student program, called ScaleUp (www.aiche.org/community/students) that incorporates industry-sponsored membership with targeted benefits, including a safety certificate program and a robust network of chapters, job resources, and conferences. While this program has evidenced an exponential growth in student membership, AIChE looked beyond this initial success to create a next step platform called ChEnected (www.aiche.org/chenected). Included in this virtual community are blog posts from a host of those early in their careers, a student/young professional of the month, and series of articles/learnings that are tailored to the early career population. To further invest in this program, AIChE created an executive student committee—a national body of leadership, many of whom then transition to leadership positions once they are in the field.

Retired Professionals

The continued exit of the Baby Boomer generation from the workplace not only is creating gaps in the workplace, but is leaving holes of knowledge, insight, and connection within their respective associations. Those who are retired may have a continued interest in the news and happenings of their long-time professions, but no longer need many of the core elements that create the value proposition to belong. Without the driver of such things as certification upkeep or cutting-edge research to best perform onsite, there is a lower likelihood of dues payment. For many associations, retired professionals are outside the gamut of their focus, and therefore very little focus is given to what is lost as they silently slip away from the organization. Specifically:

1. Along with these retirees go a host of historical perspectives and industry insights that can often serve as the answer to "why" things are the way they are.

2. Retirees have had a lifetime of relationship building. While many of their counterparts may also exit their positions, there is strength and respect that can be brought to the table simply by their knowledge of who to talk to in a given situation.

3. For those who have had successful careers and find themselves without full-time employment commitments, there is a desire to give back. Many organizations make it easy for them to volunteer and show appreciation for that time—a shortcoming of many associations.

To avoid the loss of this important segment, some associations are creating specific opportunities of involvement that often require minimal, if any, dues payments. Through low barriers to continued involvement and giving, some associations are demonstrating the value of maintaining relationships with these audience segments.

Historical Insights and Industry Insights

Video testimonials and narratives offer a compelling and engaging channel for communications beyond marketing and promotion. As a low-cost, low-technological barrier to communication, videos are a viable option for any size organization. For the first time that members select the "retired" category, there is an opportunity at that moment to thank them for their years of contribution and effort in the industry and to ask what specific insights from the field they have that could positively affect those still in the workforce.

The role of a historian or a historical committee in an association has shifted from collecting pictures and assembling a "yearbook" to the opportunity to record interviews with these retirees, no matter where they live, from the comfort of their homes. By using a similar line of questioning across interviews, compilations of insights can be created for widespread distribution. When incoming volunteer entities want to know more about a historical program or an award, or even a significant event that happened in their industry, these videos can serve as a source of insight and a connection point to reach out to the person who was interviewed. Finding ways to integrate today's means of connection and communication with the knowledge that these retirees hold preserves their valuable lessons while keeping them involved in the community that can best benefit from what they bring.

Connections

Every day associations face situations in which they are striving for deeper insight into how to best interact with vendors, internal stakeholders, or even competitors. Often, those who are retiring have had experiences both with what approaches have not worked, as well as who the key people/positions are that can get things done. Additionally, there is a mantle of respect that comes with someone who has navigated a successful career, especially those who have held leadership positions.

At a minimum, an association should keep an active reference sheet for who has had experience with which external (or even sometimes internal) entities. Those "connectors" are consulted on a regular basis, ensuring their continued engagement by recognizing who they are and what they have done. LinkedIn, or similar connection platforms, can serve in the role of a connection sheet if those retiring have complete profiles. No matter the method, an association that includes in its strategy a regular review of key connections needed for external entities opens the door for valuable retiree contributions.

Giving Back

In retirees, associations have a prime population that has deep insight into their industry, often into their organization. As retirement proceeds, the person probably has more time on his or her hands. Although traditional volunteer processes focus on professional members, there is a key opportunity to create a volunteer path to keep these retirees engaged and contributing. Opportunities may exist to contribute as a subject-matter expert to publications or professional development, or to connect as a mentor to students or emerging professionals. Others may be interested in giving back from their pockets, and association foundations that can tap into the areas of greatest interest may find their biggest supporters in their retirees.

Retirees may not be the typical member—diminishing reasons to pay dues, not part of the active workforce. Yet they possess unique time, treasure, and talent that will only continue to grow as the Baby Boomers retire. Associations that can shift their models to prioritize this segment, to make them still feel like a priority even after they depart the workforce, will see a return for their extended relationship.

Global Stage

The multifold opportunities that exist for those associations that shift focus to the global scene are significant. The opportunities for expanding an organization's community are often exponentially higher—and with that also comes expanded knowledge, industry insights, and a more vibrant global community through the acquisition of members outside of the United States and North America.

Yet, membership as a concept is not equally ingrained in every nation. To "join" or "belong" has various meanings, and whether the difference is as simple as pricing or as complex as governmental oversight of groups, a copy-paste of the American model is not going to necessarily take hold. A decision to become inclusive of international professionals, many of whom will not join as typical members, means thinking outside the box for alternative models.

Connect Where They Belong

Although the governance structure may vary, many countries have their own society counterparts. These organizations know the local issues, trends, and needs of their members better, simply for being present every day. Instead of competing for member dues with these entrenched organizations, a number of associations are looking to alternate models of partnership that are mutually beneficial. Some samples are discussed below in each category.

International Facility Management Association (IFMA)   IFMA created an "alliance" program. Through this program, IFMA and another society agree on a flat fee for which all of the partner society members become "custom" members of IFMA. In turn, any member from the global nation who wants to join IFMA must first join his or her national society for access. Although these individual members have not technically joined IFMA, nor paid direct dues, they belong to the community in a way that enhances the perspective brought to the table, the potential customer base for targeted program, products, and services, and expands the population of those who may want to engage in volunteer opportunities (www.ifma.org/community/ifma-groups).

Program Where They Are

Even as virtual presence and community continue to evolve, there is still the need for local connection. By establishing a presence in the local market, an association can become a source of learning and connection, even without the membership connection. By delivering programming on the local scale, each event can be tailored to both the needs and cultural norms of that locale.

Society of Petroleum Engineers (SPE)   SPE built their conference and workshop offerings to span the globe, building upon the global learning needs of petroleum engineers, and in the process doubling their membership. With a low barrier to entry, these efforts have expanded their own local communities (sections) and driven the need to open multiple offices. From SPE's homepage (www.spe.org), you can find on the left side SPE regions. Browse through them to see how the offerings are tailored, from content to pricing.

Recognizing Local Achievement

Connecting a local community around the world to a national association means being able to recognize the strengths and accomplishments of that community. Even without formal membership relationships, a connection with the association is going to be most possible when there is an attitude of parity—that all parties coming to the table are equal players. If an association is able to first allow the partner society to demonstrate the expertise they bring to the table and points of pride to be celebrated, that mutual recognition can pave the path to community connections that can surpass individual dues accounts.

American Society of Civil Engineers (ASCE)   ASCE celebrates achievements in civil engineering through its Landmark Program—recognizing historically significant local, national, and international civil engineering projects, structures, and sites. Civil engineers from around the world can nominate their local structure, and need only support from their own local society and not ASCE. These international landmarks are listed in the same line as domestic ones, and open the door to further connections between the professionals in each organization. (http://www.asce.org/landmarks/)

With the continued evolution and proliferation of low-cost communication technology, the geographic barriers that once existed between professionals and communities around the world will continue to disappear. Associations that are able to conceptualize models of how a professional can have a feeling of connection or belonging, without paying member dues, will best succeed at building the bridges that will create a global society for their professionals.

Additional case models that captured the attention of the authors are discussed below.

Alternative Membership Models

Trade associations have typically limited their membership structures to company memberships with a dues schedule based on some aspect of size (revenue, number of employees, level of production) to assure that members pay a dues share proportionate to the size of their organization. In addition to the struggles faced by professional societies caused by the external changing economy and other advancements, trade associations can be heavily impacted by the nuances of their industry sector. After all, it is hard to maintain membership and dues investment when a sector itself is contracting. Mergers and acquisitions also can play havoc on the traditional trade association model, especially when two or more of an association's largest members merge to become one member. If traditional methods for managing a thriving trade association have stagnated, consider the following suggestions.

Take the Top Off

If your dues schedule has a maximum dues rate based on an established number "or more" for a flat dues amount, you are especially at risk that a merger of two companies paying at or near the top amount will become one company paying at that same maximum. A relatively simple adjustment is to take the top maximum off of the schedule, replacing it with a calculation that continues the dues category based on the spirit of the dues structure. For example, a dues schedule based on number of employees that previously read "10,000 employees or more . . . $x dues" could be revised to read: "10,000 employees or more . . . $x dues plus $y per additional 100 employees."

A second method is to build a calculated schedule based on an equation that is both fair in terms of proportions and accepted (paid and retained) by your largest members. After all, mergers and acquisition are often predicated on efficiency and savings, so just as a company would expect to control human resource administration costs in a merger, it is likely to expect to see less in total dues than simply the sum of the two previous amounts, which, of course, is fair because you are now only promoting and providing benefits to one company rather than two—but a company that is larger and typically more successful than the two component parts.

An example of a calculated dues structure that takes all of these factors into account is the "square root of assets" approach utilized by some credit union associations. This approach determines the members' dues by calculating a figure based on the square root of the funds of the member credit union. As the assets rise, so does the dues amount, although in a graduated fashion such that a company may find that merger reduces the combined separate dues by a smaller amount, but still has some efficiencies.

Explore Your Value Chain and Adjust Your Membership Structure Accordingly

When the National Defense Industry Association (NDIA), a non-partisan, non-profit, educational association promoting national security through a community of corporate and individual members from across the defense and national industrial base, reviewed how it adds value to its members, it identified connecting government contractors to government employee buyers as a key element. However, an economic downturn had membership counts from government officials on the decline. In response, NDIA adjusted its model, making government employee membership free. As a result, it actually increased its relevance at a challenging time, and the decision was part of several changes that doubled revenue for the organization.

You may be able to find similar success by exploring your value chain. Begin by creating a flowchart that documents your current members at the center. To the right, add who they serve, sell to, and support. Above and below, add the suppliers, regulators, competing industries, and other organizations that assist or otherwise impact your members' operations. To the left, identify where you locate prospective members, those who influence prospective members (such as academics), and other factors that may influence the environment in which your association operates.

Add flourishes and observations to note trends, metrics, and considerations that help you understand the big picture, such as the market share your association represents and where your major association competitors are strong. Review the chart (see Figure 18.1) you have developed with a critical eye. At each noted area ask yourself:

How might our association have an increased relationship with this audience?

- Is there a financial or other growth opportunity?
- What threats to our current model must we be aware of?

Examples from Associations

Don't seek to solve every aspect of the value chain. Chances are it is evolving in the same way that your association must. Instead, seek to build a culture of awareness that allows you to experiment by introducing special offers and/or pilot programs that you can monitor for return on investment. When you find an approach like NDIA did with free government employee memberships, leverage your lessons learned! Some other ideas are discussed below.

- *Serve the organization and its professional staff through a hybrid model.* The American Alliance of Museums realized that it could build a membership structure

Figure 18.1. Sample Membership Flowchart

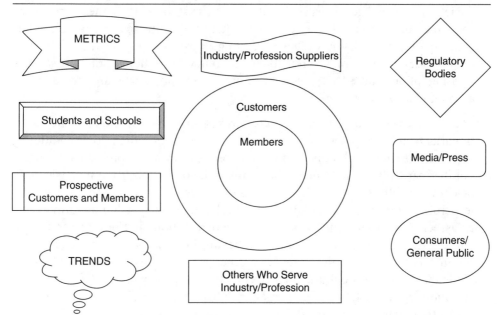

that serves both museums as institutions as well as museum professionals as individuals. Its hybrid membership structure emphasizes career management and skill-building to individuals, while highlighting accreditation and promotion for institutions. It also takes an innovative approach to the wide-ranging scope of museum funding by including even the smallest museum under a "pay what you can" dues option. (www.aam-us.org/membership)

- *Address the needs of niche or specialty areas of focus within the profession.* The American Hospital Association, a traditional trade association for hospitals, recognized that its membership employed a wide degree of professional subspecialty niches. It created 10 "personal membership groups" in these specialty areas like healthcare engineering, risk management, and human resource administration. Personal membership includes access to some (but not all) AHA benefits, such as a members-only website and hospital literature, in addition to the institutional membership.

- *Give a free experience that entices individuals to help you find prospective new organizational members.* CompTIA, an IT industry trade association, was a pretty steady organization but saw an opportunity for possible expansion. In order to stay viable in an environment in which the industry was changing, shifting to a freemium membership model allowed CompTIA to attract a much broader audience. Additionally, this shift also created opportunities for the organization to redesign its website. The freemium strategy allows for the organization to "court" potential dues-paying members and execute on a conversion strategy.

- *Provide an opportunity to upgrade to a premium level of membership.* The American Society of Travel Agents realized that, like the customers their members serve, some members prefer self-service, while others are willing to pay a premium for concierge access. ASTA innovated by creating a core membership dues of approximately $250 a year for an individual or agency that chooses the self-service website options and $2,500 a year for premium members who are served by an account management team.

- *Make it easy for members to make a bulk purchase in a single transaction.* The traditional association approach has been to reward members with multiple additional opportunities to spend money on association education and programs throughout the year. This can not only put a strain on the relationship, but it breeds inefficiency for both the association in terms of marketing costs and the member in terms of accounting costs. A more recent development is hyper-bundling, in which an association bundles a package of meeting registrations and/or other programs and services with an organizational membership. This allows easier budgeting by the member and a more efficient sales process for the association. A side benefit is that it creates a culture of engagement and typically encounters very high retention rates. ASAE has offered organizational hyper-bundles through its Circle Club program for more than 10 years. Circle Club organizations represent ASAE's top 4 percent of membership investment from associations and has been so successful that ASAE will be significantly expanding its hyper-bundling approach in January 2016. An analysis of Circle Club tells a very important tale: organizations that participate in Circle Club had the most stable revenue investment through a significant economic downturn and outpace growth and investment, as compared to associations that purchase additional programs and services via the traditional throughout-the-year model.

- *Get to know your members and increase your service to them.* The Metal Training Institute increased its retention and revenue simply by utilizing four little letters D-A-T-A. By collecting, analyzing, and utilizing data, MTI developed programs that its members could not cost-effectively develop. Moreover, the organization tracked its members' engagement by assigning participating members points. These points were then tallied and members stratified into four participation levels. A member's engagement level determined the kind of communications received. Additionally, MTI borrowed from the for-profit industry's gamification strategies for ways of creating a digital ecosystem that provides members a way they can link and track in a progressive way improvement of an action. This strategy has helped to shape the behavior of its members by creating an experience that stimulates competition, progression, and prestige in a social environment. (https://youtu.be/NHXgf4CyoAc)

- *Let your best supporters show that they are your best supporters.* Many trade associations and business leagues have found success by adding membership options that allow organizations to pay a premium dues amount to be included in a special tier that reflects their leadership above and beyond the expected dues level. For example, the Greater Durham Chamber of Commerce offers a special "Durham 2.0" membership level to allow businesses, nonprofits, and government agencies to show their leadership (and financial) commitment to the economic growth of the Durham community.

- *Use your toolbox of trade association tune-up tips to create a powerful engagement and membership engine.* There is perhaps no organization that has leveraged innovations in trade association membership in recent years better than the U.S. Chamber of Commerce. The Chamber offers a range of membership opportunities from limited investment (and limited benefits) for individual entrepreneurs through "best supporter" levels that provide a company the opportunity to participate in advisory meetings with the Chamber's CEO. In addition, there are similar dues structures for niches like associations and chambers. Not ready to join? Sign up for the "Friends of the U.S. Chamber," a social media type network that allows you to stay informed of the Chamber's programs and opportunities for involvement. Together, this network of engagement opportunities provides the Chamber with a powerful network that it can cultivate, activate, and engage, resulting in unprecedented political clout and financial success. An added benefit is the opportunity to create partnerships that facilitate business between this network and partner institutions for an additional revenue stream from affinity programs and sponsorship.

One more example from the association community is the American Nurses Association:

- *The American Nurses Association* capitalized on an opportunity to create relevance to its membership by focusing on three key strategic areas: governance, technology, and communications. Shifts in both the medical and association industries meant the American Nurses Association had to not only rethink its membership model but focus as well on its governance structure and allocate resources to renovate its overall technology strategy. By streamlining its governance structure through reduction of its board, transitioning of a committee to a working task force, and elimination of a House of Delegates as the primary governing body, the American Nurses Association created a more nimble governance structure. Additionally, the organization focused on creating an integrated business and technology platform that allowed its members to access a portfolio of products and resources that are relevant and aligned to the organization's mission and strategic plan. The technological improvements yielded opportunities of improvement in their communication strategies, which yielded enhanced online learning, e-advocacy that increased the volume of letters to Congress on important issues, free and comprehensive health-risk appraisals that provide benchmarking in an instant, and more.

Examples from the For-Profit Industry

Imitation is the best form of flattery. It comes as no surprise that the for-profit industry continues to look to the association industry to implement innovative ways to "recruit" new customers and retain existing customers using loyalty programs. Replicating the "membership" model has made Starbucks and REI two game-changers in the for-profit industry.

- Starbucks uses a dynamic relationship-based gamification strategy that keeps customers actively brewing. Using the "My Starbucks Rewards Program," customers are rewarded by using their registered cards. Customers are encouraged to create and update their profiles, link their registered cards to the app, and receive rewards and recognition through a host of different actions, ranging from purchasing coffee in grocery stores, engaging in engagement activities, taking surveys, and more—all in a user-centric way. Each experience allows the Starbucks customer to progress through three different levels of membership, Welcome, Green, and Gold. (https://www.starbucks.com/card/rewards)

- Recreational Equipment, Inc. (REI), which touts its membership base of more than five million active members and customers, began as a coop named the Recreational Equipment Cooperative. The group came together to share climbing gear with associates looking for quality equipment. Over the years, the coop grew and expanded, providing customers with not only quality equipment, but benefits such as learning opportunities, travel opportunities, and a variety of other member benefits. Members are offered 10 percent rebates annually, in-store discounts, and larger discounts for classes and travel opportunities. Additionally, program managers are offered lifetime membership after they sign up. REI's communication strategy includes supplemental content that provides best way "examples" for their members to utilize their discounts and benefits. (https://www.rei.com/membership/benefits)

Wrap-Up

While we hope the preceding examples serve as good food for thought as you think about opportunities to reinvent your membership model, we do not hold these up as templates to be duplicated in a cookie-cutter fashion. In fact, the pace of change is so fast that, as you read this, some of these practices probably are no longer even considered "innovations" and others may have been proven to be ahead of their time . . . still others having evolved further. No one change is right for every association; rather, today's association must continually re-examine its purpose, and, when needed, adjust the way in which it engages its constituency, including its membership model. Here are some questions to consider as you explore potential direction for your organization:

- What membership structure changes can expand your organization beyond its current focus?

- How will you identify membership prospects?

- Who funds membership, participation, and content?

- What is the core portion of the market? Is there a high-end subset or lower part of the market?

- How can membership growth create new product and market opportunities?

- If customers who have any interaction with the association were considered "members," even without paying dues, what would the tiers of membership look like?

- How can you redefine "belonging" to your association to account for those who have the lowest prospect of joining, but would still be additive to the larger organization?

Here are some questions of strategies that you might consider. Would looking at strategy from a slightly different angle:

- Create a portfolio of engagement options from customer to a variety of membership opportunities?

- Appeal to both individuals and organizations and maintain a connection to individuals, while providing economy of scale to organizations?

- Leverage technology to allow for targeted, customized information delivered quickly in cost-effective ways?

- Serve many niches and create a model and systems that provide value to demographic and functional niches:
  - *Expanding to adjacent horizontal markets.* Are there other individuals or companies that would have an interest in the content and activities of your organization that are not currently pursued as members? Often this includes professionals in related fields or companies that provide services as a secondary line of business.
  - *Expanding to vertical markets.* Are there other companies that would have an interest in the content and activities of your organization that are not currently pursued as members? Often this includes professionals in related fields or companies that provide services to your members, often as suppliers or distributors.
  - *Tapping into specialized niches.* Are there company or individual prospect segments that merit a specialized relationship approach? Some examples might include start-up businesses, young professionals, government officials, academics, or sole proprietorships.
  - *Create a voice space for each niche.* For each targeted segment, how will you ensure your organization has its finger on the pulse of what the specific needs are and where you can be the best-fit solution provider? Empowering leadership and dialogue from all prioritized segments will ensure that their insights are not lost.

Looking for help with the process? We recommend Sarah Sladek's *The End of Membership as We Know It: Building the Fortune-Flipping Must-Have Association of the Next Century* (ASAE, 2011). Some ideas from the book include:

- Understand what your members want and need.

- Develop member benefits that solve the problems.

- Assess the costs to provide those benefits and get rid of anything that does not provide a benefit.

- Put a membership model in place that both aligns with the way your audience wants to pay and makes it easy for your offering to sell.

- Test these offerings and revenue models with members and nonmembers. Adjust accordingly.

About the Authors

Lowell M. Aplebaum, CAE, is COO for the American Society for Parenteral and Enteral Nutrition. He is a past-chair of ASAE's Component Relations Council, serves on the CAE Commission, and led ASAE's CEO Pathways Taskforce. He has served as faculty for the Institute for Organization Management, Association Management Week, and ASAE's Online University.

Greg Melia, CAE, is chief member relations and strategy development officer for ASAE. He has been on the ASAE staff since May 2004. He holds an undergraduate degree in psychology from The College of William & Mary, a master's degree from the London School of Economics, and has completed graduate studies in creativity and change leadership from the International Center for Studies in Creativity at the State University of New York.

Melody A. Jordan-Carr is the vice president of member relations at ASAE. She holds a B.A. degree in journalism and an M.S. degree in management, concentrating on nonprofit and association management. She serves as a volunteer and board member with local organizations.

About the Executive Editor

Sheri Jacobs, FASAE, CAE, a best-selling author, keynote speaker, and association management veteran with nearly 20 years of experience, serves as the president and CEO of Avenue M Group, one of the nation's leading market research firms focused exclusively on the association community.

Sheri started her nonprofit career in the development office of the Chicago Children's Museum and moved into marketing after becoming a founding officer of Picture This Projects, a nonprofit organization that empowers underserved children in Chicago. She transitioned from the philanthropic community to the association community in 1994 when she became the director of membership and marketing at the American Academy of Implant Dentistry and joined the American Bar Association Law Practice Management Division in 1999. In 2002, Sheri joined the Association Forum of Chicagoland as the chief marketing officer and director of membership. During her tenure at the Association Forum, she built award-winning campaigns that resulted in double-digit membership and meeting attendance growth.

Over the years, Sheri has served in numerous leadership and volunteer roles, including as chair of the ASAE Foundation Development Committee, member of the Professional Development Council, chair of the ASAE Membership Council, and a member of the Marketing Council. Sheri's success in the field has led her to become an accomplished author. She is the author of the best-selling membership book, *The Art of Membership: How to Attract, Retain, and Cement Member Loyalty* (Wiley, 2014), *199 Ideas: Powerful Marketing Tactics That Sell* (ASAE, 2010) and co-editor and a contributor to *Membership Essentials* (ASAE, 2007).

In 2015, the Association Forum of Chicagoland awarded the John C. Thiel Distinguished Service Award to Sheri in recognition for her outstanding service to the association community.

Index

Page references followed by *fig* indicates an illustrated figure; by *t* indicates a table; by *e* indicates an exhibit.

Consumer Price Index, 41

Content ads, 160

Content management system (CMS), 94, 204

Copyright law, 260

Corporations: Internal Revenue Service (IRS) regulations on, 252; legal considerations related to, 252–253

CPA Institute, 40

CTIA: The Wireless Association, 24

Culture: global membership consideration of differences in, 62–63; how changes have impacted association membership, 2–3. *See also* Organizational culture

Cummings, Michael, 143

Currency issues, 64

Customer relationship management system (CRM), 94. *See also* AMS/CRM systems

Customer service: AMS/CRM system as part of, 94–102; customer relationship management system (CRM) for, 93; illustrated diagram of a membership department incorporating, 118*fig*; to international chapters, 68; member staff training on, 120; membership department role in, 115

D

Data: AMS/CRM systems for managing and using, 102–109; confidentiality of membership information, 120, 257–259; governance practices for using, 42–43; identifying best customers by using your, 107–108; measuring member engagement, 103–104; membership market, 84; order entry/processing for member, 113–114; primary versus secondary, 84; successful associations and their use of, 42

Data integrity reports, 106, 107

Data mining, 85

Databases: AMS/CRM systems features, 96–97; assessing if your database is supporting your mission, 93–94; member staff training on membership, 120; National Change of address (NICOA) services, 106; Target Market identification using your, 154

Day, John, 151

De Cagna, Jeff, 44

Deale, Charles W. L., 33

Decision-makers: deciding who the research results will go to, 78–79; presenting

membership research results to, 89–90; understanding the impact of the membership research decisions by, 80*t*–81

Decision making: AMS/CRM systems for managing and using data for, 102–109; dues increase, 41; time frame of the membership research, 79–80; understanding the impact of the membership research, 80*t*–81; venues for membership, 79

The Decision to Join (DTJ) study [ASAE], 23, 43, 44, 157–158, 175

Deferred income, 245

Direct mail marketing channel, 161*t*

Discounts: communicating membership value of, 25; international chapters and advocacy support, 69; Massachusetts Medical Society (MMS), 127; as offer strategy, 156

DOJ (Department of Justice), 255, 256

Dolci, Joel, 143

Dorsey, Mark, 14

Doyle, Kenneth A., 1

Dual memberships: description of, 39; various governance practices on, 39–40

Due process, 256

Dues: governance over rates and increase of, 40–41; governance over structure of, 37; how they are spent, 248*fig*; organizational (or enterprise) rates of, 128; paid to nonprofit organizations, 254; "square root of assets" approach to, 271–272; "take the top off" approach to, 271. *See also* Revenue

Dues increases: governance decisions on, 41; 2015 Marketing General benchmarking study on, 41

Dues payments: automatic credit card, 172; installment option for, 157, 172

Dues rates: decisions related to, 40–41; governance authority over establishing, 40

Dues reporting oversight, 41–42

Dues structures: description of, 37; as function of governance, 37

E

E-membership model, 128–129

Eadie, Douglas C., 38

Economic changes, 2–3

8 Leader Essentials for Membership Vice Presidents (AAUW), 217

Email marketing channel, 161*t*

Emotional connection, 201

The End of Membership As We Know It: Building the Fortune-Flipping Must-Have Association of the Next Century (Sladek), 39, 47–48, 277

Energy Education Council mission statement, 35, 36*e*

Engagement. *See* Member engagement

Enterprise membership. *See* Organizational (or enterprise) membership

Environmental Scanning for Associations: The Everyday Guide to Capturing, Analyzing, and Interpreting Strategic Information (ASAE), 208

Ernstthal, Henry L., 37, 39, 40

Established business relationship (EBR), 170

Explicit interest, 108–109

Exploring the Future of Membership (ASAE Foundation), 209

Extended membership offer, 156–157

F

Face-to-face sales, 161*t*

Facebook: association use of, 203*t*; decreasing reach for associations of, 192; recruitment marketing channel using, 160; "The Science of Storytelling: Why Telling a Story is the Most Powerful Way to Activate Our Brains" on, 212

Fay, Brad, 176

FCC Telephone Consumer Protection Act, 170

Federal Trade Commission (FTC), 156, 255, 256, 257–258, 259

Federation associations, 136

Financial issues: communicating how membership dollars are spent, 247–248*fig*; projecting revenue, 246*t*–247; terms to know and understand related to, 233; understand what is related to serving members vs. overhead, 234

Financial metrics: acquisition of new member, 232–233*t*; American Academy of Pediatrics example of tracking and presenting, 239–242*fig*; cost to renew a member, 234–235, 236–238*t*; cost to serve a member, 233–234*t*; lifetime value of a member (LTV), 235–236*t*; return on investment (ROI) applications, 235; terms to know and understand related to, 233

501(c)(3) nonprofit organizations, 253–254

501(c)(6) nonprofit organizations, 253–254

Focus group market research, 85–86

For-profit organizations: Recreational Equipment, Inc. (REI), 275, 276; Starbucks, 275, 276

Ford, Henry, 58

"Freemium" or open-access membership model, 129–130

"Friends of the U.S. Chamber" social media network, 275

Fulfillment of needs, 201

Full-premium (medium/high) membership model, 130

Future Perspectives (ASAE Foundation), 3

G

The gamer mentality, 8

Gammel, David, 103

Geer, Rod, 3

Generation X (born 1965 to 1980): association appeal to, 4–5; description and characteristics of, 4

Glassie, Jefferson C., 251, 261

Global MedTech Compliance Conference, 66

Global membership: additional thoughts on managing a, 73–74; association segmentation of, 269–271; case studies on, 72–73; considerations relations to managing a, 61–65*fig*; efforts to connect and recognize local achievements by, 269–271; marketing to and communication with a, 69–71*fig*, 210–211; support of chapters, 66–69; volunteer leadership role in, 65–66

Global membership consideration: cultural differences as, 62–63; differing perceptions by members, 64; legal, 63–64; local currency, 64; member and customer support, 63; when communicating with a global audience, 64

Golden, Mark, 38, 44

Good-better-best (low/medium/high) membership model, 131

Google marketing channel, 160

Governance: AMS/CRM implementation by effective project, 98, 99; differentiating between management and, 34–35; how membership staff can support, 44–45; involvement and personal perspective of members on, 43; membership functions